E. d. Nolan

Spark of Life

By Erich Maria Remarque

ALL QUIET ON THE WESTERN FRONT
THE ROAD BACK
THREE COMRADES
FLOTSAM
ARCH OF TRIUMPH
SPARK OF LIFE

Spark of Life

By
ERICH MARIA REMARQUE

Translated from the German
by
JAMES STERN

APPLETON-CENTURY-CROFTS, INC.
New York

Copyright, 1952, By
ERICH MARIA REMARQUE

All rights reserved. This book, or parts thereof, must not be reproduced in any form without permission of the publisher.

All names, characters, and events in this book are fictional, and any resemblance which may seem to exist to real persons is purely coincidental.

PRINTED IN THE UNITED STATES OF AMERICA

To the memory of my sister Elfriede.

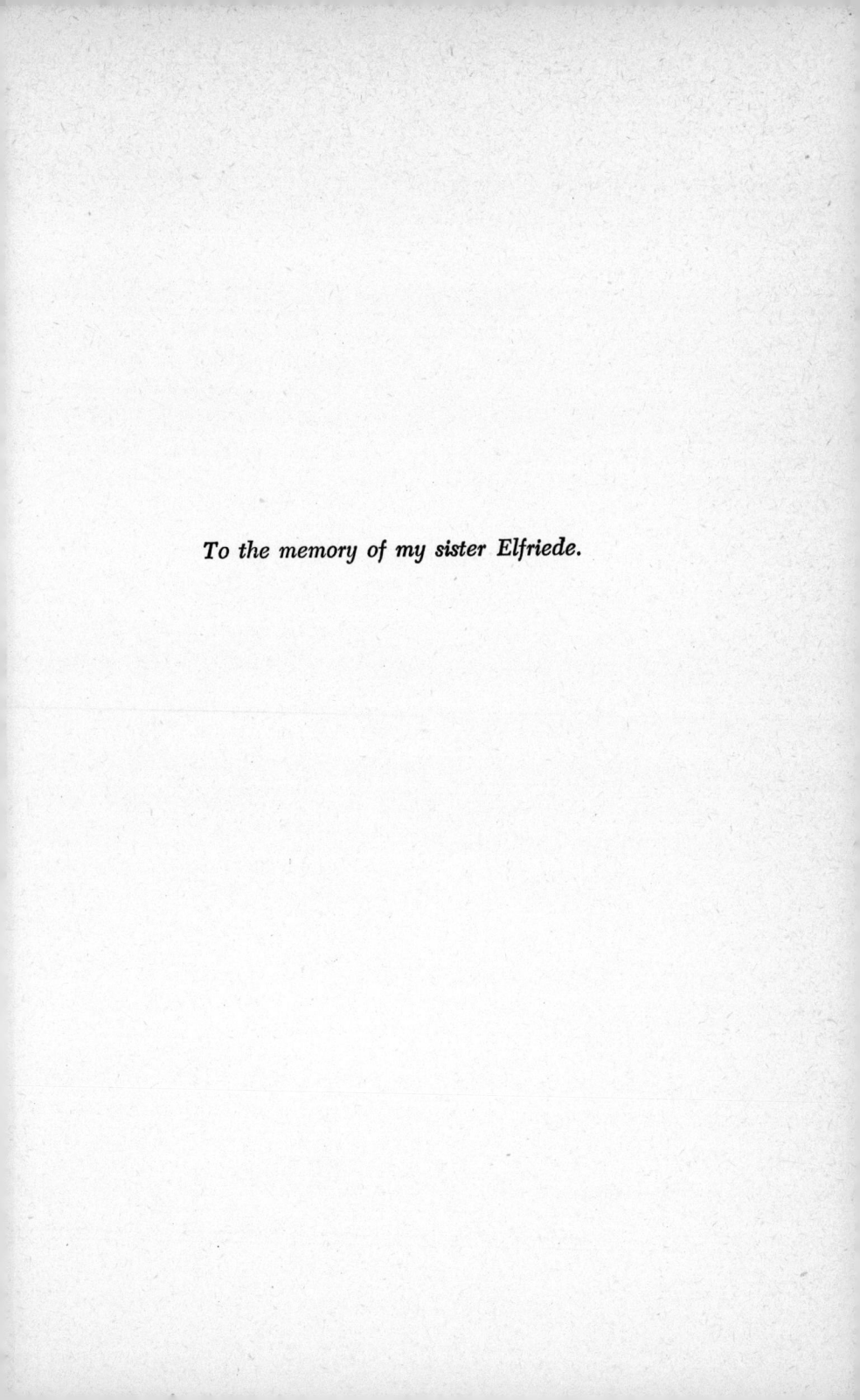

Spark of Life

CHAPTER ONE

Skeleton 509 slowly raised its skull and opened its eyes. It did not know whether it had been unconscious or merely asleep. By now there was hardly any difference between the one and the other; hunger and exhaustion had long ago seen to that. Both were a sinking into boggy depths, from which there seemed to be no more rising to the surface.

509 lay still for a while and listened. This was an old camp rule; one never knew from which side danger threatened, and as long as one remained motionless there was always the chance of being overlooked or taken for dead—a simple law of nature known to any beetle.

He heard nothing suspicious. The guards on the machine-gun tower in front of him were half asleep, and behind him, too, all remained quiet. Cautiously he turned his head and glanced back.

The Mellern concentration camp dozed peacefully in the sun. The great roll-call ground, which the SS humorously called the dance ground, was empty. Only from the strong wooden posts at the right of the entrance gate hung four men, their hands tied behind their backs. They had been strung up on ropes to a height from which their feet no longer touched the ground. Their arms were dislocated. Two stokers from the crematorium were amusing themselves by throwing small lumps of coal at them from a window; but none of the four any longer moved. They had been hanging on the crosses for half an hour and were now unconscious.

The barracks of the labor camp lay deserted; the outside gangs had not yet returned. Only a few men on room duty sneaked across the roads. To the left of the entrance gate, in front of the penal-bunker, sat the SS squad leader Breuer. He'd had a round table and wicker chair put in the sun and was drinking a cup of coffee. Real bean coffee was rare in the spring of 1945; but a little while ago Breuer had strangled two Jews who had been rotting in the bunker for six weeks, and he considered this to have been a humanitarian act worthy of reward. With the coffee the kitchen kapo had sent him a plate of dough-cake. Breuer ate it slowly and with relish; he especially liked the seedless raisins with which the dough was abundantly larded. The elder Jew hadn't given him much fun; but the younger one had been tougher; he had kicked and squawked for quite a while. Breuer grinned sleepily and listened to the scattered sounds of the camp band which was practicing behind the garden plots. The orchestra was playing the waltz "Roses from the South"— a favorite tune of the Commandant, *Obersturmbannführer* Neubauer.

509 lay on the opposite side facing the camp, close to a group of wooden barracks which were separated by a wire fence from the large labor camp. They were known as the Small camp. Here lived the prisoners who were too weak to work. They were there to die. Almost all of them died quickly; but new ones invariably arrived while the others were not yet quite dead, and so the barracks were constantly overcrowded. Often the dying lay piled on top of one another in the corridors, or they simply perished outside, in the open. Mellern had no gas chambers. Of this fact the Commandant

was particularly proud. In Mellern, he liked to explain, one died a natural death. Officially the Small camp was called the Mercy division—though there were few inmates with sufficient resistance to withstand the Mercy for longer than one to two weeks. A small tough group of these men lived in Barrack 22. They called themselves, with a remnant of grim humor, the Veterans. 509 belonged to them. He had been brought to the Small camp four months ago. It seemed a miracle even to himself that he was still alive.

The smoke blew over from the crematorium in black clouds. The wind pressed it down on the camp and the vapors swept low over the barracks; they smelled greasy and sweetish and made one want to retch. 509 had never been able to get used to them; not even after ten years in the camp. Today the remains of two Veterans would be up there; those of the watchmaker Jan Sibelski and of the university professor Joel Buchsbaum. Both had died in Barrack 22 and had been delivered to the crematorium at noon. Buchsbaum, as a matter of fact, not quite complete: three fingers, seventeen teeth, the toenails and a part of his genitals had been missing. He had lost them while being educated to become a useful human being. The subject of the genitals had provoked much laughter at the cultural evenings in the SS quarters. It had been an idea of Squad Leader Guenther Steinbrenner, who had but recently arrived at the camp. Simple, like all great inventions—an injection containing a high percentage of hydrochloric acid, that was all. With it, Steinbrenner had earned the immediate esteem of his comrades.

The March afternoon was mild and the sun already had some warmth. Even so, 509 felt cold—although he wore, apart from his own clothes, the garments of three other people: the jacket of Joseph Bucher; the overcoat of Lebenthal, a former secondhand dealer; and the torn sweater of Joel Buchsbaum which the barrack had saved before the corpse had been delivered. But to a man less than six feet tall and weighing less than eighty pounds, furs would probably not have given much warmth.

509 had the right to lie half an hour in the sun. Then he had to return to the barrack, hand over the borrowed clothes as well as his own jacket, and it was another man's turn. This was how the Vet-

erans had arranged it among themselves since the cold weather had passed. Some of them had no longer wanted it. They were too exhausted and after the sufferings of the winter had wanted only to die quietly in the barrack; but Berger, the room senior, had insisted that everyone still able to crawl should spend some time in the fresh air. The next one was Westhof; then came Bucher. Lebenthal had refused; he had better things to do.

509 turned back. The camp was situated on a hill and now he could see the town through the barbed wire. It lay in a valley, far beneath the camp, in the clear light of spring. Over the mass of roofs rose the towers of the churches. It was an old town with many churches and ramparts, with avenues of lime trees and winding alleys. To the north lay the modern section with wider streets, the main railroad station, tenement buildings, factories and copper and iron foundries where the camp's labor gangs worked. A river wound through it in a wide curve and reflected sleepily the bridges and the clouds.

509 let his head droop. He could hold it up for only a short while. A skull was heavy when the muscles of the neck had shrunk to threads—and the sight of the smoking chimneys in the valley made a man only hungrier than usual. It made him hungry in the brain— not just in the stomach. The stomach had been used to it for years and was capable of no other sensation than a dull, permanent greed. Hunger in the brain was worse. It awoke hallucinations and never grew tired. It even gnawed into sleep. In winter it had taken 509 three months to rid himself of the vision of fried potatoes. He had smelled them everywhere, even in the stench of the latrine shed. Now it was bacon. Bacon and eggs.

He glanced at the nickel watch that lay close to him on the ground. Lebenthal had lent it to him. It was a precious possession of the barrack; the Pole, Julius Silber, long since dead, had smuggled it years ago into the camp. 509 saw that he still had ten minutes left; he decided, nevertheless, to crawl back to the barrack. He didn't want to fall asleep again. One never knew if one would wake up. Once more he cautiously sent a searching glance down the main camp road. He still saw nothing that could mean danger. He didn't really expect it, either. The caution was rather more the routine of the old camp hares than real fear.

The Small camp was under a moderate kind of quarantine because of dysentery, and the SS seldom entered it. Besides, during the war years supervision in the whole camp had grown considerably less strict. The war had kept making itself more noticeable, and part of the SS guard—which until then had done nothing but heroically torture and murder defenseless prisoners—had been sent to the front. Now, in the spring of 1945, the camp held only a third of its former number of SS troops. For a long time now the internal administration had been handled almost exclusively by the inmates. Each barrack had one block senior and several room seniors; the labor gangs were subordinate to the kapos and the foremen, the whole camp to the camp seniors. All were prisoners. They were controlled by camp leaders, block leaders and labor-gang leaders. These were SS men. In the early days the camp had held only political prisoners; then, over the years, hordes of common criminals from the overcrowded jails of the town and the surrounding country had been added. The groups were distinguished by the color of the triangular patches of cloth which were sewn above the numbers on all prisoners' clothes. Those of the political prisoners were red; those of the criminals green. Jews wore a yellow patch as well, so that both triangles together formed a Star of David.

509 took Lebenthal's overcoat and Joseph Bucher's jacket, hung them over his shoulders and started crawling towards the barrack. He realized that he was more tired than usual. Even crawling he found difficult. Soon the ground beneath him began to turn. He stopped short, closed his eyes and breathed deeply. At the same moment he heard the sirens from the town.

At first there were only two. A few seconds later they had multiplied and soon after it seemed as though the whole town below were shrieking. It shrieked from the roofs and out of the streets, from the towers and out of the factories, it lay open in the sun, nothing in it seemed to stir, and yet it shrieked suddenly as if it were a paralyzed animal that sees death and cannot run away—it shrieked with sirens and steam whistles towards the sky, where all was quiet.

Instantly, 509 had ducked. It was forbidden to be outside the barrack during air-raid alarms. He could have tried to get up and run, but he was too weak to keep going fast enough and the barrack was too far; meanwhile a jittery new guard could have fired at him. He crept back a few yards as quickly as he could to a shallow fold in the ground, pressed himself into it and drew the borrowed clothes over himself. He looked just like someone who had dropped dead. This often happened and did not arouse suspicion. The alarm would not last long, in any case. During the last few months the town had had one every few days and nothing had ever happened. The planes had always flown on in the direction of Hanover and Berlin.

The camp sirens joined in. Then, after some time, came the second alarm. The howling rose and fell, as though worn-out discs were revolving on gigantic gramophones. The planes were approaching the town. 509 knew this, too. It didn't affect him. His enemy was not the one against whom the town was shrieking. His enemy was the first machine gunner to notice that he was not dead. What went on outside the barbed wire did not concern him.

He breathed with difficulty. The stuffy air under the coat turned into black cotton wool which piled itself up thicker and thicker above him. He lay in the hollow of the ground as though in a grave—and gradually it seemed to him as though it really were his grave—as if he would never be able to get up again, as if this were the end and he would have to remain lying here and die, finally overcome by the last weakness against which he had fought for so long. He tried to resist it but it helped little; he only felt it all the stronger, a strange resigned waiting which spread within him, within him and beyond him as if suddenly everything were waiting—as if the town were waiting, as if the air were waiting, as if even the light were waiting. It was like a beginning of a solar eclipse when the colors have already taken on the hue of lead and the distant foreboding of a dead sunless world—a vacuum, a waiting without breathing to discover whether or not death will once more pass by—

The blow was not violent; but it was unexpected. And it came from a side which seemed more protected than any other. 509 felt it as a hard push deep out of the ground against the stomach. At the same time the howling outside was cut through by a high, steel-like whirring, which increased furiously, similar to the sound of the sirens and yet completely different. 509 did not know which came first, the push out of the ground or the whirring and the following crash—but he knew that neither had been present in any previous alarm, and when it was repeated closer and stronger, above him and below him, he also knew what it must be—for the first time the planes had not flown on. The town was being bombarded.

The ground trembled again. It seemed to 509 as if mighty underground rubber truncheons were hitting him. Suddenly he was fully awake. The death-weariness had vanished like smoke before a storm. Each blow from the ground became a blow in his brain. For some time he continued to lie still—then, almost without realizing what he did, he carefully stretched out one hand and lifted the coat high enough in front of his face to peer down at the town.

Slowly and playfully the railroad station unfolded and lifted itself into the air. It looked almost graceful when the golden cupola sailed above the trees of the town park and disappeared. The heavy explosions didn't seem to belong to it at all—everything was far too slow. Even the noise of the flak was drowned in them like the yelping of terriers in the deep bark of a great Dane. With the next mighty crash one of the towers of St. Catherine's church began to bend. It also fell very slowly and during its fall broke calmly into several pieces—as if it were a slow-motion picture and not reality.

Fountains of vapor now grew up like mushrooms between the houses. 509 still hadn't the feeling of destruction; invisible giants were playing down there, that was all. In the undamaged sections of the town, smoke continued peacefully to rise from the chimneys; the river reflected the clouds as before, and the puffs of flak hemmed the sky as if it were a harmless cushion whose seams were everywhere bursting and ejecting flakes of gray-white cotton.

A bomb fell far outside the town into the meadows which rose up to the camp. Still 509 didn't feel any fear; all this was much too far away from the narrow world which was all he still knew. Fear one could feel about burning cigarettes on eyes and testicles, about weeks in the hunger-bunker—a stone coffin in which one could neither stand nor lie—about the rack on which one's kidneys were crushed, about the torture chamber in the left wing near the gate; about Steinbrenner, about Breuer, about the camp leader Weber—but even this had somewhat paled since 509 had been moved to the Small camp. One had to be able to forget quickly in order to find the strength to live on. Besides, after ten years the Mellern concentration camp had grown rather tired of torture; even a fresh, idealistic SS-man grew bored in time with torturing skeletons. They could not stand much and did not react enough. Only when a fresh batch of strong men capable of suffering arrived did the old patriotic zeal sometimes flare up. Then the familiar howling was heard again at night and the SS squads looked a little more animated, as after a good meal of roast pork with potatoes and red cabbage. Otherwise, the camps in Germany had become rather humane during the war years. One only gassed, clubbed and shot, or simply worked people insensible and then left them to starve. The fact that off and on in the crematorium a live man was burned with the dead was caused more by overwork and the fact that some skeletons hadn't moved for a long time than by evil intent. Actually, this happened only when it was necessary to make room quickly for new transports by mass liquidations. Even the starving to death of those incapable of work was pursued not too brutally in Mellern; in the Small camp there was always still something to eat and with it veterans like 509 had managed to create records in staying alive.

The bombardment suddenly ceased. Only the flak still raged. 509 raised the coat a little higher so that he could see the nearest machine-gun tower. The post was empty. He looked further to the right and then to the left. There, too, the towers were without guards. The SS squads had everywhere climbed down and made for safety; they had good air-raid shelters next to the barracks. 509 threw off the coat altogether and crept nearer to the barbed wire. He supported himself on his elbows and stared down into the valley.

Now the town burned everywhere. What had formerly looked playful had meanwhile changed into what it really was: fire and destruction. Yellow and black like a gigantic mollusk of annihilation, the smoke hovered in the streets and devoured the houses. Flames flared up everywhere. From the railroad station an immense sheaf of sparks shot up. The broken tower of St. Catherine's church began to blaze and along it tongues of fire licked like pale flashes of lightning. But unperturbed, as though nothing had happened, the sun stood in golden glory behind it all; and there seemed something almost ghostlike in the appearance of the blue and white sky, looking just as gay as before and the forests and mountain chains all around lying calm and unaffected in the gentle light—as if only the town had been condemned by an unknown, sinister judgment.

509 stared down. He forgot all caution and stared down. He knew the town only through the barbed wire and he had never been in it; but during the ten years he had spent in the camp it had become for him more than just a town.

At first it had been the almost unbearable image of lost freedom. Day after day he had stared down at it—he had seen it with its carefree life when, after a special treatment by the camp leader Weber, he had hardly been able to crawl any more; he had seen it with its towers and houses as he hung on the cross with dislocated arms; he had seen it with the white barges on its river and its automobiles driving into the springtime while he urinated blood from his crushed kidneys; his eyes had burned whenever he had seen it and it had been a torture, a torture that had been added to all the others of the camp.

Then he had begun to hate it. The time had passed and nothing had changed in the town, no matter what happened up here. The smoke from its cook stoves had gone on rising every day, uncontaminated by the fumes from the crematorium; its sports grounds and parks had been full of crowds while at the same time hundreds of hunted creatures had perished on the dance ground of the camp. Flocks of holiday-happy people had wandered out every summer into the woods while columns of prisoners dragged their dead and murdered back from the quarries. He had hated it because he had thought that he and the other prisoners had been forgotten forever.

Finally the hatred, too, had died down. The fight for a crust of bread had become more important than anything else, and almost equally so the knowledge that hatred and memories could destroy an endangered self as easily as pain. 509 had learned to shut himself up, to forget and no longer to worry about anything but naked existence from one hour to another. He had grown indifferent to the town, and its unchanged aspect was from now on only a sad symbol of the fact that his fate too would not change any more.

Now it was burning. He felt his arms trembling. He tried to suppress it but he couldn't; it only became stronger. Everything in him was suddenly loose and without connection. His head ached as though it were hollow and someone were drumming inside it.

He closed his eyes. He didn't want that. He didn't want anything to come up in him again. He had crushed and buried all hope and it had cost much pain to bury. He let his arms slide to the ground and laid his face on his hands. The town had nothing to do with him. He did not want it to have anything to do with him. He wanted unconcerned as before to let the sun shine on the dirty parchment that was stretched as skin over his skull, he wanted to breathe, to kill lice and not to think—as he had been doing for a long time.

He couldn't do it. The trembling in him wouldn't stop. He rolled round on his back and stretched out flat. Above him now was the sky with the little clouds of flak shot. They dissolved quickly and drifted along before the wind. Thus he lay a while; then this too he couldn't stand any more. The sky became a blue and white abyss into which he seemed to fly. He turned round and sat up. He no longer looked at the town. He looked at the camp and he looked at it, as if for the first time he expected help from there.

The barracks dozed as before in the sun. On the dance ground the four men were still hanging on the crosses. The squad leader Breuer had disappeared, but the smoke from the crematorium continued to rise; it had only become thinner. Either they were just burning children or orders had been given to cease work.

509 forced himself to observe everything carefully. This was his world. No bomb had hit it. There it lay as pitiless as ever. It alone ruled him, and all that out there on the other side of the barbed wire didn't concern him.

At that moment the flak stopped. It hit him as if a belt of noise, closed tight round him, had cracked. For a second he thought that he had only been dreaming and had just waked up. With a start he turned round.

He had not been dreaming. There lay the town, burning. There were fumes and destruction and it had something to do with him after all. He could no longer recognize what had been hit, he saw only the smoke and the fire, everything else had grown blurred, but it didn't make any difference. The town burned, the town, which had seemed unchangeable, as unchangeable and indestructible as the camp.

He started. He felt suddenly as though behind him from every tower all the camp's machine guns were turned on him. Quickly he glanced round. Nothing had happened. The towers were as empty as before. In the streets, too, no one could be seen. But it didn't help; a wild fear had suddenly seized him like a fist in the neck and shook him. He didn't want to die! Not now! Not any longer! Hastily he grabbed his clothes and crawled back. He got entangled with Lebenthal's coat and moaned and cursed and pulled it away from under his knees and crawled on towards the barracks, hastily, deeply excited and confused, as if he were fleeing from something other than death alone.

CHAPTER TWO

Barrack 22 had two wings, each of which was commanded by two room seniors. In the second section of the second wing lived the Veterans. It was the narrowest and the dampest part, but that worried them little; important to them was only that they were together. This gave each of them more power of resistance. Dying was just as contagious as typhus, and singly one easily succumbed in the general croaking, whether one wanted to or not. Several together could defend themselves better. When one man felt like giving up, his comrades helped him to hold out. The Veterans in the Small camp didn't live longer because they had more to eat; they lived because they had preserved a desperate remnant of resistance.

In the Veterans' corner at this time lay a hundred and thirty-four skeletons. There was room enough for only forty. The bunks consisted of boards, four above one another. They were bare or covered with old rotting straw. There were only a few dirty blankets over which, each time the owners died, there was a bitter fight. On each bunk lay at least three or four men. That was too close even for skeletons; for shoulder and pelvic bones didn't shrink. One gained a little more space by lying sideways, packed like sardines, but even so one heard often enough at night the hollow thud of someone falling down in his sleep. Many slept crouching and the lucky one was he whose bedfellows died in the evening. They were then carried away, and for one night he could stretch out until new arrivals came.

The Veterans had secured for themselves the corner to the left of the door. They were still twelve men. Two months ago they had been forty-four. The winter had finished them off. They all knew they were in the last stages; the rations grew steadily smaller and sometimes there was nothing whatever to eat for one or two days; then the dead lay outside in heaps.

Of the twelve one was mad and believed he was a German sheep dog. He no longer had any ears; they had been torn off when SS dogs had been trained on him. The youngest Veteran was called Karel and was a boy from Czechoslovakia. His parents were dead; they manured a pious peasant's potato field in the village of Westlage; for the ashes of the cremated were poured into sacks in the crematorium and sold as artificial manure. They were rich in phosphorous and calcium. Karel wore the red badge of the political prisoner. He was eleven years old.

The oldest Veteran was seventy-two. He was a Jew who fought for his beard. The beard belonged to his religion. The SS had forbidden it, but the man had kept on trying to let it grow. Each time in the labor camp he had been laid on the whipping block for it and given a hiding. In the Small camp he was luckier. Here the SS paid less attention to the rules and also checked up less frequently; they had too great a fear of lice, dysentery, typhoid and tuberculosis. The Pole, Julius Silber, had called the old man Ahasver because he had survived almost a dozen Dutch, Polish, Austrian and German concentration camps. Meanwhile Silber had died of typhoid and bloomed as a primrose plant in the garden of Commandant Neubauer, who received the ashes of the dead free of charge; but the name Ahasver had remained. The old man's face had shrunk in the Small camp, but the beard had grown and become the home and forest for generations of sturdy lice.

The room senior of the section was the former physician Dr. Ephraim Berger. He was important in the fight against death which closely surrounded the barrack. In winter when the skeletons had fallen on the slippery ice and broken their bones, he had been able to put on splints and save some of them. The hospital received no one from the Small camp; it existed only for those able to work and for prominent people. In the Big camp the ice in winter had also been less dangerous; during the worst days the road had been strewn with ashes from the crematorium, not out of consideration for the prisoners but to preserve the useful manpower. Since the incorporation of concentration camps into the general pooling of labor more importance had been attached to it. As compensation the prisoners of course had been worked to death faster. The losses didn't matter; every day enough new men were arrested.

Berger was one of the few prisoners who had permission to leave the Small camp. For several weeks he had been occupied in the crematorium's mortuary. In general, room seniors did not have to work, but there was a shortage of physicians; this was why he had been commandeered. It was to the advantage of the barrack; via the lazaret kapo, who had known Berger from earlier days, he could sometimes get some lysol, cotton wool, aspirin and similar things for the skeletons. He also possessed a bottle of iodine which he kept hidden under his straw.

The most important Veteran of all, though, was Leo Lebenthal. He had secret connections with the black market of the labor camp, and, so rumor had it, also with the outside. How he managed this no one exactly knew. It was known only that two whores from the establishment The Bat, which lay outside the town, belonged to it. Even an SS-man was supposed to be part of it; but of this no one really knew anything. And Lebenthal said nothing.

He traded in everything. Through him one could get cigarette ends, a carrot, sometimes potatoes, leftovers from the kitchen, a bone, and now and again a slice of bread. He didn't cheat anyone; he just kept things in circulation. The thought of secretly providing for himself never occurred to him. Trading kept him alive; not what he traded.

509 crawled through the door. The slanting sun behind him shone through his ears. For a moment they gleamed waxy and yellow on both sides of his dark head. "They have bombed the town," he said, panting.

No one answered. 509 could not yet see anything; after the light outside it was too dark in the barrack. He closed his eyes and opened them again. "They have bombed the town," he repeated. "Didn't you hear it?"

Again no one said anything. Now 509 saw Ahasver near the door. He sat on the floor and stroked the sheep dog. The sheep dog growled; he was afraid. Over his scarred face hung the matted hair and through it sparkled the frightened eyes. "A thunderstorm," murmured Ahasver. "Nothing but a thunderstorm! Quiet, wolf, quiet!"

509 crawled further into the barrack. He couldn't understand that the others were so apathetic. "Where's Berger?" he asked.

"Still in the crematorium."

He laid the coat and jacket on the floor. "Do none of you want to go out?"

He glanced at Westhof and Bucher. They didn't answer.

"You know it's forbidden," Ahasver finally said. "As long as the alarm is going."

"The alarm is over."

"Not yet."

"It is. The planes have gone. They have bombed the town."

"You've said that often enough," growled someone from the dark.

Ahasver glanced up. "Maybe they'll shoot a few dozen of us as punishment for it."

"Shoot?" Westhof coughed. "Since when do they shoot people here?"

The sheep dog barked. Ahasver held him tight. "In Holland they used to shoot ten to twenty political prisoners after an air raid. So they shouldn't get wrong ideas, they said."

"We are not in Holland here."

"I know that. All I said was that in Holland they shot people."

"Shoot!" Westhof snorted contemptuously. "Are you a soldier that you make such claims? Here they hang and club to death."

"They might shoot for a change."

"Keep your damned mouths shut," called the man from the dark.

509 squatted next to Bucher and closed his eyes. He still saw the smoke over the burning town and felt the hollow thunder of the explosions.

"D'you think we'll get any food tonight?" asked Ahasver.

"Damn it," answered the voice from the dark, "what else d'you want? First you want to be shot and then you ask for food."

"A Jew must have hope."

"Hope!" Westhof sniggered.

"What else?" asked Ahasver calmly.

Westhof gulped and suddenly began to sob. He had been stir-crazy for days.

509 opened his eyes. "Maybe they won't give us anything to eat tonight," he said. "To pay us out for the bombing."

"You with your damned bombing," shouted the man from the dark. "Do for God's sake shut up!"

"Has anyone still got something to eat?" asked Ahasver.

"Oh God!" The caller in the dark almost suffocated over this new idiocy.

Ahasver didn't pay any attention. "In Theresienstadt someone once had a piece of chocolate and didn't know it. He had hidden it when he was brought there, and forgot it. Milk chocolate from an automat. There was also a picture of Hindenburg in the wrapping."

"What else?" screamed the voice from the background. "A passport?"

"No, but we lived two days on the chocolate."

"Who's that screaming?" 509 asked Bucher.

"One of those who arrived yesterday. A new one. He'll soon stop."

Ahasver suddenly listened. "It's over—"

"What?"

"Outside. That was the All Clear. The last signal."

It suddenly became very quiet. Then steps could be heard. "Hide the sheep dog," whispered Bucher.

Ahasver pushed the madman between the bunks. "Lie down! Quiet!" He had trained him to obey commands. Had the SS found him, they would immediately have him syringed as a madman.

Bucher returned from the door. "It's Berger."

Dr. Ephraim Berger was a small man with sloping shoulders and an egg-shaped head which was completely bald. His eyes were inflamed and watered.

"The town is burning," he said, as he entered.

509 sat up. "What are they saying about it over there?"

"I don't know."

"Why not? You must have heard something."

"No," answered Berger, tired. "When the alarm came they stopped cremating."

"Why?"

"How could I know that? Orders. That's all."

"And the SS? Did you see any of them?"

"No."

Berger walked to the rear between the rows of boards. 509 followed him with his eyes. He had waited for Berger to speak to him and now he seemed as apathetic as the others. He didn't understand it. "Don't you want to go out?" he asked Bucher.

"No."

Bucher was twenty-five years old and had been seven years in the camp. His father had been editor of a Social Democratic newspaper; that had been enough to have the son locked up. If he ever gets out of here, thought 509, he can live another forty years. Forty or fifty. Whereas I'm fifty. I have maybe ten, at the most twenty years. He drew a piece of wood from his pocket and began to chew on it. Why am I suddenly thinking of that? he thought.

Berger returned. "Lohmann wants to speak to you, 509."

Lohmann lay in the rear section of the barrack on a lower bunk without straw. He had wanted it that way. He suffered from serious dysentery and could no longer get up. He thought it was cleaner that way. It wasn't cleaner. But they were all used to those things.

Almost everyone suffered more or less from diarrhea. For Lohmann it was torture. He lay on the point of death and apologized at each convulsion of his intestines. His face was so gray he could have been a bloodless Negro. He moved one hand and 509 bent over him. Lohmann's eyeballs shone yellowish. "D'you see this?" he whispered, and opened his mouth wide.

"What?" 509 looked at the blue gums.

"In back, on the right—there's a gold crown."

Lohmann turned his head in the direction of the narrow window. The sun stood behind it and the barrack on this side had now a weak, rosy light.

"Yes," said 509. "I see it." He did not see it.

"Take it out."

"What?"

"Take it out," whispered Lohmann impatiently.

509 glanced over towards Berger. Berger shook his head. "But it's fixed tight," said 509.

"Then pull the tooth out. That's not very tight. Berger can do it. He does it in the crematorium, too. The two of you can easily manage it."

"Why do you want to have it out?"

Lohmann's eyelids went slowly up and down. They looked like those of a turtle. They no longer had any lashes.

"You know why. Gold. You must buy food with it. Lebenthal can trade it."

509 didn't answer. To trade a gold crown was a dangerous job. As a rule gold fillings were registered on arrival in the camp and were later removed and collected in the crematorium. Whenever the SS noticed that a filling, registered in the lists, was missing, the whole barrack was made responsible. The inmates received no food until the filling was returned. The man on whom it was found was hanged.

"Pull it out!" panted Lohmann. "It's easy! Pliers! Or even a wire is enough."

"We haven't any pliers."

"A wire! Bend a piece of wire into shape."

"We haven't any wire, either."

Lohmann's eyes closed. He was exhausted. The lips moved, but no more words came. The body was motionless and very flat, and only the curling of the dark dry lips was still there—a tiny center of life into which quietness was already entering with a leaden flow.

509 raised himself and glanced at Berger. Lohmann could not see their faces; the boards of the upper bunks were between them.

"How is it going with him?"

"Too late for everything."

509 nodded. It had been so often like this that he no longer felt much. The slanting sun fell on five men who were crouching like withered monkeys on the top bunk. "Is he going to kick off soon?" asked one of them, scratching his armpit and yawning.

"Why?"

"We'll get his bunk, Kaiser and I."

"You'll get it all right."

509 glanced a moment into the hovering light which did not seem to belong to the stinking room. In this light the skin of the man who had asked the question looked like that of a leopard; it was sewn over with black spots. The man began to eat the rotten straw. A few bunks further on two men were quarreling in high thin voices. Feeble slappings were heard.

509 felt a slight pulling on his leg; Lohmann was plucking at his pants. He bent down again.

"Pull it out," Lohmann whispered.

509 sat down on the edge of the bunk. "We can't swap it for anything. It's too dangerous. No one will risk it."

Lohmann's mouth trembled. "They must not have it," he uttered with difficulty. "Not them! I paid forty-five marks for it. 1929. Not them! Pull it out!"

He suddenly doubled up and moaned. The skin of his face puckered up only around the eyes and the lips—elsewhere there were no muscles left to show pain.

After a while he stretched out. A pitiful sound came with the air pressed out of his chest. "Don't worry about it," Berger said to him. "We still have some water left. It doesn't matter. We'll get rid of it."

For a while Lohmann lay still. "Promise me you'll take it out—before they fetch me," he whispered. "When I'm gone. Then it'll be easy."

"All right," said 509. "Wasn't it registered when you arrived?"

"No. Promise me! For certain!"

"For certain."

Lohmann's eyes filmed over and grew calm. "What was that—just now—outside?"

"Bombing," said Berger. "The town has been bombed. For the first time. American planes."

"Oh—"

"Yes," said Berger, low and hard. "It's coming nearer! You'll be avenged, Lohmann."

509 glanced up quickly. Berger was still standing, and he could not see his face. He saw only his hands. They opened and closed as if strangling an invisible throat, letting it go and strangling it again.

Lohmann lay quiet. He had closed his eyes again and hardly breathed. 509 wasn't sure if he had still understood what Berger had said.

He got up. "Is he dead?" asked the man on the upper bunk. He was still scratching himself. The other four squatted by him like automatons. Their eyes were vacant.

"No."

509 turned toward Berger. "Why did you say that to him?"

"Why?" Berger's face twitched. "Because! Can't you understand that?"

The light veiled his egg-shaped head in a pink cloud. In the pestilential thick air it looked as though he were steaming. The eyes glittered. They were filled with water, but they were that way most of the time; they were chronically inflamed. 509 could imagine why Berger had said it. But what comfort was it for a dying man still to know that? It could as well make it even more difficult for him. He watched a fly settling on the slate-colored eye of one of the automatons. The man did not blink his lids. Perhaps it was a comfort after all, thought 509. Perhaps it was even the only comfort for a sinking man.

Berger turned round and pushed himself back along the narrow corridor. He had to climb over men lying on the ground. It looked as if a marabou were wading through a swamp. 509 followed him.

"Berger!" he whispered, as they left the corridor.

Berger stood still. 509 was suddenly out of breath. "Do you really believe it?"

"What?"

509 couldn't make up his mind to repeat it. It was as if it might then fly away. "What you said to Lohmann."

Berger looked at him. "No," he said.

"No?"

"No. I don't believe it."

"But—" 509 leaned against the nearest partition. "Then why did you say it?"

"I said it for Lohmann's sake. But I don't believe it. Nobody will be avenged, nobody—nobody—nobody."

"And the town? After all, the town's burning!"

"The town is burning. Many towns have burned already. That means nothing, nothing—"

"It does! It must—"

"Nothing, nothing," Berger whispered passionately with the despair of one who has had a fantastic hope and has immediately buried it again. The pale skull swayed to and fro and water ran out of the red eye sockets. "A small town is burning. What's that got to do with us? Nothing! Nothing will change. Nothing!"

"They'll shoot a few," said Ahasver from the floor.

"Shut up!" shouted the former voice from the dark. "Can't you for once keep your goddamned traps shut!"

509 crouched in his place near the wall. Above his head was one of the barrack's few windows. It was narrow and high up and at this hour had some sun. Then the light reached the third row of bunk boards; from there on the room lay in permanent darkness.

The barrack had been built only a year ago. 509 had helped to put it up; at that time he had still belonged to the labor camp. It was an old wooden barrack from a defunct concentration camp in Poland. One day four of them had arrived in parts at the town railroad station, had been carried on trucks to the camp where they had been put up. They had stunk of bedbugs, fear, dirt and death. Out of them the Small camp had grown. The next transport of disabled, dying prisoners from the East had been crammed into it and left to themselves. It took a few days before they could be shoveled out. Then more cripples, sick, broken-down and disabled men had been jammed into it and it had become a permanent institution.

The sun cast a distorted square of light on the wall to the right of the window. On it faded inscriptions and names became visible. They were inscriptions and names of former inmates of the barrack in Poland and Eastern Germany. They were scribbled on the wood in pencil or had been scratched in with wire ends and nails.

509 knew several of them. He knew that just now the corner of the square was lifting out of the dark a name that was framed by deep lines—Chaim Wolf, 1941. Chaim Wolf had probably written it when he knew that he had to die, and had drawn the lines around it so that no member of his family could be added to it. He had wanted to make it final so that he alone was it and would remain it. Chaim Wolf, 1941, the lines drawn tight and hard around it, so that no other name could be added to it any more; a last adjuration to fate from a father who hoped that his sons might be saved. But underneath, below the lines, close, as though they wanted to cling to it, stood two other names: Ruben Wolf and Moische Wolf. The first one upright, awkward, the writing of a schoolboy; the second slanting and smooth, resigned and without strength. Next to them another hand had written: ALL GASSED.

Diagonally underneath, above a knothole on the wall, was scratched with a nail: Jos. Meyer, and beside it: Lt.d.R. EK 1 & 2. It meant: Joseph Meyer, Lieutenant of the Reserve, owner of the Iron Cross, First and Second Class. Meyer had apparently not been able to forget this. It must have poisoned even his last days. He had been at the front in the first World War; he had been made an officer and received the distinctions; because he was a Jew he had to accomplish twice as much as anyone else. Later, again because he was a Jew, he had been imprisoned and exterminated like vermin. He had undoubtedly been convinced that the injustice done to him had been greater than that done to others because of his contributions in the war. He had been mistaken. He had only died harder. The injustice did not lie in the letters which he had added to his name. They were only a shabby irony.

The square made by the sun glided slowly on. Chaim, Ruben and Moische Wolf, whom it had only touched with one corner, disappeared again in darkness. Instead, two new inscriptions moved into the light. The one consisted of only two letters: F.M. He who had scratched it in with a nail had no longer thought as much of himself as had Lieutenant Meyer. Even his name had been almost a matter of indifference to him; nevertheless he had not wanted to succumb without leaving a sign. But under it a full name appeared again. There stood, written in pencil: Tevje Liebesch and family. And next to it, more hastily, the beginning of the Jewish Kaddish prayer: *Yis gadal—*

509 knew that in a few minutes the light would reach another blurred inscription: WRITE TO LEAH SAND—NEW YORK— The street was no longer legible, then came: FATH—and after a piece of rotten wood: DEAD. SEARCH FOR LEO. Leo seemed to have escaped; but the inscription had been made in vain. None of the many inmates of the barrack had ever been able to notify Leah Sanders in New York. No one had gotten out alive.

509 stared absent-mindedly at the wall. Silber, the Pole, while still lying in the barracks with bleeding intestines, had called it the Wailing Wall. He had also known most of the names by heart and in the beginning had even made bets as to which of them the spot of sun would reach first. Soon afterwards Silber had died; but on bright days the names had continued to wake to a ghostly life and then disappeared again into the dark. In summer when the sun stood higher others, scratched in lower down, became visible, and in winter the square moved higher up. But there were many more— Russian, Polish, Yiddish—which remained forever invisible because the light never reached them. The barrack had been put up so fast that the SS had not bothered to have the walls planed. The inmates bothered even less, least of all about the inscriptions on the dark sections of the walls. These no one even attempted to decipher. Nobody was foolish enough to sacrifice a precious match simply to grow more desperate.

509 turned away; he didn't want to see all that now. He felt suddenly alone—as if in some peculiar way the others had become estranged from him and they no longer understood one another. He still waited awhile; then he couldn't bear it any more. He groped his way to the door and crawled out again.

He was wearing now only his own rags and felt cold at once. Outside he rose to his feet, leaned against the barrack wall and looked down at the town. He wasn't quite sure why, but he no longer wanted to be on all fours; he wanted to stand. The guards on the watchtowers had not yet returned. The control on this side was never very strict; those who could hardly walk could not escape.

509 stood at the right-hand corner of the barrack. The camp was laid out in a curve which followed the range of the hills, and from here he could see not only the town but also the quarters of the SS troops. They lay outside the barbed wire behind a row of trees which were still bare. A number of SS-men were running to and fro in front of them. Others stood together in excited groups and gazed down at the town. A large gray automobile came fast up the mountain. It stopped in front of the Commandant's house which lay a short distance from the SS quarters. Neubauer already stood outside; he immediately got in and the car dashed off. From his days in the labor camp 509 knew that the Commandant owned a house in town where his family lived. His eyes followed the car so attentively that he did not see someone coming quietly along the path between the barracks. It was Handke, the block senior from Barrack 22, a squat man who always sneaked about in rubber soles. He wore the green triangular badge of the criminals and was in the camp for manslaughter. Most of the time he was harmless, but when he got his fits he had sometimes beaten people till they were cripples.

He came strolling along. 509 could still have tried to sneak out of his way—signs of fear usually satisfied Handke's simple need for superiority—but he didn't do it. He remained standing.

"What are you doing here?"

"Nothing."

"H'm, nothing." Handke spat in front of 509's feet. "You bedbug! Dreaming, eh?" His flaxen eyebrows went up. "Don't you get a swollen head! You won't get out of here! They'll send all you political dogs up the chimney first!"

He spat again and went away. 509 had held his breath. A dark curtain waved for a second behind his forehead. Handke couldn't stand him, and 509 usually avoided him. This time he had stood his ground. He watched him till he vanished behind the latrine. The threat did not frighten him; threats were daily fare in the camp. He thought only of what was behind the words. Handke must have sensed something too. Otherwise he wouldn't have said it. Maybe he had even heard it over at the SS. 509 turned round. So he was not such a fool after all.

He looked once more at the town. The smoke now lay close over the roofs. The sound of the fire brigade bells rose up thinly. From the direction of the railroad station came irregular crackling, as though ammunition were exploding. The camp Commandant's car took a curve down the mountain so fast that it skidded. 509 saw it and suddenly his face grew distorted. It screwed up into laughter. He laughed, laughed, noiselessly, convulsively, he couldn't remember when he had laughed last, he could not stop, and there was no joy in it, he laughed and looked carefully round and raised a feeble fist, clenched it and laughed, until a violent fit of coughing threw him down.

CHAPTER THREE

The Mercedes car shot down into the valley. *Obersturmbannführer* Neubauer sat next to the chauffeur. He was a heavy man with the bloated face of the beer drinker. The white gloves on his broad hands gleamed in the sun. He noticed it and took them off. Selma, he thought, Freya! The house! Nobody had answered the telephone. "Get on," he said. "Get on, Alfred! Drive on!"

In the suburbs they smelled the stench of fire. It smarted more and grew denser the further they went. Near the New Market they saw the first bomb crater. The savings bank had collapsed and was burning. The fire brigade had driven up and was trying to save the neighboring houses. But the jets of water seemed much too thin to have any effect. The crater on the Square stank of sulphur and acids. Neubauer's stomach contracted convulsively. "Drive through the Hakenstrasse, Alfred," he said. "We can't get through here."

The chauffeur turned. The car made a wide detour through the southern section of the town. Houses with small gardens lay here peacefully in the sun. The wind stood to the north and the air was clear. Then, as they crossed the river, the smell of burning returned and grew stronger until it lay in the streets like heavy fog in fall.

Neubauer tugged at his mustache which was clipped short like that of the Führer. At one time he had worn it twirled up like William II. This cramp in the stomach! Selma! Freya! The beautiful house! The whole belly, the chest, everything was stomach.

At last the car turned into the Liebigstrasse. Neubauer leaned out. There was the house! The front garden! There on the lawn stood the terra-cotta dwarf and the dachshund made of red china. Undamaged! All windows intact! The cramp in the stomach eased. He mounted the steps and opened the door. Lucky, he thought, damn lucky! So it should be! Why should anything happen just to him?

He hung his cap on the hat rack of antlers and entered the living room. "Selma! Freya! Where are you?"

No one answered. Neubauer strode to the window and pulled it open. In the garden behind the house two Russian prisoners were working. They glanced up quickly and then continued eagerly to dig.

"Hi, there! Bolsheviks!"

One of the Russians stopped working. "Where's my family?" shouted Neubauer.

The man answered something in Russian.

"Quit your swine language, idiot! You understand German! Or shall I come out and teach you?"

The Russians stared at him. "Your wife is in the cellar," said someone behind Neubauer.

He turned round. It was the servant girl. "In the cellar? Oh yes, of course. And where have you been?"

"Out there, just for a moment." The girl stood in the door, her face red and her eyes shining as though she had come from a wedding. "Already a hundred dead, they say," she began to babble. "At the station, and then in the copper foundry, and in the church—"

"Silence!" Neubauer interrupted her. "Who said that?"

"Out there, the people—"

"Who?" Neubauer took a step forward. "Such talk is hostile to the State! Who said that?"

The girl stepped back. "Out there—I didn't—someone—everyone—"

"Traitors! Brutes!" raved Neubauer. At last he could release the pent-up tension. "Skunks! Swine! Alarmists! And you? What were you doing out there?"

"I—nothing—"

"Slacking on the job, eh? Spreading lies and horror stories! We'll soon find that out! Measures must be taken here! Damn strong measures! March into the kitchen!"

The girl ran out. Neubauer breathed heavily and closed the window. Nothing has happened, he thought. They're in the cellar, of course. Might have thought of that before.

He pulled a cigar out of his pocket and lit it. Then he straightened his coat, threw out his chest, glanced in the mirror and went downstairs.

His wife and his daughter sat next to one another on a couch that stood against the wall. Above them hung a multicolored picture of the Führer in a wide gold frame.

Before the war the cellar had been turned into an air-raid shelter. It had steel girders, a concrete ceiling and massive walls; in those days Neubauer had had it built simply for show; it had been patriotic to set a good example in such matters. No one had seriously considered that Germany could be bombed. Marshal Goering's declaration that they could call him Meier if enemy planes ever brought off such a feat in the face of the Luftwaffe, had been enough for any honest German. Unfortunately it had turned out otherwise. A typical example of the treachery of the plutocrats and Jews; to pretend that they were weaker than they actually were.

"Bruno!" Selma Neubauer got up and began to sob.

She was blond and fat and wore a dressing gown of salmon-colored French silk with lace. In 1941 Neubauer had brought it back from a furlough in Paris. Her cheeks trembled and her too-small mouth chewed on words.

"It's over, Selma. Calm down."

"Over—" She continued to chew, as though the words were outsized Königsberger meatballs. "For how—how long?"

"For good. They're gone. The attack has been repulsed. They won't come back."

Selma Neubauer gathered her dressing gown tight over her breast. "Who says so, Bruno? How d'you know?"

"We have shot down at least half of them. They'll take good care not to come back."

"How d'you know?"

"I know. This time they surprised us. Next time we'll be properly on our guard."

The woman stopped chewing. "Is that all?" she asked. "Is that all you can tell us?"

Neubauer knew it was nothing. So he asked gruffly, "Isn't that enough?"

His wife stared at him. Her eyes were pale blue. "No!" she suddenly yelled. "That is not enough! That's nothing but twaddle! It means nothing! The number of stories we've heard already! First we're told we're so strong that no enemy plane could ever get into Germany, and suddenly there they are. Then it's said they won't come back because we'd shoot them all down at the border, and instead ten times as many come back and the alarm never stops. And now that they've finally caught us here, too, in you come full of yourself and say they won't come back, that we'll be sure to catch them! And you expect a sensible person to believe that?"

"Selma!" Involuntarily, Neubauer cast a glance at the picture of the Führer. Then he leapt to the door and banged it shut. "Damn it, pull yourself together!" he hissed. "D'you want to get us all into trouble? Have you gone crazy to yell so loud?"

He stood right in front of her. Above her fat shoulders the Führer continued to gaze steadfastly into the landscape of Berchtesgaden. For a moment Neubauer nearly believed he had been listening to everything.

Selma didn't see the Führer. "Crazy!" she screamed. "Who's

crazy? Not I! Before the war we had a wonderful life—and now? Now? I'd like to know who's crazy here?"

Neubauer seized her arms with both hands and shook her so that her head wobbled to and fro and she had to stop screaming. Her hair came loose, a few combs fell out, she swallowed the wrong way and coughed. He let her go. She fell like a sack onto the couch. "What's wrong with her?" he asked his daughter.

"Nothing much. Mother is very excited."

"Why? Nothing's happened."

"Nothing happened?" the woman began again. "Not to you up there, of course! But what about us alone down here—"

"Quiet! Damn it, not so loud! Have I been slaving fifteen years for you to ruin everything overnight with your yelling? Do you think there aren't already enough men waiting to snap up my job?"

"It was the first bombardment, Father," said Freya Neubauer calmly. "After all, up to now we've only had alarms. Mother'll get used to it in time."

"The first one? Of course the first one! We ought to be glad that so far nothing's happened, instead of yelling that nonsense."

"Mother's nervous. She'll get used to it."

"Nervous!" Neubauer was irritated by his daughter's calm. "Who's not nervous? D'you think I'm not nervous? We've got to control ourselves. What would happen if we didn't?"

"The same!" His wife laughed. She lay on the couch, her plump legs sprawling. Her feet were in pink silk slippers. She considered pink and silk to be very elegant. "Nervous! Get used to it! Easy for you to talk!"

"I? Why?"

"Nothing happens to you."

"What?"

"Nothing happens to you. But we're sitting here in a trap."

"That's blooming nonsense! The one's the same as the other. What d'you mean, nothing can happen to me?"

"You're safe, up there in your camp!"

"What?" Neubauer flung his cigar on the floor and trampled on it. "We've no cellar like you have here." It was a lie.

"Because you don't need one. You're outside the town."

"As if that made any difference! Where a bomb falls, there it falls."

"The camp won't be bombed."

"Really? That's a new one. How d'you know that? Have the Americans dropped a message about it? Or given you special information by radio?"

Neubauer glanced at his daughter. He expected approval of this joke. But Freya plucked at the fringes of a plush cloth which was spread over the table next to the couch. Instead, his wife answered. "They won't bomb their own people."

"Nonsense! We haven't any Americans there. No English, either. Only Russian, Poles, Balkan riffraff. And German enemies of the Fatherland—Jews, traitors and criminals."

"They won't bomb any Russians and Poles and Jews," explained Selma with blunt obstinacy.

Neubauer turned sharply round. "You seem to know a great deal," he said angrily under his breath. "But now I want to tell you something. They haven't the remotest idea what kind of camp that is up there, understand? All they can see is barracks. They can easily be taken for military barracks. They see buildings. These are our SS quarters. They see buildings with people working in them. For them they are factories and targets. Up there it's a hundred times more dangerous than here. That's why I didn't want you to live there. Down here there are no barracks and no factories. D'you understand for once?"

"No."

Neubauer stared at his wife. Selma had never been like this before. He didn't know what had gotten into her. That bit of fear alone couldn't be it. He felt suddenly deserted by his family; just when they should be standing together. Annoyed, he glanced again at his daughter. "And you," he said, "what do you think of it? Why don't you open your mouth?"

Freya Neubauer got up. She was twenty years old, thin, had a yellowish face, a jutting forehead, and resembled neither Selma nor her father. "I think Mother's calming down now," she said.

"What? Why?"

"I think she has calmed down."

Neubauer was silent for a while. He waited for his wife to say something. "All right, then," he finally declared.

"Can we go upstairs?" asked Freya.

Neubauer cast a suspicious glance at Selma. He didn't trust her yet. He had to make it clear that under no conditions should she talk to anyone. Not with the servant girl, either. Least of all with the girl. His daughter forestalled him. "Upstairs it'll be better, Father. More air."

He stood undecided. There she lies like a sack of flour, he thought. Why can't she say something sensible for once? "I've got to go over to the Town Hall. At six. Dietz phoned, the situation has to be discussed."

"Nothing will happen, Father. Everything's all right. We've also got to get dinner ready."

"All right, then." Neubauer had made up his mind. At least his daughter seemed to have kept her head. He could rely on her. His flesh and blood. He walked over to his wife. "All right, then. Let's forget all this now, Selma, eh? These things can happen. It's not really so important." He looked down at her, smiling, with cold eyes. "Eh?" he repeated.

She didn't answer.

He put his arms round her fat shoulders and fondled them. "Run along then and prepare dinner. And cook something good now that the shock is over, eh?"

She nodded listlessly.

"That's fine." Neubauer saw that it really was all over. His daughter had been right. Selma wouldn't talk any more nonsense. "Cook something specially good, children. After all, Selmachen, I'm doing it for you so you can have this beautiful house here with the safe cellar, instead of living up there near that dirty gang of thugs. And don't forget I always spend a few nights a week down here. We're all in the same boat. We must hold together. Now then, cook something tasty for supper. I trust you there. And what about bringing up a bottle of the French champagne? We still have enough of it, eh?"

"Yes," answered his wife. "Of that we still have enough."

→»› ‹«←

"Just one more thing," explained Group Leader Dietz snappily. "It has come to my ears that several gentlemen have voiced the intention of sending their families to the country. Is there something in it?"

No one answered.

"I cannot permit that. We officers of the SS must set an example. If we send our families out of town before a general order to evacuate has been given, it could be wrongly interpreted. Grumblers and alarmists would immediately jump on it. So I expect nothing of the kind to take place without my knowledge."

He stood slender and tall in his elegantly cut uniform in front of the group and gazed at them. Each man in the group looked determined and innocent. Almost all of them had considered sending their families away; but none of them betrayed it with so much as a glance. Each one thought the same: it's easy for Dietz to talk. He had no family in the town. He came from Saxony and his only ambition was to look like a Prussian officer in the Guards. That was simple. What didn't personally affect one could always be carried out with great courage.

"That is all, gentlemen," said Dietz. "Remember once more: our newest secret weapons are already in mass production. The V.1.'s are nothing in comparison, however effective they may be. London lies in ashes. England is being blasted all the time. New York's skyscrapers are heaps of rubble. We occupy the major ports of France. The invasion armies are having the greatest difficulties with reinforcements. The counteroffensive is going to sweep the enemy into the sea. It is in immediate preparation. We have accumulated powerful reserves. And our new weapons—I'm not allowed to say more about them—but I have it from the highest authority: victory is ours in three months. We've got to hold out that long." He stretched up his arm. "Back to work! Heil Hitler!"

"Heil Hitler!" thundered the group.

Neubauer left the Town Hall. About Russia he hadn't said a word, he thought. Nor about the Rhine. Least of all about the broken West Wall. Hold out—that's easy for him. He doesn't own anything. He's a fanatic. He hasn't an office building near the railroad station. He doesn't own shares in the Mellern newspaper. He doesn't even own any building ground. I have all that. Supposing it all goes up in the air—who'll give me anything for it?

Suddenly there were people in the street. The Square in front of the Town Hall was packed. On its steps a microphone was being installed. Dietz was going to speak. Smiling, unmoved, the stone faces of Charlemagne and Henry the Lion stared down from the façade. Neubauer climbed into the Mercedes. "To the Hermann Goeringstrasse, Alfred."

Neubauer's office building lay on the corner of the Hermann Goeringstrasse and the Friedrich's Allee. It was a large building with a fashion store on the street level. The two upper floors consisted of offices.

Neubauer had the car stopped and walked round the building. Two display windows were cracked; otherwise nothing was damaged. He looked up at the offices. They lay in the fog of fumes from the station; but nothing was burning. There could be a few cracked windowpanes there, too; but that was all.

He stood for a while. Two hundred thousand marks, he thought. It was worth at least that, if not more. He had paid five thousand for it. In 1933 it had belonged to the Jew, Max Blank. He had demanded a hundred thousand for it and had made a fuss and complained that he was losing enough on it as it was, and wouldn't let it go for less. After two weeks in the concentration camp he had sold it for five thousand. I have been decent, thought Neubauer. I could have got it for nothing. Blank would have made me a present of it after the SS had had their fun with him. I gave him five thousand marks. Good money. Not all at once, of course; at the time I didn't have that much. But I did pay it after the first rents came in. Blank was also satisfied with that. A legal sale. Of his own free will. Attested by the notary. The fact that Max Blank had accidentally fallen down in the camp, lost an eye, broken an arm, and otherwise hurt himself had been a regrettable incident. People with flat feet fell easily. Neubauer hadn't seen it. He hadn't even been present. He hadn't given any orders. He had only arranged to have Blank taken into protective custody, so that overzealous SS-men couldn't do him any harm. What happened after that had been Weber's business.

He turned round. Why was he suddenly thinking of this old story? What was the matter with him? All this had been forgotten long ago. One had to live. If he hadn't bought the house, then someone else in the Party would have done so. For less money. For nothing. He had acted legally. According to the law. The Führer himself had said that his faithful followers ought to be rewarded. And what was this trifle he, Bruno Neubauer, had gotten hold of compared to what the big shots were getting? Goering, for instance, or Springer, the Gauleiter who had risen from a hotel porter to a millionaire? Neubauer hadn't stolen anything. He had only bought cheap. He was covered. He had receipts. Everything was officially certified.

A flame shot up from the railroad station. Explosions followed. Probably ammunition wagons. Red reflections fluttered above the building—as if it were suddenly sweating blood. Ridiculous, thought Neubauer. I'm actually nervous. The Jewish lawyers who had been dragged out from up there at the time had been long ago forgotten. He got back into his car. Too close to the station—perfect place for business but damn dangerous in bombardments; no wonder it made one nervous.

"To the Grosse Strasse, Alfred."

The Mellern newspaper building was completely undamaged. Neubauer had already heard about it by telephone. They were just bringing out an extra edition. Copies were being snatched from the sellers' hands. Neubauer watched the white stacks disappear. One pfennig in every paper was his. New sellers arrived with new stacks. They dashed away on their bicycles. Extra editions meant extra income. Each seller had with him at least two hundred. Neubauer counted seventeen sellers. That meant thirty-four extra marks. At least something good to come out of it all. He could pay for some of the cracked show windows out of it. Nonsense—they were insured. That is, if the insurance paid. Could pay, with all the damage. They would pay! At least him. The thirty-four marks were net earnings.

He bought one of the extra papers. A short appeal by Dietz was already in it. Quick work. With it came a report that two flyers had been shot down over the town, half of the others over Minden, Osnabrueck and Hanover. An article by Goebbels about the inhuman barbarism of bombing peaceful German towns. A few pithy words from the Führer. A report that the Hitler Youth was in search of flyers who had dropped by parachute. Neubauer threw away the paper and entered the cigar store on the corner. "Three Deutsche Wacht," he said.

The salesman produced the box. Neubauer chose without interest. The cigars were bad. Pure beech leaves. He had better ones at home, imports from Paris and Holland. He asked for the Deutsche Wacht simply because the shop belonged to him. Before the Rising, it had belonged to Lesser & Sacht, a firm of Jewish exploiters. Then Storm Leader Freiberg had snapped it up. Had owned it until 1936. A gold mine. Neubauer bit the end off a Deutsche Wacht. What could he have done about the fact that Freiberg, in his cups, had made treasonable remarks against the Führer? It had been his duty as an upright Party member to notify the authorities. Shortly afterwards Freiberg had disappeared and Neubauer had bought the shop from the widow. He had advised her urgently to sell. He had let her know that he had information, that Freiberg's possessions were about to be confiscated. Money would be easier to hide than a shop. She had been grateful. Had sold the shop. For a quarter of its value, of course. Neubauer had pointed out that he wasn't flush and it had to be done fast. She had seen the point. The confiscation had never taken place. Neubauer had explained that to her, too. He had used his influence on her behalf. In this way she could keep the money. He had acted decently. Duty was duty—and the shop might really have been confiscated. Besides, the widow would have been unable to run it. She would have been squeezed out for less money.

Neubauer took the cigar from his mouth. It didn't draw. Filthy stuff. But the people paid for it. Were crazy about anything that could be smoked. Pity it was rationed. The turnover would have been ten times as much. He glanced once more at the shop. Damn lucky. Nothing had happened. He spat. He suddenly had a bad taste in his mouth. It must be the cigar. Or what else? After all, nothing had happened. Nerves? Why was he suddenly thinking of all these old stories? That old business from way back! He threw away the cigar as he got into the car again and gave the other two to the chauffeur. "Here, Alfred. Something special for tonight. And now let's be off—to the garden."

The garden was Neubauer's pride. It was a large plot of land on the outskirts of the town. Most of it was under vegetables and fruit; there was also a flower garden and a shed for livestock. A number of Russian slave laborers from the camp kept everything in order. They cost nothing and in fact should have paid Neubauer. Instead of working hard from twelve to fifteen hours in the copper foundry, with him they had fresh air and light work.

Dusk lay over the garden. On this side the sky was clear and the moon hung in the crowns of the apple trees. The freshly broken earth smelled strong. In the furrows sprouted the first vegetables and the fruit trees had sticky swelling buds. A small Japanese cherry tree which had spent the winter in the greenhouse was already sprayed over with a hue of white and pink—shy blossoms just opening.

The Russians were working in the section opposite to the plot. Neubauer saw their dark bent backs and the silhouette of the guard with his rifle, its fixed bayonet seemingly piercing the sky. The guard was there only because of regulations; the Russians didn't run away. Where could they have run to, anyhow, in their uniforms, without knowing the language? They had with them a large paper bag filled with ashes from the crematorium which they were strewing along the furrows. They were working in the beds of asparagus and strawberries for which Neubauer had a special predilection. He couldn't eat enough of them. The paper bag contained the ashes of sixty people, among them twelve children.

The first primroses and narcissus shimmered pale through the early, plum-colored dusk. They were planted along the south wall and covered with glass. Neubauer opened one of the horizontal windows and bent down. The narcissus did not smell. Instead, there was a scent of violets, invisible violets in the dusk.

He took a deep breath. This was his garden. He had paid for it himself and properly. Old-fashioned and honest. The full price. He hadn't taken it away from anyone. This was his place. The place where one became a human being after hard service for the Fatherland and concern for the family. He looked around, filled with satisfaction. He saw the arbor overgrown with honeysuckle and rambler roses, he saw the box hedge, he saw the artificial grotto of tufa stone, he saw the lilac bushes, he smelled the acrid air in which there was already a touch of spring, he felt with tender hand the straw-covered trunks of the peach and pear trees on the trellis work against the wall, and then he opened the door to the shed.

He didn't go to the chickens which were squatting like old women on the perch—nor did he go to the two young pigs which slept in the shed—he went to the rabbits.

They were white and gray Angora rabbits with long silky hair. They were asleep when he turned the light on and then they began slowly to move. He stuck a finger through the wire mesh and scratched their fur. They were softer than anything he knew. He took cabbage leaves and pieces of turnip from a basket and pushed them into the cages. The rabbits came over and began to nibble with pink snouts, gently and slowly. "Mucki!" he crooned. "Come here, Mucki—"

The warmth of the shed made him drowsy. It was like a faraway sleep. The smell of the animals brought with it a forgotten innocence. It was a small world in itself of almost vegetative life, far away from bombs and intrigues and the struggle for existence—cabbage leaves and turnips and furry mating and being shorn and giving birth. Neubauer sold the wool; but he never allowed an animal to be slaughtered. "Mucki!" he crooned again.

With gentle lips a great white buck took the leaf out of his hand. The red eyes gleamed like bright rubies. Neubauer stroked its neck. His boots creaked as he bent down. What did Selma say? Safe? There in the camp you are safe? Who was safe anyway? When had he ever really been?

He pushed more cabbage leaves through the wire mesh. Twelve years, he thought. Before the Revolution I was a post-office clerk with hardly two hundred marks a month. Could neither live nor die on it. Now I have something. I am not going to lose that again.

He looked into the buck's red eyes. Today everything had gone well. It would continue to go well. The bombing could have been a mistake. Such things happened with newly appointed formations. The town was unimportant; otherwise they would have tried to destroy it before. Neubauer felt himself growing calmer. "Mucki!" he said, and thought: Safe? Of course, safe! After all, who wants to pop off at the last moment?

CHAPTER FOUR

"Filthy swine! Count again!"

The labor gangs of the Big camp stood in columns of ten, according to blocks, in strict formation on the roll-call ground. It was already dark and the prisoners in their striped garb looked like an immense herd of dead-tired zebras.

The roll call had already lasted more than an hour, but it still didn't tally. It was due to the bombing. The labor gangs which worked in the copper foundry had suffered losses. One bomb had fallen into their division and a number of men had been killed and wounded. On top of this, after the first shock, the supervising SS-men had started firing on the prisoners who sought cover; they had feared they might escape. Thus a further half-dozen had perished.

After the bombing the prisoners had dragged out their dead from under the rubble and wreckage—or rather what was left of them. It was important for the roll call. Little as the life of a prisoner was valued and indifferent as the SS were to it, dead or alive the numbers at the roll call had to tally. Bureaucracy did not stop short at corpses.

The labor gangs had carefully taken along everything they could find; some had carried an arm, others legs and torn-off heads. The few stretchers they had managed to improvise had been used for the wounded whose limbs were missing or whose bellies had been ripped to pieces. The rest of the wounded had been supported and dragged along by their comrades as best they could. It had been possible to make only a few bandages; there had been hardly anything to make them with. Those bleeding to death had been tied off hastily with wire and cord. Those wounded in the stomach had to hold in their intestines with their own hands while lying on the stretchers.

The procession had climbed painfully up the mountain. Two more men had died on the way. They were dragged along dead. This led to an incident in which Squad Leader Steinbrenner had made rather a fool of himself. At the camp's entrance gate the band had been standing as usual playing the Fridericus Rex March. The march-past had been ordered and with eyes-right and legs thrown high the labor gangs had marched past SS Camp Leader Weber and his staff. Even the severely wounded on the stretchers had turned their heads to the right and tried to assume a somewhat more military posture while dying. Only the dead had no longer saluted. At this moment Steinbrenner had noticed how a man, while being lugged along by two others, had allowed his head to droop. He had not observed that the man's feet also trailed, but had promptly leapt into the line and hit him between the eyes with his revolver. He was young and eager and in his haste had assumed him merely to be unconscious. The dead man's head had been flung back by the blow and the lower jaw had fallen down; it had looked as though the bloody mouth, with a last grotesque movement of the skull, were snapping at the revolver. The other SS-men had roared with laughter and Steinbrenner had been furious; he had realized that some of the respect he had earned with the hydrochloric-acid cure on Joel Buchsbaum had been lost again.

The march up from the copper foundry had taken a long time and it was later than usual when the roll call began. According to custom, the dead and wounded had been laid out in strict military order, rank and file next to the block formations to which they belonged. Even the severely wounded had neither been taken to hospital nor had their wounds dressed; the roll call count was more important.

"Get on! Again! If it doesn't work this time you'll get assistance!"
Weber, the SS camp leader, sat astride a wooden chair which had been placed on the roll-call ground. He was thirty-five years old, of average height, and very powerfully built. His face was broad and brown, and a deep scar ran from the right corner of his mouth down across his chin—it was a souvenir of an indoor brawl with a Reichsbanner crowd in the year 1929. Weber had his arms propped on the back of his chair and stared with boredom at the prisoners among whom SS-men, block seniors and kapos ran excitedly to and fro, clubbing and shouting.

The block seniors sweated and gave the order to number again. The voices sounded monotonous: "One—two—three—"

The confusion arose as a result of those who had been torn to shreds in the copper foundry. The prisoners had collected heads, arms and trunks as best they could; but not everything had been found. No matter how they tried, it seemed that two men were missing.

In the twilight there had already been a battle between the labor gangs over the different limbs; especially, of course, over the heads. Each block wanted to be as complete as possible to avoid the severe penalties meted out for incomplete reports. They had snatched and fought over the bloody pieces until the command "Halt!" had sounded. In the general haste the block seniors had not been able to organize anything; as a result, two bodies had been missing. The bomb had probably smashed them to smithereens which had been blown over the walls or were lying in scraps on the roof of the copper foundry.

The report leader came over to Weber. "Now only one and a half are missing. The Russians had three legs for one man and the Poles one arm too many."

Weber yawned. "Call the names and make sure who is missing."

A barely perceptible swaying passed through the lines of prisoners. The name-calling meant that they would have to stand for another hour or two, if not longer—among the Russians and the Poles, who understood no German, errors involving their names continuously occurred.

The calling began. Voices fluttered up; then revilings and beatings were heard. The SS were irritated and started flogging because they were losing their free time. The kapos and block seniors flogged out of fear. Here and there men toppled over and black pools of blood spread slowly under the wounded. Their gray-white faces grew more pointed and gleamed deathly in the deep dusk. They glanced up resignedly at their comrades, who stood at attention, hands to their sides, and could not help those bleeding to death. For some, this forest of dirty zebra legs was the last they saw of the world.

The moon crept up behind the crematorium. The air was turbid, and the moon had a wide halo. For a while it stood immediately behind the chimney and its light shimmered above it so that it looked as if ghosts were being burned in the ovens and cold fire was flaring out of it. Then it slowly became more and more visible, and now the blunt chimney was a mine thrower firing a red ball straight into the sky.

In Block Thirteen's first column of ten stood the prisoner Goldstein. He was the last man on the left wing, and near him lay the block's wounded and dead. One of the wounded was Goldstein's friend Scheller. He lay close beside him. Out of the corner of his eye, Goldstein noticed that the black pool under Scheller's shattered leg was suddenly spreading much faster than before. The scanty bandage had come undone and Scheller was bleeding to death. Goldstein nudged his neighbor, Muenzer; then he let himself topple over sideways as if he had fainted. He arranged it so that he fell half across Scheller.

What he did was dangerous. The enraged SS block leader circled around the lines like a snapping police dog. One good kick of his heavy boot against the temple could finish Goldstein off. The prisoners at close quarters stood motionless; but everyone noticed what was happening.

Just now the block leader happened to be with the block senior at the other end of the group. The block senior was reporting something there. He, too, had noticed Goldstein's maneuver and tried to detain the squad leader for several moments.

Goldstein groped beneath him for the cord with which Scheller's leg had been tied off. Right in front of his eyes he saw the blood and smelled the raw flesh.

"Oh, leave it," Scheller whispered.

Goldstein found the knot which had slipped off and loosened it. The blood gushed stronger. "They'll finish me off with a syringe, anyhow," whispered Scheller. "With that leg—"

The leg hung from only a few sinews and scraps of skin. Goldstein's fall had changed its position and it lay there askew and strange with the foot twisted as though the leg had a third joint. Goldstein's hands were wet with blood. He pulled the knot tight but once more the cord slipped off. Scheller twitched. "Why don't you leave it—"

Goldstein had to untie the knot again. He felt the splintered bone against his fingers. His stomach rose. He swallowed, searched in the slippery flesh, found the cord again, moved it higher up and gasped. Muenzer had kicked his foot. It was a warning; the SS block leader came snorting up. "Another of these swine! Now what's wrong with this one?"

"Collapsed, Herr Squad Leader." The block senior was beside him. "Get up, you lazy bastard!" he shouted at Goldstein and kicked him in the ribs. The kick looked much harder than it was. At the last moment the block senior had put a break on it. He kicked once more. Thus he prevented the squad leader from doing it himself. Goldstein didn't move. Scheller's blood welled up against his face.

"Get on! Let him lie there!" The block leader passed on. "Damn it, when are we going to be through here?"

The block senior followed him. Goldstein waited a second; then he seized the cord round Scheller's leg, pulled it together, made a knot and tied the woolder, which had previously fallen loose, tightly into it again. The blood stopped gushing. Now it only trickled. Carefully Goldstein removed his hands. The bandage held fast.

The roll call was over. It had been agreed that three-quarters of one Russian and the upper half of the prisoner Sibolski from Barrack 5 were missing. This was not quite correct. Of Sibolski the arms existed. They were actually in the possession of Barrack 17, which had passed them off as the remains of Josef Binswanger of whom nothing had been recovered. In return, two men from Barrack 5 had stolen the lower half of the Russian which was passed off there as Sibolski, since it was difficult to distinguish between legs. Fortunately, apart from these, there were also a few odd remnants of limbs which could make up for the missing man and a quarter. Thus it was clear that none of the prisoners had escaped in the confusion of the bombardment. Nevertheless, it could have happened that everyone would have been kept standing on the roll-call ground until morning in order to continue the search for the remains in the copper foundry. Once, a few weeks ago, the camp had stood for two days until one man had been found who had committed suicide in the pigsty.

Weber sat calmly on his chair, his chin still supported by his hands. During the whole time he had hardly moved. After the report, he rose slowly and stretched.

"The men have stood long enough. They need movement. Practice geography!"

Commands resounded across the ground. "Clasp hands behind the head! Knees bend! Leapfrog! Forward—leap!"

The long lines obeyed. They leapt slowly forward with bent knees. Meanwhile the moon had risen higher and shone brighter. It now illuminated a section of the roll-call ground. The rest of it lay in the shadow thrown by the buildings. The contours of the crematorium, of the gate and even of the gallows were sharply outlined on the grounds.

"Leap back!"

The lines leapt back out of the light into the dark. Men toppled over. SS-men, kapos and block seniors beat them until they got up again. The yelling could hardly be heard above the scraping of the innumerable feet.

"Forward! Back! Forward! Back! Halt!"

Now began the real geography lesson. It consisted of the prisoners having to throw themselves down, crawl along the ground, jump up, throw themselves down again and go on crawling. In this manner they received a painfully exact knowledge of the earth on the dance ground. After a short while the ground was a mass of huge swarming striped maggots which seemed to have few human traits left. They protected the wounded as best they could; but in the haste and fear it was not always possible.

After a quarter of an hour Weber ordered a halt. But the quarter hour had wrought havoc among the exhausted prisoners. Everywhere men lay around who couldn't go on.

"Fall in line according to blocks!"

The men dragged themselves back. They fetched the ones who had broken down and between them supported those still able to stand. The others they laid down next to the wounded.

The camp stood still. Weber stepped forward. "What you have just been doing has taken place in your own interest. You have learned how to take cover during an air raid."

A few SS-men sniggered. Weber cast a glance across at them and continued: "Today you have learned in the flesh about the sort of inhuman enemy with whom we have to deal. Germany, who has always only desired peace, has been attacked in a brutal way. The enemy, who has been beaten all along the front, is resorting in his despair to extreme measures; he is violating all international law by bombing open, peaceful German towns in the most cowardly manner. He is destroying churches and hospitals. He is murdering helpless women and children. Nothing else could be expected from subhuman brutes and monsters. We shall not keep them waiting for an answer. Beginning tomorrow, the camp Command orders an increase in the performance of work. The labor gangs will march out one hour earlier in order to clear up. Until further notice there will be no more free time on Sundays. Jews will receive no bread for two days. For all this you can thank the enemy incendiaries."

Weber was silent. The camp did not move. Up the mountain

came the high humming of a powerful car, approaching fast. It was Neubauer's Mercedes.

"Sing!" Weber commanded. *"Deutschland, Deutschland über alles!"*

The blocks did not start at once. They were surprised. During recent months the order to sing had not often been given any more—and when it was, it had always been for folk songs. As a rule the command to sing was given when corporal punishment was under way. While the tortured men screamed, the other prisoners had to accompany them by singing lyrical songs. The old national anthem from pre-Nazi days had not been ordered for years.

"Start, you bastards!"

In Block 13, Muenzer began to sing. The others joined in. Those who no longer knew the words went through the motions. The main thing was that all mouths should keep moving.

"Why?" Muenzer whispered, after some time, without turning his head toward his neighbor Werner and yet giving the impression of continuing to sing.

"What?"

The melody turned into a thin squawking. They hadn't started in a low enough key and now the voices, unable to reach the high jubilating notes of the last line, broke off. Besides, the prisoners hadn't much breath left.

"What kind of filthy yelping is that?" shouted the second camp leader. "Start again from the beginning. If it doesn't work out this time, you'll stay here the whole night!"

The prisoners started in a lower key. Now the song went better.

"What?" Werner repeated.

"Why just *Deutschland, Deutschland über alles?*"

Werner screwed up his eyes. "Maybe they no longer trust—their own Nazi songs—after what happened today."

The prisoners stared straight ahead and sang. Werner sensed a strange tension rising in him, and he suddenly had the impression that he was not the only one to sense it—as if Muenzer also sensed it, as if Goldstein on the ground sensed it, as if many others sensed it, including even the SS. The song sounded suddenly different from the way the prisoners usually sang. It grew louder and almost defiantly ironical and the words had no longer anything to do with it. I hope Weber doesn't notice it, thought Werner, while he glanced at the camp leader—or we'll have even more dead than are lying there already.

Goldstein's face on the ground was close to that of Scheller. Scheller's lips were moving. Goldstein couldn't understand what he said; but he saw the half-open eyes and guessed what it was. "Nonsense!" he said. "We can count on the lazaret kapo. He'll wangle it. You'll pull through."

Scheller answered something. "Shut your trap!" Goldstein shouted back through the noise. "You'll pull through—that's that." In front of him he saw the gray porous skin. "They won't syringe you off!" he howled as text into the last bar of the anthem. "We can count on the lazaret kapo. He'll grease the doctor."

"Attention!"

The song broke off. The camp Commandant had arrived on the ground. Weber reported. "I've given these boys a short sermon and struck an extra hour's work on them."

Neubauer was uninterested. He sniffed the air and glanced up at the night sky. "Do you think the gangsters'll be coming back tonight?"

Weber grinned. "According to the last radio reports, we shot down ninety per cent."

Neubauer didn't find that funny. One more with nothing to lose, he thought. A little Dietz, a hireling, that's all. "Let the men break ranks when you're through," he suddenly declared, grumpy.

"Fall out!"

The blocks marched off to the barracks. They took with them their wounded and dead. Scheller's face was pointed like that of a dwarf when Werner, Muenzer and Goldstein picked him up. He looked as if he would not survive the night. During the geography practice Goldstein had received a kick in the nose. As he marched off it began to bleed. In the pale light the blood shone dark on his chin.

They turned into the road leading to their barracks. The wind, blowing up from the town, had increased and hit them square as they turned the corner. It brought up with it the smoke of the burning town.

The faces of the prisoners changed. "Do you smell it, too?" asked Werner after a while.

"Yes." Muenzer raised his head.

Goldstein felt the sweet taste of the blood on his lips. He spat and tried to taste the smoke with open mouth.

"It smells as if it were burning here too."

"Yes."

Now they could even see it. It blew up from the valley through the streets like a light white mist and soon it hung everywhere between the barracks. For a moment it struck Werner as strange and almost incomprehensible that the barbed wire did not keep it back—as though the camp were suddenly no longer so cut off and inaccessible as it had been before.

They walked down the road. They walked through the smoke. Their steps grew firmer and their shoulders straighter. They carried Scheller with great care. Goldstein bent low over him. "Smell it! Do smell it, too!" he said quietly, desperate and imploring, into the pointed face.

But Scheller had fainted long ago.

CHAPTER FIVE

The barrack was dark and stank. It was a long time since there had been any light in the evenings. "509," whispered Berger. "Lohmann wants to speak to you."

"Has it got that far?"

"Not yet."

509 groped along the narrow passages to the wooden partitions near which was outlined the dim square of the window. "Lohmann?"

Something rustled. "Is Berger there, too?" asked Lohmann.

"No."

"Get him."

"What for?"

"Get him!"

509 groped his way back. Curses followed him. He trod on bodies lying in the corridors. Someone bit him in the calf. 509 beat on the unknown head until the teeth let go.

After a few minutes he returned with Berger. "Here we are. What is it?"

"Here!" Lohmann stretched out his arm.

"What?" asked 509.

"Put your hand under mine. Flat. Careful."

509 felt Lohmann's thin fist. It was as dry as a lizard's skin. Slowly it opened. Something small and heavy fell into 509's hand. "Got it?"

"Yes. What is it? Is it—?"

"Yes," whispered Lohmann. "My tooth."

"What?" Berger shuffled nearer. "Who did it?"

Lohmann began to chuckle. It was an almost soundless, ghostlike chuckle. "I did."

"You? How?"

They felt the satisfaction of the dying man. He seemed childish and proud and deeply reassured. "Nail. Two hours. Small iron nail. Found it and bored the tooth loose with it."

"Where's the nail?"

Lohmann reached out beside him and handed it to Berger. Berger held it up to the window and then fingered it. "Filth and rust. Did it bleed?"

Lohmann chuckled again. "Berger," he said, "I can risk blood poisoning."

"Wait." Berger searched his pocket. "Has anyone a match?"

Matches were precious. "Not me," answered 509.

"Here," said someone from the center bunk.

Berger struck the box. The match flared up. Berger and 509 had kept their eyes closed so as not to be blinded. This way they could see for several seconds longer. "Open your mouth," said Berger.

Lohmann stared at him. "Don't be foolish," he whispered. "Sell the gold."

"Open your mouth."

Across Lohmann's face flitted something that could have been meant as a smile. "Let me alone. Good to have seen you once more in the light."

"I'm going to put iodine on it. I'll get the bottle."

Berger gave 509 the match and groped towards his bunk. "Lights out!" someone squawked.

"Shut up!" answered the man who had produced the match.

"Lights out!" squawked the other voice again. "D'you want the guards to mow us down?"

509 stood in such a way that his bent body was between the wall and the match. The man in the center bunk held his blanket against the window while 509 protected the little flame sideways with his jacket. Lohmann's eyes were very clear. They were too clear. 509 glanced at the stub of match that had not yet burned out, and then at Lohmann, and he thought how he had known Lohmann for seven years and he knew this was the last time that he would see him alive. He had seen too many such faces not to know it.

He felt the heat of the flame on his fingers, but he held it till he could no longer stand it. He heard Berger return. Then darkness was suddenly there, as though he had been struck blind. "Got another match?" he asked the man in the center bunk.

"Here—" The man gave him another. "The last one."

The last one, thought 509. Fifteen seconds of light. Fifteen seconds for the forty-five years that still were called Lohmann. The last ones.

The little flickering circle. "Lights out, damn it! Knock the light out of his hand."

"Idiot! No swine can see anything!"

509 held the match lower. Berger stood close to him, the bottle of iodine in his hand. "Open your mouth—"

He stopped. Now he too saw Lohmann clearly. There had been no point in getting the iodine. He had really fetched it only in order to be doing something. He put the bottle slowly into his pocket. Lohmann looked calmly at him without blinking. 509 glanced away. He opened his hand and saw gleaming in it the little lump of gold. Then he glanced again at Lohmann. The flame scorched his fingers. From the side a shadow struck at his arm. The light went out.

"Good night, Lohmann," said 509.

"I'll be back again later," said Berger.

"Just leave me," whispered Lohmann. "This now—is easy—"

"Maybe we'll find a few more matches."

Lohmann didn't answer any more.

→»> «<-

509 felt the gold crown hard and heavy in his hand. "Come out," he whispered to Berger. "We better talk it over outside. We're alone there."

They groped their way to the door and went to the side of the barrack that was protected against the wind. The town was blacked out and the fires to a large extent extinguished. Only the tower of St. Catherine's church still burned like a gigantic torch. It was very old and full of dry timber; the fire-brigade hoses were powerless against it; there was nothing to be done but to let it burn itself out.

They squatted down. "What'll we do?" asked 509.

Berger rubbed his inflamed eyes. "If the crown is registered in the office, we're lost. They'll investigate and hang a few of us—me first."

"He says it wasn't registered. When he arrived, they hadn't started that here. He's been in the camp seven years. At that time gold teeth were knocked out, but not registered. That came later."

"Are you sure of that?"

509 shrugged his shoulders.

They were silent for a while. "Of course we can still tell the truth and hand over the crown. Or stick it in his mouth when he's dead," explained 509 at last. His hand closed tightly round the little lump. "You want to do that?"

Berger shook his head. That gold was life for several days. Both knew that now they had it, they wouldn't give it up.

"Couldn't he have broken the tooth out years ago and sold it himself?" asked 509.

"Do you think the SS would fall for that?"

"No. Certainly not if they discovered the fresh wound in his mouth."

"That's the least worry. If he holds out a bit longer, the wound will heal. Besides, it's a molar in the back; that makes checking more difficult, if the corpse is already stiff. If he dies this evening, he'll be that far by the morning. If he dies early tomorrow we'll have to keep him here till he's stiff. That should work. We can fool Handke at the morning roll call."

509 looked at Berger. "We've got to risk it. We need the money. Especially now."

"Yes. There's nothing else left for us to do. Who's going to get rid of the tooth?"

"Lebenthal. He's the only one who can do it."

Behind them the barrack door opened. A few men dragged out a figure by its arms and legs and lugged it to a heap beside the road. Here lay the dead who had died since the evening roll call.

"Is that Lohmann already?"

"No. Those aren't our people. They're Mussulmen."

The men who had dropped the dead staggered back to the barrack.

"Did anyone notice that we got the tooth?" asked Berger.

"I don't think so. They're almost all Mussulmen lying there. The only chance is the man who gave us the match."

"Did he say anything?"

"No. Not yet. But he can always come and ask for his share."

"That's our least worry. The question is if he considers it a better business to betray us."

509 thought for a while. He knew there were people capable of doing anything for a crust of bread. "He didn't look like it," he said finally. "Why else would he have given us the match?"

"That hasn't anything to do with it. We must be careful. Otherwise, we're both done for. And Lebenthal as well."

509 knew that too, well enough. He had seen many a man hang for less. "We must watch him," he declared. "At least until Lohmann is cremated and Lebenthal has got rid of the tooth. After that he won't be able to do anything."

Berger nodded. "I'll go in again. Maybe I'll find out something."

"Okay. I'll stay here and wait for Leo. He must still be in the labor camp."

Berger got up and went over to the barrack. He and 509 would have risked their lives without hesitating if anything could have saved Lohmann. But he could not be saved. So they talked about him as about a stone. The years in the camp had taught them to think realistically.

509 crouched in the shadow of the latrine. It was a good place; here no one paid any attention to him. For all the barracks together

the Small camp had only one large communal latrine which was built on the boundary between the two camps and to which an endless procession of skeletons, continuously moaning, shuffled to and from the barracks. Practically everyone had diarrhea or worse and many lay around in a state of collapse, waiting until they had once more gathered sufficient strength to stumble on. From both sides of the latrine ran the barbed-wire fence separating the Small camp from the labor camp.

509 crouched in such a way that he could watch the gate which had been cut into the barbed wire. It was there for the SS block leaders, the block seniors, the corpse carriers and the hearses. Berger was the only one in Barrack 22 allowed to use it when he went to the crematorium. To all others it was strictly forbidden. The Pole, Silber, had called it the croak-gate because the prisoners committed to the Small camp returned through it only as corpses. Any guard was allowed to fire at a skeleton trying to get into the labor camp. Almost no one tried it. Nor from the labor camp did anyone cross over except those on duty. The Small camp was not only under a moderate quarantine; it was also generally considered hopeless by the other prisoners and regarded merely as a kind of cemetery in which for a short while the dead still staggered about.

Through the barbed wire 509 could see a part of the labor camp's roads. They teemed with prisoners making the most of what was left of their free time. He watched them talking to one another, standing together in groups and wandering along the roads—and although it was just another section of the concentration camp, it seemed to him as though he were separated from them by an unbridgeable gulf and as though over there were something like a lost home in which life and comradeship still existed. Behind him he heard the soft shuffling of the prisoners staggering to the latrine and he didn't need to glance around to see their dead eyes. They hardly spoke any more; at most they moaned or squabbled in weary voices; they didn't think any longer; camp humor dubbed them Mussulmen because they were utterly resigned to their fate. They moved like automatons and no longer had any will of their own; save for a few physical functions everything in them was extinct. They were living corpses and died like flies in frost. The Small camp was full of them.

They were broken and lost and nothing could save them—not even freedom.

509 felt the coolness of the night deep in his bones. The murmuring and moaning behind him was like a gray flood in which one could drown. It was the temptation to surrender the self—the temptation against which the Veterans desperately fought. 509 moved his shoulders involuntarily and turned his head so as to feel he was still alive and had a will of his own. Then he heard the final whistle in the labor camp. The barracks there had their own latrines and were locked up at night. The groups on the roads broke up. The men disappeared. In less than a minute everything over there was empty, and only the cheerless procession of the shadows in the Small camp remained—forgotten by the comrades on the other side of the barbed wire; written off, isolated—a remnant of lost trembling life in the territory of certain death.

Lebenthal did not come through the gate. 509 saw him suddenly walk diagonally in front of him across the ground. He must have entered from somewhere behind the latrine. No one knew how he smuggled himself through; it wouldn't have surprised 509 if he had used a foreman's armband or even that of a kapo for the purpose.

"Leo!"

Lebenthal stood still. "What's happening? Look out! The SS are still over there. Come away from here."

They went over to the barrack. "Did you get something?" asked 509.

"What?"

"Food. What else?"

Lebenthal raised his shoulders. "Food! What else!" he repeated irritably. "What d'you think? Am I the kitchen kapo?"

"No."

"Well! What d'you want from me, then?"

"Nothing. I merely asked if you got hold of something to eat."

Lebenthal stood still. "Food," he said bitterly. "Do you know that every Jew in the camp is to have two breadless days? Weber's orders."

509 stared at him. "Is that a fact?"

"No. I made it up. I always invent things like that. It's funny."

"My God! That'll make corpses!"

"Sure. Heaps. And you still want to know if I got some food—"

"Be quiet, Leo. Sit down here. This is a bloody story. Just now! Now, when we need all the grub we can lay our hands on!"

"Do we? So perhaps it's all my fault, eh?" Lebenthal began to tremble. He always trembled when excited, and he got easily excited; he was very touchy. With him it meant about as much as drumming one's fingers on the table would mean with another. It came from the permanent hunger. It magnified and diminished all emotions. In the camp, hysteria and apathy were twins.

"I've done what I could," wailed Lebenthal softly in a high breaking voice. "I've lugged things along and taken chances and provided, and now you come and declare we need—"

His voice drowned suddenly in a boggy, incomprehensible gargle. It sounded as though one of the camp's loudspeakers had broken down. Lebenthal's hands fumbled over the ground. Now his face looked no longer like an offended skull; it was merely a forehead with a nose and frog-eyes and underneath a lot of flabby skin with a hole in it. At last he found his false teeth on the ground, wiped them on his jacket and pushed them into his mouth. The loudspeaker was working again and the voice was back, high and wailing.

509 let him wail without listening. Lebenthal noticed it and stopped. "We've often had breadless days," he said feebly at last. "And more than two at a time. What's the matter with you that you're making such a fuss about it today?"

509 looked at him for a while. Then he pointed at the town and the burning church. "What's the matter? That there, Leo—"

"What?"

"That down there. What was that in the Old Testament?"

"What have you got to do with the Old Testament?"

"Wasn't there something like this in the time of Moses? A pillar of fire that led the people out of slavery?"

Lebenthal blinked his eyes. "A cloud of smoke by day and a pillar of fire by night," he said without wailing. "Is that what you mean?"

"Yes. And wasn't God in it?"

"Jehovah."

"All right, Jehovah. And that down there—you know what that is?" 509 waited a moment. Then he said: "It's a little something like that. It's hope, Leo, hope for us! Damn it, can't any of you see that?"

Lebenthal didn't answer. He sat shrunk into himself and gazed down at the town. 509 let himself sink back. At last, for the first time, he had pronounced it. One can hardly say it, he thought, it almost kills one, it's such an enormous word. I've avoided it throughout all these years; it would have eaten me up had I thought it—but now today it has returned, one doesn't yet dare to think it quite out, but it is there, and now it will either shatter me or come true.

"Leo," he said. "That down there means that this here will also go smash."

Lebenthal moved. "If they lose the war," he whispered. "Only then! But who can know that?" Automatically he glanced around in fear.

During the first years the camp had been fairly well informed about the course of the war. Later, however, when victories ceased, Neubauer had forbidden the bringing in of newspapers and the reporting over the camp radio of news concerning the retreat. Since then the wildest rumors had spread through the barracks until finally no one any longer knew what really to believe. The war was going badly, that everyone knew; but the revolution, for which many had been waiting for years, had never come.

"Leo," said 509. "They're losing it. It's the end. If that down there had happened during the first year, it wouldn't have meant anything. That it's happening now, after five years, means that the others are winning."

Lebenthal glanced back again. "Why are you talking about it?"

509 was aware of the superstition of the barracks. What was said aloud lost in certainty and power, and a disappointed hope was always a serious loss in energy. This was also the reason for the caution of the others.

"I'm talking about it because now we've got to talk about it," he said. "The time for it has come. Now it'll help us to pull through. This time it's no latrine password. It can't last much longer. We must—" He stopped.

"What?" asked Lebenthal.

509 was not sure himself. Pull through, he thought. Pull through and even more. "It's a race," he said finally. "A race, Leo, with—" With death, he thought; but he didn't say it aloud. He pointed in the direction of the SS quarters. "With them over there! We can't afford to lose now. The end's in sight, Leo." He seized Lebenthal's arm. "Now we've got to do everything—"

"But what can we do?"

509 felt his head swim as though he had been drinking. He was no longer accustomed to think or speak much. And for a long time he hadn't thought as much as today. "Here's something," he said, and produced the gold tooth from his pocket. "From Lohmann. Probably not registered. Can we sell it?"

Lebenthal weighed the lump in his hand. He didn't show any surprise. "Dangerous. Can be done only through someone who can leave the camp or has connection with the outside."

"How, doesn't matter. What can we get for it? It must be done fast."

"It can't be done so fast. A thing like this must be carefully figured out. That requires brains, otherwise we're on the gallows or it's gone without a penny."

"Can't you still do it tonight?"

Lebenthal let the hand with the tooth drop. "509," he said, "yesterday you were still reasonable."

"Yesterday is long ago."

A crash came up from the town and immediately afterwards a clear reverberating sound of a bell. The fire had eaten through the beams of the church tower and the bell had collapsed.

Lebenthal had ducked in terror. "What was that?" he asked.

"A sign." 509 drew in his lips. "A sign, Leo, that yesterday is long ago."

"It was a bell, wasn't it? Why was it never melted into cannons?"

"I don't know. Maybe they've forgotten it. Now how about tonight? We need grub for the breadless days."

"It can't be done tonight. Today's Thursday. Community evening in the SS quarters."

"I see. Today the whores come?"

Lebenthal looked up. "So you knew that? How?"

"That's neither here nor there. I know it, Berger knows it, Bucher knows it and Ahasver knows it."

"Who else?"

"No one."

"So you all know that! I hadn't realized you'd been watching me. Must be more careful. Okay, that's what's going to happen tonight."

"Leo," said 509. "Try to get rid of the tooth tonight. That's more important. This other I can do for you. Give me the money; I know my way about. It's simple."

"You know how it's done?"

"Yes, from the pit—"

Lebenthal reflected. Then he said: "There's somebody in the truck column. Tomorrow he's driving into town. I could try and see if he bites. Okay. I will. And maybe I'll be back in time to do this business here myself."

He held the tooth out to 509.

"What'll I do with it?" asked 509, surprised. "Mustn't you take it with you?"

Lebenthal shook his head with slight contempt. "Now we see what you know about business! D'you imagine I'd get anything for it once one of those brothers got his paws on it? It's not done that way. If all goes well I'll come back and fetch it. Meanwhile you hide it. And now listen—"

509 lay in a hollow in the ground a short distance from the barbed wire. Here the palisades made a turn and the spot could not easily be seen from the machine-gun towers—even less at night and in fog. The Veterans had discovered this long ago, but only Lebenthal, several weeks back, had managed to make capital out of it.

The entire territory for several hundred yards outside the camp was a forbidden zone which could be entered only by special permission from the SS. A broad strip of it had been cleared of all underbrush and the range of the machine guns was adjusted to it.

Lebenthal, who had a sixth sense for everything connected with food, had observed that on Thursday evenings during the last few months, two girls took the wide part of the road leading past the Small camp. They belonged to The Bat, a low dive lying outside the town, and came as guests to the informal parties on the SS cultural evenings. The SS had gallantly permitted them to pass through the forbidden zone; in this way they were spared a detour of almost two hours. During the short time it took them to pass through the zone the electric current alongside the Small camp was turned off as a precaution. The camp administration knew nothing about it; the SS-men, during the general confusion of the last months, had done this on their own hook. They didn't risk anything; no one in the Small camp was capable of escaping.

In a fit of kindheartedness one of the whores had once thrown a piece of bread through the wire as Lebenthal happened to be nearby. A few words whispered in the dark and the offer to pay had been sufficient—since that day the girls had sometimes brought something with them, especially when the weather was rainy or foggy. They threw it through the wire while pretending to fix their stockings or shake sand out of their shoes. The camp was completely blacked out and on this side the guards were often asleep, but even should a guard have grown suspicious, he would not have fired at the girls and by the time someone had arrived to investigate, all traces would long ago have vanished.

509 heard the crash as the bell tower in the town collapsed. A sheath of fire shot up and was blown away. Then came the distant signals of the fire brigade.

He wasn't sure how long he had waited; in the camp, time was a meaningless concept. But suddenly through the uneasy dark he heard voices and then steps. From under Lebenthal's coat he crept out closer to the wire and listened. They were light steps coming from the left. He looked back; the camp was very dark and he could no longer see even the Mussulmen tottering to the latrine. Instead, he heard one of the guards call after the girls, "Going to be relieved at twelve. Meet you then, eh?"

"Sure, Arthur."

The steps came closer. It still took some time before 509 could recognize the vague outlines of the girls against the sky. He looked over to the machine-gun towers. It was so turbid and dark that he couldn't see the guards—nor they him. Cautiously he began to hiss.

The girls stood still. "Where are you?" whispered one of them.

509 raised one arm and beckoned.

"Oh, there! Got the money?"

"Sure. What have you got?"

"First hand over the dough. Three marks."

With a long stick Lebenthal had pushed the money in a bag with a string attached under the barbed wire onto the road. One of the girls bent down, took out the money and quickly counted it. Then she said, "Here! Look out!"

Both of them took potatoes from their coat pockets and flung them through the wire. 509 tried to catch them in Lebenthal's coat.

"Now comes the bread," said the fatter girl.

509 watched the slices sail through the wire. He gathered them quickly together.

"Well, that's all!" The girls were about to move on.

509 hissed.

"What?" asked the fatter one.

"Can you bring more?"

"Next week."

"No. When you come back from the SS quarters. They surely give you what you want there."

"Are you the same one as usual?" asked the fatter girl, bending forward.

"They all look the same, Fritzi," said the other.

"I can wait here," whispered 509. "I've still got some money."

"How much?"

"Three."

"We must be off, Fritzi," said the other girl. All this time she had been feigning steps on the spot so that the guards shouldn't hear that the two of them were not walking on.

"I can wait all night. Five marks."

"You're a new one, what?" asked Fritzi. "Where's the other? Dead?"

"Sick. He sent me here. Five marks. Maybe even more."

"Come on, Fritzi. We can't go on standing here."

"Okay. We'll see. You can wait here for all I care."

The girls went on. 509 heard their skirts rustle. He crawled back, dragged the coat after him and lay down exhausted. He had the sensation of sweating, but he was quite dry.

As he turned round, he saw Lebenthal. "Did it work?" asked Leo.

"Yes. The potatoes here and the bread."

Lebenthal bent down. "Those beasts," he said. "What bloodsuckers! Those prices are almost as bad as here in the camp! One mark fifty would have been enough. For three marks there ought to have been sausage as well. That's what happens when you don't do things yourself!"

509 wasn't listening. "Let's divide it, Leo," he said.

They crawled behind the barrack and sorted out the potatoes and bread. "I need the potatoes," said Lebenthal. "For trading tomorrow."

"No. We now need everything ourselves."

Lebenthal glanced up. "So? And where am I to get money for the next time?"

"Surely you have some left."

"The things you don't know!"

They suddenly crouched opposite one another on all fours like animals and gazed into each other's sunken faces.

"They'll come back tonight and bring more," said 509. "Stuff from over there which will be easier for you to trade. I told them we still have five marks."

"Listen—" began Lebenthal. Then he shrugged his shoulders. "If you have the cash it's your business."

509 stared at him. At last Lebenthal looked away and let himself sink onto his elbows. "You're ruining me," he wailed softly. "What do you really want? Why are you suddenly meddling into everything?"

509 resisted the overwhelming greed to stuff a potato in his mouth and then another, quickly, all of them, before anyone could prevent him. "How d'you imagine the whole thing?" Lebenthal continued to whisper. "Bolt everything down, spend the money like idiots—how are we to get any more?"

The potatoes. 509 smelled them. The bread. Suddenly his hands would no longer obey his thoughts. His stomach was nothing but greed. Eating! Eating! Wolfing! Quick, quick! "We have the tooth," he said with difficulty, and turned his head away. "What about the tooth? We'll surely get something for it. What about it?"

"There wasn't much doing today. That takes time. Isn't certain, either. One has only what one holds in one's hand."

Isn't he hungry? thought 509. What's he saying? Isn't it tearing his stomach to pieces? "Leo," he said with a thick tongue. "Think of Lohmann. When we've got that far, it'll be too late. Now each day counts. We no longer have to think for months ahead."

From the direction of the women's camp came a thin high scream —as from a frightened bird. A Mussulman stood there on one leg, stretching his arms towards the sky. A second one was trying to hold him up. It looked as though these two were dancing a grotesque *pas de deux* against the horizon. An instant later they toppled to the ground like dry timber and the screaming ceased.

509 turned back again. "When we're like them, nothing will help us any longer. Then we're through forever. We've got to resist, Leo—"

"Resist—how?"

"Resist," said 509 more calmly. The attack had passed. He could see again. The smell of the bread no longer blinded him. He brought his head near to Lebenthal's ear. "For afterwards," he said almost without sound. "To avenge ourselves—"

Lebenthal shrank back. "I don't want to have anything to do with that."

509 smiled feebly. "You won't have to, either. You just see to the grub."

Lebenthal fell silent for a while. Then he groped in his pocket, counted some coins close before his eyes and gave them to 509. "Here are three marks. The last. Now are you satisfied?"

509 took the money without answering.

Lebenthal sorted out the bread and potatoes.

"Twelve lots. Damn little for each." He began counting them out.

"Eleven. Lohmann doesn't want any more. Doesn't need it any more, either."

"Okay. Eleven."

"Take it inside to Berger, Leo. They're waiting."

"Yes. Here's yours. Are you going to stay here till the two of them come back?"

"Yes."

"You've still time. They won't come before one or two."

"That's okay. I'll stay here."

Lebenthal shrugged his shoulders. "If they bring no more than before, there's no point whatever in your waiting. For that much I can even get something in the Big camp. Outrageous prices, the beasts!"

"Yes, Leo. I'll see that I get more."

509 crawled back under the coat. He felt cold. He still held the potatoes and the piece of bread in his hand. He stuck the bread in his pocket. I won't eat anything tonight, he thought. I will wait until tomorrow. If I can do that, then—he didn't know what would happen then. Something. Something important. He tried to think it out. He couldn't. He still held the potatoes in his hand. A big one and a very small one. They were too strong. He ate them. He devoured the small one at one gulp, the big one he chewed and chewed. He hadn't expected his hunger to become worse afterwards. He should have known it. It always happened, but one never believed it. He licked his fingers and then bit into his hand to keep it from the bread in his pocket. I don't want to bolt down the bread immediately as I did before, he thought. I won't eat it until tomorrow. This evening I won out against Lebenthal. I half convinced him. He didn't want to; but he gave me three marks. I'm not done in yet. I still have a will. If I can hold out with the bread until tomorrow—he felt as though black rain were dripping in his head—then—he clenched his fists and stared at the burning church—there it was at last—then I'm not an animal. Not a Mussulman. Not merely a wolfing machine. Then I have, it is—once more came the weakness, the greed—it is—I told Lebenthal just now, but then I hadn't any bread in my pocket—to talk is easy—it is—resistance—it is—to become a human being again—a beginning—

CHAPTER SIX

Neubauer sat in his office. Opposite him sat the surgeon-major Wiese, a small monkeylike man with freckles and a straggly reddish mustache.

Neubauer was in a bad mood. He was having one of those days when everything seemed to go wrong. The news in the papers had been more than cautious; at home Selma had grumbled around; Freya had crept through the house with red eyes; two lawyers had given up their offices in his business building—and now on top of all that came this lousy pillmonger with his requests.

"How many men do you want, then?" he asked, sulkily.

"Six will be enough for the time being. Physically rather run down."

Wiese did not belong to the camp. He owned a small hospital outside the town and had the ambition to be a man of science.

Like some other physicians he made experiments on living human beings, and several times the camp had put prisoners at his disposal for this purpose. He had been on friendly terms with the former gauleiter of the province and for this reason no one had asked many questions as to what the men were to be used for. Later on the corpses had always been duly handed over to the crematorium; this had been sufficient.

"And you need the men for clinical experiments?" asked Neubauer.

"Yes. Experiments for the army. Secret, for the moment, of course." Wiese smiled. The teeth under his mustache were surprisingly large.

"So, secret—" Neubauer breathed heavily. He couldn't stand these superior academicians. They meddled into everything and supplanted the old fighters with their pomposity. "You can have as many as you want," he said. "We're only too glad if these men can be made some use of. All we need for it here is an order of assignment."

Wiese looked up surprised. "An order of assignment?"

"Certainly. An order of assignment from my superior board."

"But why—I don't understand that—"

Neubauer suppressed his satisfaction. He had expected Wiese's surprise. "I really don't understand—" said the surgeon-major once more. "Up to now I've never needed such a thing!"

Neubauer knew this. Wiese had not needed it because he had known the gauleiter. Meanwhile, however, the gauleiter had been sent to the front on account of some unsavory affair; this now gave Neubauer a welcome opportunity to make difficulties for the surgeon-major.

"The whole thing is purely a matter of form," he explained affably. "If the army proposes an assignment for you, you'll get them without any further trouble."

Wiese had little interest in that; he had used the army merely as a pretext. Neubauer knew this, too. Wiese tugged nervously at his mustache. "I don't understand all this. Up to now I always got men without any difficulty."

"For experiments? From me?"

"From the camp here."

"There must have been a mistake." Neubauer seized the telephone. "I'll just make inquiries."

He didn't need to; he knew all about it. After a few questions he put down the receiver. "Exactly as I expected, Herr Doctor. You formerly requested men for light work and got them. Our labor board does such things without formalities. Every day we supply dozens of factories with labor gangs. In this case the men remain under the supervision of the camp. Your case today is different. Now you are demanding them for clinical experiments. That makes an assignment necessary. In this case the men leave the camp officially. For that I need an order."

Wiese wagged his head. "But surely that comes to the same thing," he declared irritably. "The men were used for experiments as much before as now."

"Of that I know nothing." Neubauer leaned back. "I know only what the documents state. And I think it's better to leave it at that. You doubtless have no interest in drawing the attention of the authorities to such an error."

Wiese remained silent for a moment. He realized that he had trapped himself. "Had I claimed men for light work, would I have got them?" he asked then.

"Certainly. That's what our labor board is there for."

"Good. Then I demand six men for light work."

"But Herr Surgeon-Major!" Neubauer enjoyed the situation with reproachful triumph. "Frankly, I'm at a loss to comprehend so sudden a change in your requests. First you want men as physically run down as possible, and then you demand them for light work. This is surely a contradiction! Men here as physically run down as that can no longer even darn stockings, you can take that from me. This is an education and labor camp run on the lines of Prussian discipline—"

Wiese swallowed, got up briskly and took his cap. Neubauer also rose. He was content at having annoyed Wiese. He was not interested in making a real enemy of the man. One could never be sure whether one day the old gauleiter wouldn't be reinstated. So he said: "I have another suggestion, Herr Doctor."

Wiese turned round. He was pale. The freckles stood out sharp from his cheese-white face. "Yes?"

"If you need the men so urgently, you could ask for volunteers. That disposes of formalities. If a prisoner wishes to render a service to science, we have nothing against it. It's not entirely official, but I'll take that on my shoulders, especially with those useless gluttons in the Small camp. The men will sign a declaration to that effect, that's all."

Wiese didn't answer at once. "In a case like this a payment for work done is not even necessary," said Neubauer warmly. "Officially the men stay in the camp. You see, I'm doing what I can."

Wiese remained suspicious. "I don't know why you're suddenly so difficult. I'm serving the Fatherland—"

"We're all doing that. Nor am I being difficult. Just orderly. Office rules. To a scientific genius like you it seems unnecessary; but for us it's half the world."

"So I can have six volunteers?"

"Six and more, if you wish. I'll even give you our first camp leader to accompany you on your tour; he can show you round the Small camp. Storm Leader Weber. Thoroughly capable man."

"Fine. Thanks."

"Not at all. Was a pleasure."

Wiese left. Neubauer picked up the telephone and gave Weber instructions. "Let him wear himself out. No orders! Only volunteers. So far as I'm concerned he can talk himself into consumption. If nobody volunteers, we just can't help him."

He smirked and laid down the receiver again. His bad mood had vanished. It had done him good to show one of these culture-Bolsheviks for once that his word counted for something. That business with the volunteers had been an especially fine idea. Wiese would find it difficult to lay his hands on anyone. Almost all the prisoners knew what it meant. Even the camp doctor, who also considered himself a scholar, had to scrape his victims together from the roads when he needed healthy people for experiments. Neubauer grinned and decided to inquire later on as to how the whole thing had turned out.

→»→ ←«←

"Can the wound be seen?" Lebenthal asked.

"Hardly," said Berger. "The SS certainly couldn't. It was the last molar but one. The jaw is stiff by now."

They had laid Lohmann's corpse in front of the barrack. The morning roll call was over. They were waiting for the truck to pick up the dead.

Ahasver stood next to 509. His lips were moving. "You don't need to say Kaddish for him, old man," 509 explained. "That one was a Protestant."

Ahasver looked up. "It won't do him any harm," he said calmly and continued to murmur.

Bucher appeared. Behind him came Karel, the boy from Czechoslovakia. His legs were as thin as sticks and the face tiny as a fist beneath the far too large skull. He staggered.

"Go back, Karel," said 509. "It's too cold for you here."

The boy shook his head and came closer. 509 knew why he wanted to stay. Lohmann had occasionally given him some of his bread. And this was Lohmann's funeral; it meant the way to the cemetery, it meant wreaths and flowers with bitter scent, it meant praying and wailing, it meant everything they still could do for him—this: to stand here and gaze with dry eyes at the body that lay in the early sun.

"There comes the truck," said Berger.

During the early years the camp had had only corpse bearers; then, as the dead became more numerous, a cart with a white nag had been added. The nag had died, and now there was a flat discarded truck such as is used for the transporting of slaughtered cattle. It went from barrack to barrack, collecting the dead.

"Are the corpse bearers there?"

"No."

"Then we'll have to load him on ourselves. Get Westhof and Meyer."

"The shoes," whispered Lebenthal, suddenly excited. "Damn it, we forgot them. They can still be used!"

"Yes. But he must have something on his feet. Have we anything?"

"There's still a torn pair belonging to Buchsbaum in the barrack. I'll get them."

"Stand around here in a circle," said 509. "Quick! Make sure I can't be seen."

He knelt down beside Lohmann. The others stood in such a way that he was protected from the truck which stopped in front of Barrack 17 and from the guards on the nearby towers. He found it easy to pull off the shoes; they were far too big. Lohmann's feet consisted of nothing but bones.

"Where's the other pair? Quick, Leo!"

"Here—"

Lebenthal returned from the barrack. He had the torn shoes under his jacket. He stepped between the others and turned in such a way that he could let the shoes drop in front of 509, who handed him Lohmann's. Lebenthal pushed them high up under his jacket till they were hidden in his armpit, and then returned to the barrack. 509 slipped Buchsbaum's torn shoes over Lohmann's feet and stood up, reeling. The car stopped now in front of Barrack 18.

"Who's driving it?"

"The kapo himself. Strohschneider."

Lebenthal returned. "How could we ever have forgotten them!" he said to 509. "The soles are still good."

"Can they be sold?"

"Traded."

"Okay."

The truck came closer. Lohmann lay in the sun. His mouth was torn askew and slightly open, and one of his eyes gleamed like a yellow horn button. No one said anything more. They all looked at him. He was infinitely far away.

The corpses in front of Sections B and C had been loaded. "Get on!" shouted Strohschneider. "D'you want a sermon as well? Chuck those stinkers up!"

"Come," said Berger.

This morning Section D had only four corpses. There was still enough space for the first three. But then the truck was full. The Veterans were at a loss to know where to put Lohmann. The other corpses lay on top of each other as high as they could go. Most of them were rigid.

"On top!" shouted Strohschneider. "Shall I help you find your legs? A few of you climb up, you lazy swine! That's the only work you still have to do. To load and to croak."

They could not lift Lohmann onto the truck from below. "Bucher! Westhof!" said 509. "Come on!"

They laid the corpse back on the ground. Lebenthal, 509, Ahasver and Berger helped Bucher and Westhof to climb up onto the truck. Bucher was almost up when he slipped and swayed. He groped for a hold; but the corpse to which he held was not yet rigid. It gave, and they slid down together. The corpse sliding down without resistance looked terribly submissive, as though it consisted of nothing but joints.

"Damn it!" shouted Strohschneider. "What kind of a stinking mess is this?"

"Quick, Bucher! Once more!" whispered Berger.

They panted and pushed Bucher up again. This time he succeeded in holding on. "First the other one," said 509. "It's still soft. It's easier to push up."

It was the body of a woman. It was heavier than corpses in the camp usually were. She also still had lips. She had died, not starved. She still had breasts, not skinny sacks. She was not from the women's division that bordered on the Small camp; in that case she would have been thinner. She probably came from the exchange camp for Jews with South American immigration papers; there, families were still together.

Strohschneider had climbed down from his seat and seen the woman. "Getting randy, you rams, eh?"

He bellowed with laughter at his joke. As a kapo of the corpse-bearing gang he didn't have to drive the car himself; he did it simply because it was an automobile. He had formerly been a chauffeur and drove whenever he could. He was always in good humor when sitting at the wheel.

It took eight of them to get the soft body finally up again. They trembled with exhaustion. Then, while Strohschneider spat tobacco juice at them, they lifted Lohmann up. After the woman, he was very light.

"Fasten him tight," whispered Berger to Bucher and Westhof. "Hook his arm through one of the others." They succeeded in pushing one of Lohmann's arms through the laths on the truck's side. As a result the arm hung out, while the body was held fast under the armpit by the crossbar.

"Done," said Bucher and let himself fall down.

"Done, you grasshoppers!"

Strohschneider laughed. The ten hurrying skeletons had reminded him of giant grasshoppers dragging around a stiff eleventh one. "You grasshoppers!" he repeated, looking at the Veterans. They didn't laugh. They just panted and stared at the end of the truck from which the feet of the dead stuck out. Many feet. Among them a pair of child's feet in dirty white shoes.

"Now," said Strohschneider, climbing back into his seat. "Which of you typhus brothers is going to be the next?"

No one answered. Strohschneider's good humor vanished. "Shits!" he snarled. "And you're even too dumb for that!"

He stepped suddenly on the gas. The motor rattled like a machine-gun salvo. The skeletons leapt out of the way. Strohschneider nodded with glee and turned the car.

They stood in the blue smoke of the oil. Lebenthal coughed. "That fat bloated swine!" he cursed.

509 remained standing in the fumes. "Maybe it's good against lice."

The truck drove down to the crematorium. Lohmann's arm jutted out sideways. The truck rocked on the uneven road and the arm swayed as though beckoning.

509 gazed after it. He felt the gold crown in his pocket. For a moment it seemed to him as though the tooth should also have disappeared with Lohmann. Lebenthal was still coughing. 509 turned round. Now he also felt in his pocket the piece of bread from the previous evening. He still had not eaten it. He felt it, and it struck him as a senseless consolation. "What about the shoes, Leo?" he asked. "What are they worth?"

Berger was on his way to the crematorium when he saw Weber and Wiese. He limped back at once. "Weber's coming! With Handke and a civilian. I think it's the guinea-pig doctor. Look out!"

In the barracks a turmoil started. High-ranking SS officers hardly ever came to the Small camp. Everyone knew there must be a special reason. "The sheep dog, Ahasver!" called 509. "Hide him!"

"Do you think they'll inspect the barracks, too?"

"Maybe not. There's a civilian with him."

"Where are they?" asked Ahasver. "Is there still time?"

"Yes. Quick!"

The sheep dog lay down obediently while Ahasver stroked him and 509 tied his hands and feet so that he could not run outside. He actually never tried it but this visit was out of the ordinary and it seemed wiser not to take any risks. Ahasver stuffed a rag into his mouth so that he could breathe, but not bark. Then they pushed him into the darkest corner.

"Stay there!" Ahasver raised his hand. "Quiet! Sit!" The sheep dog had tried to get up. "Lie down! Quiet! Stay there!" The madman sank back.

"Step out!" Handke shouted outside. The skeletons hustled out and lined up. Those unable to walk were supported or carried and laid on the ground.

It was a miserable heap of half-dead, dying and starving men. Weber turned to Wiese. "Is this what you need?"

Wiese's nostrils sniffed the air as though he were smelling a roast. "Excellent specimens," he muttered. Then he put on his horn-rimmed spectacles and looked benevolently at the lines.

"D'you want to make a choice?" asked Weber.

Wiese coughed slightly. "Yes—well—there was some talk—of volunteers—"

"All right," answered Weber. "As you wish. Six men forward for light work!"

No one moved. Weber turned red. The block seniors repeated the shouted command and began hastily pushing the men forward. Weber walked along the lines with a bored expression and suddenly discovered Ahasver in the rear rank of Barrack 22. "That one! The one with the beard!" he shouted. "Step out! Don't you know it's forbidden to run around like that? Block senior! How is this possible? What are you here for? Fall out, that man there!"

Ahasver stepped forward. "Too old," muttered Wiese, and held

Weber back. "Just a moment. I think we must handle this differently."

"Men," he then said gently. "You should be in hospital. All of you. There's no more room in the camp lazaret. I can provide quarters for six of you elsewhere. You need soup, meat and nourishing food. The six of you who need it most, step forward."

No one stepped forward. No one in the camp believed such fairy tales. Besides, the Veterans had recognized Wiese. They knew he had taken men away several times before. None had returned.

"It seems you've still too much to eat, eh?" snapped Weber. "That will be changed. Six men step forward, but snappy!"

From Section B a skeleton staggered forward and stood still. "Good," said Wiese and inspected it. "You are sensible, dear man. We'll feed you up all right."

A second one followed. Then another. They were newcomers.

"Come on! Three more!" shouted Weber angrily. He considered Neubauer's suggestion about the volunteers a crazy idea. One gave orders in the office and six men were supplied, that was that.

The corners of Wiese's mouth twitched. "I personally guarantee you good food, men. Meat, cocoa, nourishing soups."

"Herr Surgeon-Major," said Weber. "These tramps don't understand being talked to like that."

"Meat?" asked the skeleton Wassya, who stood as though hypnotized beside 509.

"Of course, my dear man." Wiese turned towards him. "Every day. Meat every day."

Wassya chewed. 509 gave him a warning shove with his elbow.

Though it had been hardly a movement, Weber had nevertheless noticed it. "Filthy bastard!" He kicked 509 in the belly. It was not an excessively vicious kick; it was a kick of warning, not a punishing one, in Weber's opinion. But 509 promptly fell over.

"Get up, you swindler!"

"Not like that, not like that," muttered Wiese, holding Weber back. "I must have them intact."

He bent over 509 and examined him. After a while 509 opened his eyes. He did not look at Wiese. He looked at Weber.

Wiese straightened himself. "You've got to go to hospital, dear man. We'll take care of you."

"I'm not hurt," panted 509, getting up with difficulty.

Wiese smiled. "As a physician, I know better." He turned toward Weber. "That makes two more. Now the last, a younger one." He pointed at Bucher who had been standing on the other side of 509. "This one, perhaps—"

"March! Step out!"

Bucher stepped up to 509 and the others. Through the gap thus caused, Weber now saw the Czech boy, Karel. "There's still half a portion. Would you like it as a supplement?"

"Thanks. I need full-grown people. These will do. Many thanks."

"All right. You six report in the office in fifteen minutes. Block senior! Take down the numbers! Get washed, you dirty swine!"

They stood as though a flash of lightning had struck them. No one spoke. They knew what it meant. Only Wassya grinned. He was feeble-minded from hunger and believed what Wiese had said. The three new ones stared apathetically into the void; they would have followed any order without resisting; even the order to run into the electrically charged wire. Ahasver lay on the ground and moaned. After Weber and Wiese had gone Handke had beaten him with a club.

"Josef!" A weak voice came over from the women's camp.

Bucher did not move. Berger nudged him. "There's Ruth Holland."

The women's camp lay to the left of the Small camp, separated from it by a double strand of uncharged barbed wire. It consisted of only two small barracks which had been installed during the war, when the new mass arrests had started. Formerly there had been no women in the camp.

Two years ago Bucher had worked over there for several weeks as a carpenter. This was how he had met Ruth Holland. Off and on they had been able to meet and speak secretly for a short while; then Bucher had been transferred to another gang. They had seen one another again only when Bucher had been handed over to the Small camp. Then, occasionally at night or in fog, they had whispered to each other.

Ruth Holland stood behind the barbed wire separating the two camps. The wind blew her striped smock around her thin legs. "Josef!" she called again.

Bucher raised his head. "Get away from the wire! They'll see you."

"I've heard everything. Don't do it!"

"Get away from the wire, Ruth! The guard might fire!"

She shook her head. Her hair was short and entirely gray. "Not you! Stay here! Don't go! Stay here, Josef!"

Bucher looked helplessly over at 509. "We'll come back," 509 said for him.

"He won't come back. I know it. And you know it, too." She pressed her hands against the wire. "No one ever comes back."

"Go back, Ruth." Bucher glanced towards the watchtowers. "It's dangerous to stand there."

"He won't come back! You all know it!"

509 did not reply. There was nothing to be said. He was deaf within himself. He no longer had any feelings left. Neither for others nor for himself. Everything was over; he knew it but he didn't feel it yet. He felt only that he didn't feel anything.

"He won't come back," Ruth Holland repeated. "He must not go."

Bucher stared at the ground. He was too dazed to go on answering.

"He must not go," said Ruth Holland. It was like a litany. Monotonous, without emotion. It was already beyond all emotion. "Someone else must go. He's young. Someone else must go for him—"

No one answered. Everyone knew that Bucher had to go. The numbers had been written down by Handke. And who would have gone for him, anyway?

They stood and looked at each other. Those who had to go and those who stayed behind. They looked at each other. Had a flash of lightning struck and killed 509, it would have been more bearable. It was unbearable because in this last glance was still the lie, the unspoken: *Why I? Just I?* on the one side—and the: *Thank God. Not I! Not I!* on the other.

Ahasver got up slowly from the ground. For one more moment he stared dazed before him; then he remembered. He whispered something.

Berger turned round. "It's my fault," squawked the old man suddenly. "I—my beard—that's why he came here! Otherwise he'd have stayed over there. Oi—"

He began tugging with both hands at his beard. Tears poured over his face. He was too weak to pull his hair out. He sat on the ground and jerked his head to and fro.

"Get back into the barrack," Berger said sharply.

Ahasver stared at him. Then he let himself fall flat on his face and wailed.

"We must go," said 509.

"Where's the tooth?" asked Lebenthal.

509 groped in his pocket and held it out to Lebenthal. "Here—"

Lebenthal took it. He trembled. "Your God!" he stammered, and made a vague gesture down toward the town and the burned-out church. "Your signs! Your pillar of fire!"

509 fumbled again for his pocket. He had felt the piece of bread while getting the tooth. What good had it done now not to eat it? He held it out to Lebenthal.

"Eat it yourself," said Lebenthal, furious and helpless. "It's yours."

"It's no longer any use to me."

A Mussulman had seen the piece of bread. He stumbled fast towards him, his mouth wide open, clutched 509's arm and snapped at the bread. 509 shoved him away and pushed the bread into the hand of Karel, who all this time had been standing silently beside him. The Mussulman clutched at Karel. The boy kicked him calmly and precisely on the shin. The Mussulman reeled and the others pushed him away.

Karel looked at 509. "Are you going to be gassed?" he asked in a matter-of-fact tone.

"There aren't any gas chambers here, Karel. You should know that," said Berger angrily.

"That's what they said in Birkenau, too. When they give you towels and tell you to take a bath, then it's gas."

Berger shoved him aside. "Go and eat your bread, or someone'll take it from you."

"I'll watch out." Karel crammed the bread into his mouth. He had enquired as one does after a traveler's destination, and had not meant any harm. He had grown up in concentration camps and knew nothing else.

"Let's go—" said 509.

Ruth Holland began to sob. Her hands hung like bird-claws on the barbed wire. She bared her teeth and moaned. She had no tears.

"Let's go—" said 509 once more. He let his eyes wander over those remaining behind. Most of them had crawled back indifferently into the barrack. Only the Veterans and a few others stood there. Suddenly it seemed to 509 as if he still had something of enormous importance to say, something on which everything depended. He tried as hard as he could but he was unable to put it into thoughts and words. "Don't forget this," was all he finally said.

No one answered. He knew they would forget it. They had seen similar things too often. Perhaps Bucher would not have forgotten it; he was young enough; but he had to go with him.

They stumbled along the road. They had not washed. That had been one of Weber's jokes. The camp never had enough water. They walked ahead. They did not look round. They passed through the barbed-wire gate which fenced off the Small camp. The croak-gate. Wassya smacked his lips. The three new ones walked like automatons. They passed the first barracks of the labor camp. The gangs had marched out long ago. The barracks were empty and dismal; but to 509 they appeared now to be the most desirable place in the world. They were suddenly security, life and safety. He would have liked to crawl in and hide himself away from this merciless walk into death. Two months too early, he thought apathetically. Maybe only two weeks too early. Everything in vain. In vain.

"Comrade," said someone suddenly next to him. It was in front of Barrack 13. The man stood in front of the door and had a face black with stubble. 509 looked up. "Don't forget this," he murmured. He didn't know the man.

"We won't forget it," answered the man. "Where are you going?"

Those who had stayed behind in the labor camp had seen Weber and Wiese. They knew this must mean something special.

509 stood still. He looked at the man. All of a sudden he was no

longer apathetic. He felt again the importance of what he still had to say, of that which must not be allowed to get lost. "Don't forget it," he whispered insistently. "Never! Never!"

"Never!" repeated the man with a firm voice. "Where have you got to go?"

"To a hospital. As guinea pig. Don't forget it. What's your name?"

"Lewinsky, Stanislaus."

"Don't forget it, Lewinsky," said 509. With the name, it seemed to him to have more force. "Lewinsky, don't forget it!"

"I won't forget it."

Lewinsky touched 509's shoulder with his hand. 509 felt it spread further than his shoulder. He looked once more at Lewinsky. Lewinsky nodded. His face was not like those in the Small camp. 509 was aware that he had been understood. He walked on.

Bucher had waited for him. They joined the group of the four others who had trudged on.

"Meat," muttered Wassya. "Soup and meat!"

The office smelled of stale air and boot polish. The office senior had prepared the papers. He looked blankly at the six men. "You've got to sign this."

509 glanced at the table. He didn't understand why there should be anything to sign. Prisoners were usually commandeered and that was the end. Then he became aware that someone was looking at him. It was one of the clerks sitting behind the kapo. He had carrot-red hair. When he saw that 509 had noticed him he moved his head almost imperceptibly from right to left and promptly looked down again at his desk.

Weber came in. Everyone stood at attention.

"Carry on!" he commanded and took the papers from the table. "Not through yet? Get on. Sign this!"

"I don't know how to write," said Wassya, who stood nearest.

"Then make three crosses."

Wassya made three crosses.

"Next!"

The three new ones stepped forward one after the other. 509 tried desperately to collect himself. It seemed to him that somewhere there must still be a way out. He glanced once more at the clerk; but he didn't look up again. "Now your turn!" growled Weber. "Come on! Dreaming, eh?"

509 picked up the form. His eyes were dim. The few typewritten lines wouldn't stand still. "Even want to read, what?" Weber gave him a kick. "Sign, you lousy dog!"

509 had read enough. He had read the words, *I herewith declare myself a volunteer*—He let the paper drop onto the table. This was the last desperate opportunity! This was what the clerk had meant.

"Get on, you quivering hog! Shall I guide your hand?"

"I'm not volunteering," said 509.

The office senior stared at him. The clerks raised their heads and immediately ducked again over their papers. For one moment it was very quiet.

"What?" asked Weber incredulously.

509 took a deep breath. "I'm not volunteering."

"You refuse to sign?"

"Yes."

Weber licked his lips. "So you won't sign this?" He took 509's left hand, twisted it and jerked it up across his back. 509 fell forward to the floor. Weber still held on to the twisted hand, pulled 509 up by it, rocked and kicked him in the back. 509 screamed and fell silent.

Weber seized him by the collar with his other hand and put him back on his legs. 509 collapsed.

"Weakling!" growled Weber. Then he opened a door.

"Kleinert! Michel! Just take this wretch in there and wake him up. Leave him there. I'll come over."

They dragged 509 out.

"Now you?" said Weber to Bucher. "Sign!"

Bucher trembled. He did not mean to tremble, but he had no control over himself. He was suddenly alone. 509 was no longer there. Everything in him gave way. He had to do fast what 509 had done, or else it would be too late and he would carry out like an automaton what he was bid.

"I won't sign, either," he stammered.

Weber grinned. "Imagine! Another one! This is just like the good old days!"

Bucher hardly felt the blow. A crashing darkness broke down over him. When he came to, Weber was standing above him. 509, he thought numbly. 509 is twenty years older than me. He did the same with him. I've got to pull through! He felt the jerking, the fire, the knife in his shoulders, he didn't hear that he yelled—then came the darkness again.

When he came to for the second time he lay wet beside 509 on the concrete floor of another room. Through a roar came Weber's voice.

"I could easily have that signed for you, and the thing would be settled; but I'm not going to do it. I will break your stubbornness. You will sign this yourselves. You will beg me on your knees to be allowed to sign it, provided you're still able to."

509 saw Weber's head dark against the window. The head seemed very big with the sky behind it. The head was death and the sky behind it was suddenly life, life no matter where and how, beaten, bleeding, louse-ridden—life in spite of everything for one fierce moment—then the numbness broke over him again, the nerves became mercifully dim once more and nothing was left but the dull roaring. Why am I resisting, something in him thought dejectedly when he came to again—what's the difference whether I'm clubbed to death here or I sign and am finished off with an injection, quicker than this, less painful. Then he heard a voice beside him, his own voice, with which someone else seemed to be speaking. "No! I won't sign—and if you beat me to death—"

Weber laughed. "That's what you'd like, you carcass! To get it over, eh? With us, beating to death takes weeks. We're only just beginning."

He picked up the belt again. The blow caught 509 across the eyes. It did not harm them; they were sunk too deep. The second one got his lips. They split open like dry parchment. After a few more cracks across the skull with the belt buckle, he fainted again.

Weber shoved him aside and started on Bucher. Bucher tried to duck; but he was far too slow. The blow hit him across the nose.

He doubled up and Weber kicked him between the legs. Bucher screamed. He was still aware of the belt buckle crashing several times into the back of his neck, then once more he fell into the storm of darkness.

He heard confused voices; but he didn't move. As long as he appeared unconscious they wouldn't continue beating him. The voices passed over him, endlessly. He tried not to listen, but they came closer and pierced his ears and his brain.

"I regret, Herr Doctor, but if the men won't volunteer—Weber, as you see, has done his best to persuade them."

Neubauer was in excellent spirits. His expectations had been far surpassed. "Are you responsible for this?" he asked Wiese.

"Of course not."

Bucher tried carefully to blink. But he could not control his eyelids. They snapped open like those of a mechanical doll. He saw Wiese and Neubauer. Then he saw 509. 509's eyes were also open. Weber was no longer there.

"Of course not," declared Wiese once more. "As a man of culture—"

"As a man of culture," Neubauer interrupted him, "you need these men for your experiments, isn't that so?"

"That is a matter of science. Our experiments save the lives of ten thousand others. Perhaps you don't quite understand it—"

"Oh yes, indeed. But perhaps you don't understand this situation here. It's a simple matter of discipline. Eminently important, too."

"Every man to his taste," declared Wiese haughtily.

"Certainly, certainly. I regret that I cannot be more helpful to you. But we don't coerce any of our protégés. And the people here seem to have an aversion to leaving the camp." He turned to 509 and Bucher. "You'd rather remain in the camp?"

509 moved his lips. "What?" asked Neubauer sharply.

"Yes," said 509.

"And you there?"

"Me, too," whispered Bucher.

"You see, Herr Surgeon-Major?" Neubauer smiled. "The people like it here. There's nothing to be done."

Wiese did not smile. "Louts!" he said contemptuously in the direction of 509 and Bucher. "This time we really didn't intend to do anything but make feeding experiments."

Neubauer blew his cigar smoke away. "All the better. Double punishment for insubordination. If you'd still like to try and find others in the camp—it's at your disposal, Herr Doctor."

"Thanks," said Wiese coldly.

Neubauer closed the door behind him and came back into the room. The blue, aromatic clouds of tobacco smoke hovered round him. 509 smelled them and he suddenly felt a tearing greed in his lungs. It had nothing to do with him; it was a strange, independent greed which clawed itself into his lungs. Unconsciously he breathed deep and tasted the smoke, all the while watching Neubauer. For a moment he couldn't understand why he and Bucher hadn't been sent out with Wiese; but then he knew. There was only one explanation. They had disobeyed an SS officer and would be punished for it in the camp. The punishment could be foreseen—men had been hanged for disobeying a mere kapo. It had been wrong not to sign, he suddenly thought. With Wiese they might perhaps still have stood a chance. Now they were lost.

A choking remorse welled up in him. It pressed on his stomach, it stood behind his eyes, and simultaneously, sharp and inexplicable, he felt the raving greed for the tobacco smoke.

Neubauer contemplated the number on 509's chest. It was a low number. "How long have you been here?" he asked.

"Ten years, Herr *Obersturmbannführer.*"

"Ten years." Neubauer had not realized that prisoners from the early days still existed. Actually a sign of my leniency, he thought. I'll bet there aren't many camps with anything like that. He pulled on his cigar. One day something like this might come in quite handy. One never knew what might happen.

Weber came in. Neubauer took the cigar from his mouth and belched. He had eaten scrambled eggs and sausage for breakfast—one of his favorite dishes. "Storm Leader Weber," he said, "this was not ordered."

Weber glanced at him. He waited for the joke. The joke didn't come. "We'll hang them tonight at the roll call," he said finally.

Neubauer belched once more. "It was not ordered," he repeated. "By the way, why do you do such things yourself?"

Weber did not answer at once. He couldn't see why Neubauer should waste so much as a word on such trifles. "There are surely enough people here for that kind of thing!" said Neubauer. Weber had lately become rather independent. It would not do any harm to make him realize who gave orders here. "What's the matter with you, Weber? Lost your nerve?"

"No."

Neubauer turned again to 509 and Bucher. Hang them, Weber had said. He was right, of course. But why? The day had taken a better turn than could have been expected. And besides, it was just as well to show Weber that not everything had to happen his way.

"It wasn't a direct refusal to obey," he declared coldly. "I had given orders for volunteers. This doesn't look like it. Give those men two days' bunker, nothing else. Nothing else, Weber. You understand? I want my orders to be carried out."

"Very well."

Neubauer left. He felt superior and contented. Weber followed him with a contemptuous glance. Nerves, he thought. Who has nerves here? And who turns soft here? Two days' bunker! He turned round angrily. A shaft of sun fell across 509's smashed face. Weber looked at him more carefully.

"I'm sure I know you. Where from?"

"I don't know, Herr Storm Leader."

509 knew perfectly well. He hoped Weber wouldn't remember.

"I know you from somewhere. I'll find out. Where did you get those wounds?"

"I fell down, Herr Storm Leader."

509 sighed with relief. This was the old routine again. Still a joke from the early days. No one was ever allowed to admit that he had been flogged.

Weber looked at him once more. "I know that mug from somewhere," he muttered. Then he opened the door. "Throw these two here into the bunker. Two days." He turned again to 509 and Bucher. "Don't you think you're getting away with this, you muckworms! I'll hang you yet!"

They were lugged out. 509 closed his eyes from pain. Then he felt the air outside. He opened his eyes again. There was the sky. Blue and endless. He turned his head over towards Bucher and looked at him. They had gotten away. So far, at least. It was hard to believe.

CHAPTER SEVEN

They fell out of the bunkers when Squad Leader Breuer had the doors opened two days later. During the last thirty hours both of them had tumbled from semiconsciousness into unconsciousness. During the first day they had still been able to communicate off and on by knocking; then no more.

They were carried out. They lay on the dance ground close to the wall surrounding the crematorium. Hundreds of men saw them; no one touched them. No one took them away. No one acted as though he saw them. No orders had been given as to what should be done with them; thus they didn't exist. Anyone touching them would himself have ended up in the bunker.

Two hours later the last dead of the day were brought to the crematorium.

"What about these?" the SS-man on duty asked lazily. "Are they going in, too?"

"They're two out of the bunker."

"Have they kicked off?"

"It looks like it."

The SS-man watched 509's hand closing slowly into a fist and opening again. "Not quite," he said. His back hurt him. Last night with Fritzi in The Bat had been a tough round. He closed his eyes. He had won out against Hoffmann. Hoffmann and Wilma. A bottle of Hennessy. Good brandy. But he was pooped out. "Ask in the bunker or the office where they belong," he said to one of the corpse bearers.

The man returned. With him the red-haired clerk came hurrying along. "These two are discharged from the bunker," he announced. "They belong to the Small camp. Supposed to have been discharged today at noon. Orders from the Commandant's quarters."

"Then take them away from here." The SS-man looked lazily at his list. "I have thirty-eight goners." He counted the corpses which were lined up in rank and file before the entrance. "Thirty-eight. Correct. Get these two out, or there'll be a mix-up again."

"Four men! Take these two to the Small camp!" called the corpse kapo.

Four men seized them. "Over here," whispered the red-haired clerk. "Quick! Away from the dead. Over here!"

"They're already as good as gone," said one of the bearers.

"Shut your trap! Get on!"

They carried 509 and Bucher away from the wall. The clerk bent over them and listened. "They're not dead. Get some stretchers. Quick!"

He looked around. He was afraid Weber might arrive, might remember, and have them both hanged. He remained on the spot until the men came with the stretchers. They were boards roughly fitted together on which corpses were usually transported.

"Load them on! Quick!"

The ground around the gate and the crematorium was always dangerous. SS-men loafed about there and Squad Leader Breuer was nearby. He didn't like the idea of someone getting out of the bunker alive. Neubauer's order had been executed and settled with the discharge, and 509 and Bucher were once more at large. Anyone could vent his bad temper on them; especially Weber whose honor, had he known they still lived, would almost have required him to have them liquidated.

"Crazy idea!" said one of the bearers, annoyed. "Here we are, dragging them all the way to the Small camp and tomorrow morning they're bound to have to be brought back again. They won't even last a few more hours."

"What's that got to do with you, you idiot?" the red-haired clerk suddenly snarled in anger. "Pick them up! Get on! Isn't there one man with any sense among you?"

"Here," said an older man, lifting the stretcher on which 509 was lying. "Who are they? Something special?"

"They are a couple from Barrack 22." The clerk looked round and stepped close to the bearer. "These are the men who refused to sign the day before yesterday."

"Sign what?"

"The declaration for the guinea-pig doctor. The other four he took along."

"What? And they're not going to be hanged?"

"No." The clerk continued to walk several steps beside the stretcher. "They must get back to the barracks. That was the order. So make it snappy before something happens."

"Oh, I see."

Suddenly the bearer took such vigorous strides that he shoved the stretcher into the back of the knee of the man in front of him. "What the hell!" the other said angrily. "Have you gone crazy?"

"No. Let's first of all get these two away from here. I'll tell you why later."

The clerk stayed behind. The four bearers now walked fast and in silence until they had passed the administration buildings. The sun was setting. 509 and Bucher had spent half a day longer in the bunker than had been ordered. Breuer hadn't allowed himself to be deprived of this little variation.

The leading bearer turned around. "Say, what's up? Are these here special big shots?"

"No. But they are two of the six whom Weber had lugged out of the Small camp on Friday."

"What's happened to them? They look as if they've been simply battered to bits."

"So they have. They refused to go with the surgeon-major who wanted them. Experiment station outside the town, so the red-haired clerk said. He has often taken people before."

The leading bearer let out a whistle. "Good God, and they're still alive?"

"See for yourself."

The first man shook his head. "And now they're even being sent back from the bunkers! Not hanged! What's it all about? I've not seen anything like this for years!"

They came to the first barrack. It was Sunday. The labor gangs had worked through the day and had just marched in. The roads were filled with prisoners. The news spread like lightning.

The camp knew why the six men had been taken away. It also knew that 509 and Bucher had been in the bunker; this had soon been discovered via the office and forgotten again. No one had expected them to return alive. But now they were coming—and even those not in the know could see that they were not returning because they had been useless, otherwise they wouldn't be so beaten up.

"Come," said someone out of the crowd to the rear bearer. "I'll give you a hand. It'll make it easier."

He seized one of the stretcher's handles. Another man came up and took the other front handle. Soon each stretcher was being carried by four prisoners. It wasn't necessary; 509 and Bucher were not heavy, but the prisoners wanted to do something for them, and at the moment there was nothing else they could do. They carried the stretchers as though they were made of glass, and the news ran ahead of them as on ghostly feet; two men who had disobeyed an order were returning alive. Two from the Small camp. Two from the barrack of the dying Mussulmen. It was unheard of. No one realized that it was due simply to a whim of Neubauer's—but that wasn't important. The important thing was that they had disobeyed and were returning alive.

Lewinsky stood in front of Barrack 13 long before the stretchers approached. "Is it true?" he asked from afar.

"Yes. Is that them—or not?"

Lewinsky came closer and bent over the stretchers.

"I believe, yes—yes, that's the one I spoke to. Are the other four dead?"

"There were only these two in the bunker. The clerk says the others went along. These didn't. They refused."

Lewinsky slowly straightened himself. He saw Goldstein beside him. "Refused. Would you have believed that?"

"No. Not of people from the Small camp."

"I don't mean that. I mean that they were let out again."

Goldstein and Lewinsky looked at one another. Muenzer joined them. "Seems like the Thousand Year brothers are getting soft," he said.

"What?" Lewinsky turned round. Muenzer had expressed precisely what he and Goldstein had been thinking. "What put that in your head?"

"The old man himself ordered it," said Muenzer. "Weber wanted them hanged."

"How d'you know that?"

"The red clerk said so. He heard it."

For a moment Lewinsky stood very still—then he turned to a small gray man. "Go to Werner," he whispered. "Tell him. Tell him that he who wanted us not to forget it is one of them."

The man nodded and crept along close to the barrack. Meanwhile the bearers had walked on with the stretchers. More and more prisoners appeared from the doors. A few came up shyly and quickly and glanced at the two bodies. One of 509's arms had fallen down and it trailed along the ground; two men sprang up to him and laid it carefully back.

Lewinsky and Goldstein followed the stretchers with their eyes. "Hell of a lot of courage for two living corpses just to refuse like that, eh?" said Goldstein. "Would never have expected that from any of the croak division."

"Nor would I." Lewinsky still stared down the road. "They must be kept alive," he said. "They must be kept from croaking. You know why?"

"I can imagine. You mean that only then would it become important for us."

"Yes. If they croak, by tomorrow it'll be forgotten. If not—"

If not, then it'll be a proof for the camp that something has changed, thought Lewinsky. He did not say it aloud. Instead he said, "We can use that. Especially now. For the morale of the camp."

Goldstein nodded.

The bearers walked on towards the Small camp. In the sky stood a fierce red sunset. Its reflection fell on the right wing of the labor camp barracks; the left-hand one lay in blue shadows. The faces at the windows and doors on the shaded side were as usual pale and blurred; but those on the other side were flooded by the strong light as by a sudden burst of borrowed life. The bearers walked straight through the light. It fell on the bodies that lay smeared over with blood and dirt on the stretchers, and suddenly it seemed as though these were not just two beaten-up prisoners being dragged back—it seemed to be almost something like a pitiful triumphal march. They had resisted. They still breathed. They had not been defeated.

Berger worked on them. Lebenthal had provided some turnip soup. They had drunk some water and, half-unconscious, had gone to sleep again. Then, at some time out of gradually dissolving torpor, 509 felt something warm on his hand. A shy, fleeting memory. Far away. Warmth. He opened his eyes.

The sheep dog was licking his hand.

"Water," whispered 509.

Berger was applying iodine to his chafed joints. He looked up, fetched the mug of soup and held it to 509's mouth.

"Here, drink this."

509 drank. "How is Bucher?" he asked wearily.

"He's lying beside you."

509 wanted to ask more. "He's alive," said Berger. "Get some rest."

For the roll call they had to be carried out. They were laid on the ground in front of the barrack with the sick who could no longer walk. It was already dark and the night was clear.

Squad Leader Bolte was taking the roll call. He contemplated the faces of 509 and Bucher as one inspects crushed insects. "Those two are dead," he said. "Why are they lying here with the sick?"

"They are not dead, Herr Squad Leader."

"Not yet," declared Block Senior Handke.

"Tomorrow, then. They'll go up the chimney. You can bet your heads on that."

Bolte left in a hurry. He had money in his pocket and wanted to risk a game of skat. "Break ranks!" shouted the block seniors. "Food-carriers out!"

The Veterans carried Bucher and 509 back with great care. Handke saw it and grinned. "Are those two made of china, what?"

No one answered him. He stood around for a while; then he also left.

"That swine!" growled Westhof and spat. "That filthy swine!"

Berger watched him attentively. Westhof had been stir-crazy for quite a while. He was restless, brooded around, talked to himself and picked fights. "Be quiet," said Berger sharply. "Don't make a row. We all know what's wrong with Handke."

Westhof stared at him. "A prisoner like us. And such a swine. That's—"

"We all know what it is. There are dozens even worse. Power makes brutes of people, you should have learned that long ago. And now lend a hand."

They had made a bed free for both Bucher and 509. As a result six men were going to sleep on the ground. One of them was Karel, the boy from Czechoslovakia. He helped carry the two men in. "The squad leader's all wrong," he said to Berger.

"Really?"

"They won't go up the chimney. Certainly not tomorrow. We could safely have made a bet."

Berger looked at him. The small face was utterly blank.

"Look here, Karel," said Berger. "You can make bets with SS-men only if you're sure of losing. Even then, it's better not to."

"They won't go up the chimney tomorrow. Not these two. Those three over there, yes." Karel pointed at three Mussulmen lying on the floor.

Berger looked at him again. "You're right," he said.
Karel nodded without pride. He was an expert.

The following evening they were able to speak. Their faces were so thin there wasn't much in them to swell. They were black and blue, but the eyes were free and only the lips torn.

"Don't move them when you speak," said Berger.

It wasn't difficult. They had learned it during the years in the camp. Everyone who had been there for some time could talk without moving a muscle.

After the food had been fetched there was suddenly a knock at the door. For an instant every heart stopped beating—each man asked himself if they were still coming to take the two away.

The knock came again, cautious, barely audible. "509! Bucher!" whispered Ahasver. "Act as though you were dead."

"Open the door, Leo," said 509. "That's not the SS. They come—differently—"

The knocking stopped. Several seconds later a shadow appeared in front of the pale light of the window and moved a hand.

"Open the door, Leo," said 509. "That's someone from the labor camp."

Lebenthal opened the door and the shadow slipped in. "Lewinsky," it said in the dark. "Stanislaus. Who's awake?"

"Everyone. Here."

Lewinsky groped in the direction of Berger, who had spoken. "Where? I don't want to tread on anyone."

"Stand still."

Berger came over. "Here. Sit down here."

"Are they both alive?"

"Yes. They are lying to your left."

Lewinsky pushed something into Berger's hand. "Here's something—"

"What?"

"Iodine, aspirin and cotton. Here's a roll of gauze, too. And this is peroxide."

"That's a real pharmacy," said Berger, astounded. "Where did you get it all from?"

"Stolen. From the hospital. One of us cleans up there."

"Fine. We can use it."

"Here's sugar. In lumps. Give it to them in water. Sugar is good."

"Sugar?" asked Lebenthal. "Where did you get that from?"

"From somewhere. You're Lebenthal, aren't you?" asked Lewinsky into the darkness.

"Yes, why?"

"Because you asked about it."

"I didn't ask for that reason," said Lebenthal, offended.

"I can't tell you where it came from. Someone from Barrack 9 brought it. For these two. Here's some cheese, too. These six cigarettes are from Barrack 11."

Cigarettes! Six cigarettes! An unimaginable treasure. For a while they all fell silent.

"Leo," Ahasver said then. "He's better than you."

"Rot!" Lewinsky spoke abruptly and fast as though he were out of breath. "They brought it before the barracks were locked up. They knew I'd come over here as soon as the camp was safe."

"Lewinsky," whispered 509, "is it you?"

"Yes—"

"You can get out?"

"Sure. How else could I be here? I'm a mechanic. Piece of wire. Very easy. I'm good with locks. Besides, one can always get through the window. How do you manage it here?"

"Here they don't lock up. The latrine is outside," answered Berger.

"I see, yes. Had forgotten that." Lewinsky paused. "Did the others sign?" he asked then, in the direction of 509. "Those who were with you?"

"Yes—"

"And you didn't?"

"We didn't."

Lewinsky leaned forward. "We wouldn't have believed that you could pull that off."

"Nor would I," said 509.

"I don't mean only that you could stand it, but that nothing more happened to you."

"That's what I mean, too."

"Leave them alone," said Berger. "They're weak. Why d'you want to know everything so exactly?"

Lewinsky moved in the dark. "That's more important than you think." He got up. "I must be off. Will come back soon. Bring some more. Also want to talk something else over with you."

"Okay."

"Do you often have check-ups here at night?"

"No," said Berger. "What for? To count the dead?"

"So you don't."

"Lewinsky—" whispered 509.

"Yes—"

"Sure you're coming back?"

"Sure."

"Listen—" 509 searched excitedly for words. "We are—we are not yet finished—we can still—be used for something—"

"That's why I'm coming back. Not out of charity, you can take that from me."

"Okay. Then it's all right—you're sure to come back—"

"Sure—"

"Don't forget us—"

"You already told me that once. I didn't forget it. That's why I came here. I'll come back."

Lewinsky groped his way to the entrance. Lebenthal pulled the door to behind him. "Stop," whispered Lewinsky, from outside. "Forgot something else. Here—"

"Can't you find out where the sugar came from?" asked Lebenthal.

"Don't know. Will see." Lewinsky still spoke abruptly and as though out of breath. "Here, take this—read it—we got it today—"

He thrust a folded paper into Lebenthal's fingers and glided out into the shadow of the barrack.

Lebenthal closed the door. "Sugar," said Ahasver. "Let me touch a lump. Only touch, nothing else."

"Is there any water left?" asked Berger.

"Here—" Lebenthal handed him a mug.

Berger took two lumps and dissolved them. Then he crept over to 509 and Bucher. "Drink this. Slowly. A gulp each, in turn."

"Who's eating there?" asked someone from the center bunk.

"No one. Who would be eating?"

"I hear swallowing."

"You're dreaming, Ammers," said Berger.

"I'm not dreaming! I want my share! You're wolfing it down there! I want my share!"

"Wait till tomorrow."

"By tomorrow you'll have wolfed it all. It's always the same. Every time I get the least. I—" Ammers began to sob. No one paid any attention. He had been sick for several days and was convinced the others were always cheating him.

Lebenthal groped his way over to 509. "That about the sugar just now," he whispered, embarrassed. "I didn't ask about it for trading. I only meant to try and get more for you."

"Yes—"

"I also still have the tooth. I haven't sold it yet. I waited. Now I'll soon make the deal."

"Okay, Leo. What else did Lewinsky give you? At the door?"

"A piece of paper. It's not money." Lebenthal fingered it. "Feels like a piece of newspaper."

"Newspaper?"

"Feels like it."

"What?" asked Berger. "You have a piece of newspaper?"

"Look at it," said 509.

Lebenthal crept to the door and opened it. "Correct. It's a piece of newspaper. Torn."

"Can you read it?"

"Now?"

"When else?" asked Berger.

Lebenthal raised the scrap high. "There isn't enough light."

"Open the door wider. Crawl out. There's a moon outside."

Lebenthal opened the door and crouched down outside. He held the torn piece of newspaper into the uncertain weaving light. He studied it for a long time. "I think it's an army report," he said then.

"Read!" whispered 509. "Read, for God's sake, man!"

"Hasn't anyone a match?" asked Berger.

"Remagen—" said Lebenthal. "On the Rhine—"

"What?"

"The Americans are at Remagen—crossed the Rhine!'

"What, Leo? Are you reading right? Crossed the Rhine? Doesn't it say something else? A French river?"

"No—Rhine—at Remagen—Americans—"

"Don't talk rot! Read properly! For God's sake read properly, Leo!"

"It's correct," said Lebenthal. "That's what it says here. I can see it now quite clearly."

"Across the Rhine? The Rhine? But how's that possible? Then they must be in Germany! Go on reading! Read! Read!"

They all began talking at once. 509 was not aware that his lips were splitting. "Across the Rhine! But how? In planes? In boats? How? By parachute? Read, Leo!"

"Bridge," Lebenthal spelled out. "They have—crossed—a bridge—the bridge is—under heavy German fire—"

"A bridge?" asked Berger, incredulous.

"Yes, a bridge—at Remagen—"

"A bridge," repeated 509. "A bridge—across the Rhine? Then the army must—read on, Leo! It must say something more."

"I can't read the part in small print."

"Has no one a match?" asked Berger in despair.

"Here," someone answered from the dark. "Here are a couple."

"Come in, Leo."

They formed a group close to the door. "Sugar," wailed Ammers. "I know you have some sugar. I've heard it. I want my share."

"Give the damn dog a lump, Berger," whispered 509 impatiently.

"No."

Berger fumbled for the abrasive strip on the box. "Hold the blankets and coats in front of the windows. Crawl into the corner under the blanket, Leo. Read!"

He lit the match. Lebenthal began to read as fast as he could. There was the usual hushing-up of facts. The bridge was worthless, the Americans were under the heaviest fire and cut off on the bank they had reached, martial law awaited the troops who had failed to destroy the bridge—

The match went out. "The bridge not destroyed," said 509. "So they crossed it—intact. Do you realize what that means?"

"They must have been taken by surprise—"

"That means that the West Wall has been broken through," said Berger cautiously, as though he believed he was dreaming. "The West Wall broken! They have gotten through!"

"It must be the army. Not parachute troops. Parachute troops would have dropped behind the Rhine."

"My God—and we didn't know anything about it! We've been thinking that the Germans were still holding a part of France!"

"Read it once more, Leo," said 509. "We must be sure. When was that? Is there a date on it?"

Berger lit the second match. "Light out!" someone shouted.

Lebenthal was already reading. "When was it?" interrupted 509.

Lebenthal searched. "March 11, 1945."

"Eleventh of March, '45. And what's today?"

No one knew exactly whether it was the end of March or the beginning of April. In the Small camp they had lost the habit of counting. But they knew that March 11th was quite a while in the past. "Let me see it, quick!" said 509.

Despite his pains, he had crawled over to the corner where they were holding the blanket. Lebenthal moved aside. 509 looked at the piece of paper and read. The small circle of the dying match threw light only on the headline. "Light a cigarette, Berger, quick!"

Berger lit one while kneeling down. "Why did you crawl over here?" he asked, and shoved the cigarette into 509's mouth. The match went out.

"Give me the paper," said 509 to Lebenthal.

Lebenthal handed it to him. 509 folded it and thrust it into his shirt. He felt it on his skin. Then he took a pull on the cigarette. "Here—hand it on."

"Who's smoking there?" asked the man who had produced the matches.

"Your turn will come. Each man a pull."

"I don't want to smoke," wailed Ammers. "I want sugar."

509 crawled back into his bunk. Berger and Lebenthal helped him. "Berger," he whispered after a while. "Do you believe it now?"

"Yes."

"So it was true about the town and the bombardment—"

"Yes."

"You too, Leo?"

"Yes."

"We must—"

"We'll talk about all this tomorrow," said Berger. "Go to sleep now."

509 let himself sink back. He felt dizzy. He thought it came from the pull on the cigarette. The little red spot of light, shielded by hands, wandered through the room.

"Here," said Berger, "drink what's left of the sugar water."

509 drank. "Hold on to the other lumps," he whispered. "Don't dissolve them. We can trade them for food. Real food is more important."

"There are some more cigarettes," squawked someone. "Pass the others round!"

"There aren't any more," answered Berger.

"Sure! You still have some. Hand them over."

"Everything that was brought in is for the two out of the bunker!"

"Rot. It's for all of us. Hand it over!"

"Look out, Berger," whispered 509. "Take a stick. We've got to trade the cigarettes for food. You watch out too, Leo."

"I'll watch out, all right."

The Veterans could be heard crowding together. Men groped through the dark, fell, cursed, hit out and screamed. Others on the bunks began growling and raging.

Berger waited a moment. Then he shouted: "The SS are coming!"

A flitting about and crawling and pushing and moaning—then it grew quiet.

"We shouldn't have started smoking," said Lebenthal.

"Right. Have you hidden the other cigarettes?"

"Long ago."

"We should have saved the first one, too. But when something like this happens—"

Suddenly 509 was utterly exhausted. "Bucher," he still managed to ask. "Did you hear it, too?"

"Yes."

509 felt the soft dizziness grow stronger. Across the Rhine, he thought, and felt the cigarette smoke in his lungs. He had felt the same thing a short while ago, he remembered—but when? Smoke, forcing its way greedily into the lungs, tormenting and irresistible. Neubauer, yes, the cigar smoke, while he lay on the wet floor. It seemed already far away, and only for an instant fear flashed through it; then it grew blurred and became a different smoke, the smoke of the town which had come through the barbed wire and which he had also inhaled, smoke from the town, smoke from the Rhine—and suddenly it seemed as though he were lying in a misty meadow that sloped down and down, and everything grew very gentle and for the first time dark without fear.

CHAPTER EIGHT

The latrine was overcrowded with skeletons. They were standing in a long line, shouting to the others to hurry up. A number of those waiting lay on the ground, writhing with cramps. Anxiously, others crouched close to the walls and evacuated when they could no longer contain themselves. One man stood upright like a stork, one bony leg raised high, one arm propped against the barrack wall, and stared open-mouthed into the distance. He stood thus for a while, then he fell over dead. This occasionally happened: skeletons hardly able to crawl any more suddenly raised themselves laboriously, stood there a few moments with vacant eyes, then fell down dead—as though their last wish had been to stand once more before the end, upright like a human being.

Lebenthal stepped cautiously over the dead skeleton and walked toward the entrance. An excited cackling started immediately. The waiting men believed he was trying to push himself forward in the line. They dragged him back and pummeled him with thin fists. No one dared leave the line; the others wouldn't have let him return to his place. The skeletons succeeded, nevertheless, in knocking Lebenthal down and trampling on him. It didn't do him much harm; they had no strength.

He stood up. He hadn't intended to cheat. He was looking for Bethke, who belonged to the transportation gang. He had been told Bethke had come here. He waited awhile near the exit, at a safe distance from the grumbling line. Bethke was a customer for Lohmann's tooth.

He did not come. As a matter of fact, Lebenthal didn't understand what he would be doing in this lice-infested latrine. True, business was carried on here, too; but for such deals a big shot like Bethke had much better opportunities elsewhere.

Finally, Lebenthal gave up waiting and walked over to the wash barrack. It consisted of a smaller section attached to the latrine and contained long concrete troughs over which water pipes with small openings were fixed. Clusters of prisoners crowded round them, most of them in order to drink or catch some water in tin mugs to take away with them. There was never enough for a man to wash properly, and anyone undressing to try to do so would have had the permanent fear that his clothes would be stolen in the meantime.

The washroom was a place for the slightly better black market. In the latrine, at best bread crusts, refuse and a few cigarette stubs were traded. The washroom was already a haunt for the minor capitalists. Even men from the labor camp came here.

Lebenthal slowly forced his way through. "What've you got?" someone asked him.

Leo threw the man a quick glance. He was a ragged prisoner with only one eye. "Nothing."

"I've some carrots."

"Not interested." In the washroom Lebenthal suddenly appeared more determined than he ever did in Barrack 22.

"Fathead!"

"One yourself!"

Lebenthal knew several of the dealers. He would have tried to bargain for the carrots if he hadn't been counting on Bethke this evening. He was offered sauerkraut, a bone and a few potatoes at outrageous prices; he declined and walked on. In the furthest corner of the barrack he noticed a young fellow with feminine features who didn't look as if he belonged here. He was greedily eating something out of a tin can, and Lebenthal realized that it wasn't just thin soup; he was chewing, too. Beside him stood a well-nourished prisoner of about forty who didn't seem to fit into the place, either. He belonged undoubtedly to the camp's aristocracy. His bald fat head gleamed and his hand slid slowly down the young man's back. The youth's hair was not shaven; it was well combed and had a parting. Nor was he dirty.

Lebenthal turned round. He was about to return disappointed to the carrot dealer when he suddenly saw Bethke coming, forcing his way ruthlessly toward the corner where the youth was standing. Lebenthal stepped in his path. Bethke pushed him aside and placed himself in front of the youth. "So, this is where you're hiding, Ludwig, you whore! Now I've caught you for once!"

The boy stared at him and gulped quickly. He didn't say a word.

"With a foul baldhead of a kitchen bull!" Bethke added viciously.

The kitchen bull ignored Bethke. "Eat, my boy," he said indolently to Ludwig. "If you're still hungry, then you can have more."

Bethke turned red. He hit the tin can with his fist. The contents splashed up into Ludwig's face. A piece of potato fell to the ground. Two skeletons flung themselves at it, tore it away and came to blows. Bethke kicked them aside. "Don't you get enough from me?" he asked.

Ludwig held the can pressed tight with both hands against his chest. Anxiously he screwed up his face and glanced from Bethke to the baldhead. "Evidently not," exclaimed the kitchen bull in the direction of Bethke. "Don't you worry," he then said to the boy. "Go on eating, and if you haven't enough, there's more. You won't get a hiding from me, either."

Bethke looked as though he were about to fling himself at the baldhead; but he didn't dare. He didn't know how much protection the other had. Such things were extremely important in the camp.

If the baldhead had the full protection of the kitchen kapo, a fight could turn out badly for Bethke. The kitchen had excellent connections and was known to make deals with the camp seniors and various SS-men. Bethke's own kapo, on the other hand, distrusted him. Bethke knew he wouldn't do much for him; he hadn't been sufficiently greased. The camp was full of such intrigues. If he wasn't careful Bethke could lose his job without further ado and become an ordinary prisoner again. That would be the end of the profitable business deals he made outside the camp while driving to the railroad station and the depot.

"What does all this mean?" he asked the baldhead, more calmly.

"What's it got to do with you?"

Bethke swallowed. "It has something to do with me." He turned toward the boy. "Didn't I get that suit for you?"

Ludwig had gone on hastily eating while Bethke was talking to the baldhead. Now he let the can drop, thrust himself with a quick unexpected movement between the two men and made for the exit. A few skeletons were already wrestling for the can to scrape it out. "Come again!" the kitchen bull called after the boy. "I'll always have enough for you."

He laughed. Bethke had tried to stop the boy but had tripped over the skeletons on the floor. He got up raging and trod on their snatching fingers. One of the skeletons squealed like a mouse. The other got away with the can.

The kitchen bull began whistling the waltz "Roses from the South" and walked past Bethke with provocative slowness. He had a large stomach and was well nourished. His fat posterior wobbled. Almost all the prisoners in the kitchen were well fed. Bethke spat after him. But he spat so cautiously that he only hit Lebenthal. "And you?" he said insolently. "What do you want? Come along. How did you know I'd be here?"

Lebenthal didn't answer any of the questions. He was here on business. There was no time for superfluous explanations. He had two serious prospective customers for Lohmann's tooth: Bethke and a foreman from one of the outside gangs. Both needed money. The foreman was enslaved to a certain Mathilde, who worked in the same factory as he and whom he managed, through bribery, to meet alone from time to time. She weighed almost two hundred pounds and seemed to him divinely beautiful; in the camp of permanent hunger, weight was the yardstick for beauty. He had offered Lebenthal several pounds of potatoes and one pound of fat. Lebenthal had declined and now congratulated himself on it. He had interpreted the recent scene with lightning speed and now expected more from the pansy Bethke. He considered abnormal love more willing to make sacrifices than the normal. After the scene he had witnessed he had immediately raised his price in his mind. "Have you got the tooth on you?" asked Bethke.

"No."

They stood outside. "I don't buy what I don't see."

"A crown is a crown. Molar. Heavy, solid, prewar gold."

"Muck! I've got to see first. Otherwise there's nothing doing."

Lebenthal knew that the far-stronger Bethke would simply take the tooth from him if he saw it. He wouldn't be able to do anything about it. If he complained, he'd be hanged. "Okay, then nothing doing," he said calmly. "Other people are not so difficult."

"Other people! Fool! First find some."

"I know some. One was here just now."

"So? I'd like to see that one!" Bethke glanced contemptuously round. He knew the tooth could be of use only to someone who had connections with the outside.

"You saw my customer yourself a minute ago," said Lebenthal. It was a lie.

Bethke was taken aback. "Who? The kitchen bull?"

Lebenthal shrugged his shoulders. "There must be a good reason for my being here just now. Maybe someone's trying to buy a present for someone else and needs the money for it. Gold is very much in demand outside. He certainly has enough food for trading."

"You crook!" said Bethke furiously. "You archcrook!"

Lebenthal raised his heavy eyelids once, then shut them down again.

"Something that can't be had in the camp," he continued, unmoved. "Something made of silk, for instance."

Bethke almost suffocated. "How much?" he bellowed.

"Seventy-five," Lebenthal declared firmly. "A special price." He had meant to demand thirty.

Bethke looked at him. "D'you know that one word from me could put you on the gallows?"

"Sure. If you can prove it. And what would you get out of it? Nothing. You want the tooth. So let's talk business."

Bethke was silent for a moment. "No money," he said then. "Food."

Lebenthal didn't answer. "A hare," said Bethke. "A dead hare. Run over. How's that?"

"What kind of hare? Dog or cat?"

"A hare, I tell you. I ran over it myself."

"Dog or cat?"

They stared at one another for some time. Lebenthal didn't blink. "Dog," said Bethke.

"Sheep dog?"

"Sheep dog! Why not an elephant? Medium size. Like a terrier. Fat."

Lebenthal didn't betray anything. The dog was meat. A magnificent windfall. "We can't cook it," he said. "Not even skin it. We haven't anything to do it with."

"I can deliver it skinned."

Bethke became more eager. He knew that in the procuring of food the kitchen bull could easily outdo him in Ludwig's eyes. He had to get something from outside the camp in order to be able to compete. Underpants of artificial silk, he thought. That would make an impression and give himself some pleasure, too. "Good, I'll even cook it for you," he said.

"Still difficult. We'd have to have a knife as well."

"A knife? Why a knife?"

"We haven't any knives in our place. We'd have to cut it up. The kitchen bull told me—"

"All right, all right," Bethke interrupted him impatiently. "A knife, too, then."

The underpants should be blue. Or mauve. Mauve would be better. There was a shop near the depot that carried such things. The kapo would let him go there. The tooth he'd sell to the dentist next door. "You can have the knife, too, for all I care. But that's going to be all."

Lebenthal realized he wouldn't be able to squeeze out much more at the moment. "A loaf of bread, of course," he said. "That goes with it. When?"

"Tomorrow evening. After dark. Behind the latrine. Bring the tooth along. Otherwise—"

"Is it a young terrier?"

"How could I know? Are you crazy? Medium. Why?"

"If not, it should be cooked longer."

Bethke looked as though he were about to leap at Lebenthal's face. "Anything else?" he asked quietly. "Cranberry sauce? Caviar?"

"The bread."

"Who said anything about bread?"

"The kitchen bull—"

"Shut your trap. I'll see." Bethke was suddenly in a hurry. He wanted to whet Ludwig's appetite for the underpants. The kitchen bull could feed him for all he cared, but once he had the underpants in store that would clinch the matter. Ludwig was vain. A knife he could steal. The bread wasn't so important, either. And the terrier was only a dachshund. "Tomorrow evening, then," he said. "Wait behind the latrine."

Lebenthal went back. He didn't yet fully believe in his luck. A hare, he would say in the barrack. Not because it was a dog, that wouldn't shock anyone—there had been people who had tried to eat the flesh of corpses—but because it was part of the joy of business to exaggerate. Besides, he had been fond of Lohmann—so he would like to have gotten something out of the ordinary for his tooth. The knife could easily be sold in the camp; that would mean more money for trading.

The deal was settled. The evening had turned misty and white waves of fog spread through the camp. Lebenthal slunk back through the dark. He carried the dog and the bread hidden under his jacket.

A short distance from the barrack he noticed a shadow swaying across the middle of the road. He saw at once that it was not one of the ordinary prisoners; they didn't move like that. An instant later he recognized the block senior of 22. Handke walked as though he were aboard ship. Lebenthal knew at once what it meant. It was Handke's day; he must have gotten alcohol somewhere. Lebenthal saw that it was no longer possible to get past him into the barrack unnoticed, to hide the dog and warn the others. So he sneaked behind the rear wall of the barrack and hid in the shadows.

Westhof was the first whom Handke ran across. "Hi there, you!" he shouted.

Westhof stood still.

"Why aren't you in the barrack?"

"I'm on my way to the latrine."

"Latrine yourself! Come here!"

Westhof stepped closer. In the fog he could see Handke's face only indistinctly.

"What's your name?"

"Westhof."

Handke reeled. "Your name's not Westhof. You're a filthy stinking Jew. What's your name?"

"I'm not a Jew."

"What?" Handke struck him in the face. "Which block are you from?"

"Twenty-two."

"That, too! From my own! Swine! Which room?"

"Room D."

"Lie down."

Westhof did not throw himself down. He remained standing. Handke came one step closer. Now Westhof saw his face and tried to run away. Handke kicked him on the shin. As a block senior he was well fed and much stronger than anyone else in the camp. Westhof fell down and Handke kicked him in the chest. "Lie down, Jewish swine!"

Westhof lay flat on the ground.

"Room D, step out!" shouted Handke.

The skeletons came out. They already knew what was going to happen. One of them would be beaten up. Handke's boozing days always ended this way. "Are these all?" he said thickly. "Room duty!"

"All present!" Berger reported.

Handke stared through the misty dark at the lines. Bucher and 509 stood among the others. With great difficulty they could once more stand and walk. Ahasver was missing. He had remained in the barrack with the sheep dog. Had Handke asked for him, Berger would have reported him dead. But Handke was drunk, and even had he been sober he wouldn't have known who was in front of him. He disliked going into the barrack for fear of typhus and dysentery.

"Anyone else here want to disobey orders?" Handke's voice grew thicker. "Lous—lousy Jews!"

No one answered. "Shtand—shtand at attention! Like men—men of culture!"

They stood at attention. Handke gaped at them for a while. Then he turned round and began trampling on Westhof, who still lay on the ground. Westhof tried to protect his head with his arms. Handke went on kicking him for some time. It was quiet, and nothing could be heard but the muffled thumping of Handke's boots against Westhof's ribs. 509 was aware of Bucher moving beside him. He seized his wrist and held it tight. Bucher's hand twitched. 509 didn't let it go. Handke continued to trample senselessly. At last he grew tired of it and jumped several times on Westhof's back. Westhof didn't move. Handke came back. His face was wet with sweat. "Jews," he said. "You've got to be trodden on like lice. What are you?"

He pointed a shaking finger at the skeletons. "Jews," answered 509.

Handke nodded and for several seconds stared pensively at the ground. Then he turned round and walked over to the barbed wire which fenced off the women's barracks. He stood there and could be heard breathing heavily. He had formerly been a printer and had come to the camp for indecent assault; he had been block senior for a year. After several minutes he returned and without paying heed to anyone strode back down the camp road.

Berger and Karel turned Westhof over. He was unconscious.

"Did he break his ribs?" asked Bucher.

"He kicked him in the head," answered Karel. "I saw it."

"Shall we carry him in?"

"No," said Berger. "Leave him here. He'll be better here for the moment. There's not enough room inside. Is there any water left?"

They had a tin can of water. Berger opened Westhof's jacket. "Hadn't we better take him in?" asked Bucher. "That brute might come back."

"He won't come back. I know him. He's had his fling."

Lebenthal sneaked round the corner of the barrack. "Is he dead?"

"No. Not yet."

"He trampled on him," said Berger. "Mostly he only beats people up. He must have gotten more schnapps than usual."

Lebenthal pressed his arm against his jacket. "I have some food."

"Quiet! Or the whole barrack will hear. What have you got?"

"Meat," whispered Lebenthal. "For the tooth."

"Meat?"

"Yes. A lot. And bread."

He didn't mention the hare. It was no longer suitable. He looked at the dark figure on the ground beside which Berger was kneeling. "Maybe he can still eat some of it," he said. "It's cooked."

The fog had grown denser. Bucher stood at the double fence of barbed wire which separated them from the women's barrack. "Ruth," he whispered. "Ruth!"

A shadow approached. He stared across but could not recognize the figure. "Ruth," he whispered again. "Are you there?"

"Yes."

"Can you see me?"

"Yes."

"I've got something to eat. Can you see my hand?"

"Yes, yes."

"It's meat. I'll throw it over. Now."

He took the small piece of meat and threw it over both barbed-wire fences. It was half the portion he had received. He heard it fall on the other side. The shadow bent down and searched on the ground. "Left! To your left," whispered Bucher. "It must be about a yard to your left. Have you found it?"

"No."

"Left. Another yard further. Cooked meat! Look for it, Ruth." The shadow halted. "Have you got it?"

"Yes."

"Fine. Eat it right away. Is it good?"

"Yes. Got any more?"

Bucher started. "No. I've already had my share."

"You've still got some! Throw it over!"

Bucher stepped so close to the wire that the spikes pricked his skin. The camp's inner fences were not electrically charged. "You are not Ruth! Are you Ruth?"

"Yes—Ruth. More! Throw!"

He suddenly realized it wasn't Ruth. Ruth wouldn't have said all that. The fog, the excitement, the shadow and the whispering had deceived him. "You're not Ruth! Say my name!"

"Psst! Quiet! Throw!"

"What's my name? What's my name?"

The shadow didn't answer. "The meat is for Ruth! For Ruth!" whispered Bucher. "Give it to her! You understand? Give it to her!"

"Yes, yes. Have you any more?"

"No! Give it to her! It's hers. Not yours! Hers!"

"Yes, of course—"

"Give it to her, or I—I—"

He stopped. What could he do? He knew the shadow had devoured the piece of meat long ago. In despair he let himself fall to the ground as though an invisible fist had knocked him down. "Oh, you—damned bitch—drop dead—drop dead for that—"

It was too much. A piece of meat after so many months, and to lose it so idiotically! He sobbed without tears.

The shadow opposite was whispering. "Bring more—I'll show you something—here—"

It seemed to raise its skirt. The movements were distorted by the white waves of fog, as if a grotesque inhuman figure were doing a witch's dance there.

"You bitch!" whispered Bucher. "You bitch, drop dead! Idiot—I—idiot—"

He should have made certain before throwing the meat; or he should have waited until it cleared up; but by then he might have eaten the meat himself. He had meant to give it to Ruth at once. The fog had appeared to him as a stroke of good luck. And now—he moaned and struck the ground with his fists. "What a fool I am! What have I done!" A piece of meat was a piece of life. He could have vomited with misery.

The cool of the night woke him up. He staggered back. In front of the barrack he stumbled over someone. Then he saw 509. "Who's this here? Westhof?" he asked.

"Yes."

"Is he dead?"

"Yes."

Bucher bent close over the face on the ground. It was moist from the fog and had dark blotches from Handke's kicks. He saw the face and thought of the lost piece of meat and both seemed to belong together. "Damn it," he said. "Why didn't we help him?"

509 glanced up. "Why d'you talk such rot? How could we?"

"We could. Maybe. Why not? We've managed other things."

509 was silent. Bucher let himself drop beside him. "We managed with Weber," he said.

509 gazed into the fog. There it was again, he thought. The false heroism. The old trouble. For the first time in years this boy had experienced a desperate bid for revolt, which had turned out well—and within a few days the imagination was already beginning to work with the romantic falsification that forgot the risk.

"You think that just because we managed to cope with the camp leader himself, it would also have had to work out with the drunken block senior, eh?"

"Yes. Why not?"

"And what ought we to have done?"

"I don't know. Something. But not have allowed Westhof simply to be trampled to death."

"Six or eight of us should have attacked Handke? Is that what you mean?"

"No. That wouldn't have been any use. He's stronger than us."

"What should we have done, then? Talked to him? Told him he ought to be reasonable?"

Bucher didn't answer. He knew that too wouldn't have been of any use. 509 contemplated him for a while. "Listen," he said then. "With Weber we had nothing to lose. We refused and were inconceivably lucky. But if we'd done something to Handke this evening, he'd have simply killed one or two more and reported the barrack for mutiny. Berger and a few others would have been hanged. Westhof, in any case. Very likely you, too. Next thing would have been several days without food. That would have meant a few dozen more dead. Correct?"

"Maybe."

"Can you think of anything else?"

Bucher thought for a while. "No," he said then, reluctantly.

"Nor can I. Westhof was stir-crazy. Just as much as Handke. Had he said what Handke wanted him to, he'd have gotten away with a few kicks. He was a good man. We could have used him. He was a fool." 509 turned toward Bucher. His voice was filled with bitterness. "Do you imagine you're the only one sitting here and thinking of him?"

"No."

"Maybe he would have kept his mouth shut and still be alive if we two hadn't managed to pull through with Weber. Maybe it was just that which made him reckless today. Did you ever think of that?"

"No." Bucher stared at 509. "Do you believe that?"

"It's possible. I've seen worse foolishness. And from better men. And the better the men the greater sometimes the foolishness, when they thought they had to show courage. Damn schoolboy twaddle! Do you know Wagner from Barrack 21?"

"Yes."

"He's a wreck. But he was a man and had courage. Too much. He hit back. For two years he was the delight of the SS. Weber almost loved him. Then he was through. Forever. And what for? We could have made good use of him. But he couldn't control his courage. And there were many like him. Few of them are left. And fewer who are not done for. That's why I held on to you this evening when Handke was trampling on Westhof. Do you understand at last?"

"You think Westhof—"

"It doesn't matter. He's dead—"

Bucher fell silent. He now saw 509 more clearly. The fog had lifted a little and in one spot the moonlight filtered through. 509 had raised himself. His face was black and blue and green with bruises. Bucher suddenly remembered some old stories he had heard about him and Weber. He himself must once have been one of those men about whom he had been talking.

"Listen," said 509. "And listen carefully. It's a damn fallacy that spirit cannot be broken. I've known good men who were no longer anything but howling animals. Nearly all resistance can be broken; all that's needed is enough time and opportunity. Those over there," he gestured in the direction of the SS quarters, "they know it very well. And they've always kept after it. The only important thing about resistance is what one achieves by it; not what it looks like. Senseless courage is certain suicide. Our little bit of resistance is the only thing still left to us. We've got to hide it so they can't find it— use it only in case of extreme necessity—as we did with Weber. Otherwise—"

The moonlight had reached Westhof's body. It hovered over his face and neck. "A few of us must last out," said 509. "For afterwards. All this must not have been in vain. A few who are not completely finished."

He leaned back exhausted. Thinking was as exhausting as running. Most of the time it was impossible because of hunger and weakness; but sometimes, in between, a strange lightness appeared, everything became extra clear and for a short while one could see far—until once more the fog of weariness crept over everything.

"A few who are not completely finished and who don't want to forget," said 509.

He looked at Bucher. He's more than twenty years younger than I, he thought. He can still do a great deal. He's not yet through.

And I? Time, he thought, suddenly desperate. It devoured and devoured. One would know it only when all this was over. One would know fully whether one was finished only when one tried to make a fresh beginning outside. These ten years in the camp counted twice and three times longer than ordinary years. Who would still have enough strength left? And a great deal of strength would be needed.

"When we get out of here they won't fall on their knees before us," he said. "They'll try to deny and forget everything. Us, too. And many of us will also want to forget it."

"I'm not going to forget it," answered Bucher glumly. "Neither this, nor any of it."

"All right." The wave of exhaustion returned stronger. 509 closed his eyes but immediately opened them again. There was still something he had to say before he lost it again. Bucher had to know it. Perhaps he'd be the only one to pull through. It was important for him to know it. "Handke is not a Nazi," he said with difficulty. "He's a prisoner like ourselves. Outside he would probably never have killed a man. He does it here because he has the power to do it. He knows it doesn't do us any good to complain. He's protected. He has no responsibility. That's it. Power—too much power in the wrong hands—too much power altogether—in anyone's hands—do you understand?"

"Yes," said Bucher.

509 nodded. "This and the sloth of hearts—the fear—the shirking of conscience—that is our misery—that's what I've been thinking about—today."

The weariness was now like a black cloud approaching noisily. 509 pulled a piece of bread out of his pocket. "Here, I don't need this—had my meat—give it to Ruth—"

Bucher looked at him and did not stir. "Heard everything over there just now," said 509 with a heavy voice already sinking down. "Give it to her—it is—" his head fell forward, but he raised it once more, and the skull, colored with bruises, was suddenly smiling, "also important—to give—"

Bucher took the bread and went over to the fence surrounding the women's camp. Now the fog floated shoulder-high. Below everything was clear. It produced a ghostly effect, as if the Mussulmen were stumbling headless to the latrine. After some time Ruth appeared. She, too, had no head. "Bend down," whispered Bucher.

Both crouched on the ground. Bucher threw the bread over. He wondered if he should tell her that he'd had meat for her. He didn't do it. "Ruth," he said. "I think we'll get out of here—"

She could not answer. Her mouth was full of bread. Her eyes were wide open and she looked at him. "I now really believe it," said Bucher.

He didn't know why he suddenly believed it. It had something to do with 509 and with what he had said. He went back. 509 was fast asleep. His head lay close to Westhof's. Both faces were covered with bruises, and Bucher could hardly distinguish which of them was still breathing. He didn't wake 509. He knew he had been waiting out here for two days for Lewinsky. The night was not too cold but Bucher stripped Westhof of his jacket and laid it over 509.

CHAPTER NINE

The next air raid came two days later. The sirens began howling at eight in the evening. Shortly afterwards the first bombs fell. They fell fast like a shower; and the explosions sounded only slightly louder than the firing of the flak. Only toward the end came the blockbusters.

The Mellern newspaper building was on fire. The machines were melting. The rolls of paper crackled into the black sky and the building slowly collapsed.

A hundred thousand marks, thought Neubauer. There go a hundred thousand marks belonging to me. A hundred thousand marks. I never knew that so much money could burn so easily. Those swine! Had I known it, I'd have bought shares in a mining concern. But mines burn, too. They are also bombed. No longer safe, either. They say the Ruhr district is devastated. What is still safe?

His uniform was gray with paper soot. His eyes were red from smoke and tears. The cigar store opposite, which had also belonged to him, was a ruin. Yesterday still a gold mine, today an ash heap. Another thirty thousand marks. Maybe even forty. One could lose a lot of money in one evening. The Party? Each one of them thought only of himself. The insurance? Would go bankrupt if it had to pay out for all that had been destroyed tonight. Besides, he had insured everything too low. Economy in the wrong place. Anyway, it was unlikely that bomb damage would be acknowledged. After the war the great compensation would begin, so it had always been said; after the victory the enemy would have to pay for everything. That was a likely story! A long time one would have to wait for that. And now it was too late to start something new. What for, anyhow? What would be on fire tomorrow?

He stared at the black cracked walls of the store. Five thousand Deutsche Wacht cigars had burned with it. Oh, well. Didn't make any difference. But what had been the good of denouncing Storm Leader Freiberg at that time? Duty? Nonsense! There was his duty burning. Burning to cinders. In all, a hundred and thirty thousand marks. One more fire like that, a few bombs into Max Blank's office building, a few on his garden and on his own house—that could happen tomorrow—and back he'd be where he had started. Or not even that! Older! Worse off! For—soundlessly something suddenly came over him which had always been lurking somewhere in the corners, banished, driven away, not allowed to break through as long as his own property had remained untouched—the doubt, the fear which until now had been kept in check by a stronger counterfear—suddenly now they were breaking out of their cages and staring at him, they sat in the ruins of the cigar store, they rode on the walls of the newspaper building, they grinned at him and their claws pointed threateningly into the future. Neubauer's fat red neck grew wet, he stepped uncertainly back and for an instant saw nothing and knew it and yet didn't want to admit it to himself: that the war could no longer be won.

"No!" he said aloud. "No, no—there must still—the Führer—a miracle—in spite of everything—of course—"

He looked round. No one was there. Not even anyone to put out the fire.

Selma Neubauer at last grew silent. Her face was swollen, the French silk dressing gown was covered with tearstains and her fat hands trembled.

"They won't come again tonight," said Neubauer without conviction. "The whole town's already on fire. What else could they bomb?"

"Your house, your office building. Your garden. They're still standing, aren't they?"

Neubauer conquered his anger and the sudden fear that it could happen. "Nonsense! They won't come specially for that!"

"Other houses. Other shops. Other factories. There are still enough standing."

"Selma—"

She interrupted him. "You can say what you like! I'm coming up." Her face flushed. "I'm coming up to you in the camp, even if I have to stay with the prisoners! I'm not going to remain here in the town! In this rattrap! I don't want to die! You don't care, of course, as long as you're safe. Well out of harm's way! As usual! We can stew in our own juice! You were always like this!"

Neubauer looked at her, offended. "I was never like this. And you know it! Look at your clothes! Your shoes! Your dressing gowns! Everything from Paris! Who got them for you? I! Your lace! The best stuff from Belgium! I bought them for you. Your fur coat! The fur rug! I had them sent you from Warsaw. Look at your stock in the cellar! Your house! I've taken good care of you."

"You forgot one thing. A coffin. You can still hurry and buy it now. By tomorrow morning coffins won't be cheap. There are scarcely any left in Germany. But up there in your camp you could have one made! After all, you have enough people for that."

"So? That's your gratitude! The gratitude for all the chances I've taken. That's the gratitude I get."

Selma didn't listen to Neubauer. "I don't want to burn! I don't want to be ripped to pieces." She turned to her daughter. "Freya, you have been listening to your father! Your own father! All we ask is to sleep up there in his house at night. Nothing else. To save our lives. He refuses. The Party. What's Dietz going to say? What's Dietz saying about the bombs? Why doesn't the Party do something about it? The Party—"

"Quiet, Selma!"

"*Quiet, Selma!* Hear that, Freya? *Quiet! Stand still! Die quietly! Quiet, Selma*—that's all he knows."

"Fifty thousand people are in the same position," said Neubauer warily. "All of them—"

"Fifty thousand people don't concern me. Fifty thousand people don't give a damn if I die. Save your statistics for Party speeches."

"My God—"

"God? Where's God? You people have driven Him out. Don't mention God to me—"

Why don't I give her a box on the ear? thought Neubauer. Why am I suddenly so tired? I should give her one! Show authority! Energy! A hundred and thirty thousand marks gone! And this screaming woman! Take the situation in hand! Yes! Save! What? Save what? Where to?

He sat down in an armchair. He wasn't aware that it was an exquisite 18th century Gobelin *fauteuil* from the house of the Comtesse Lambert—for him it was simply a chair that looked rich. That's why he had bought it several years ago with a few other pieces of furniture from a major returning from Paris.

"Bring me a bottle of beer, Freya."

"Bring him a bottle of champagne, Freya! He should drink it before it goes up in the air. Pop, pop, pop! Let the corks shoot into the air! Victories must be celebrated!"

"Lay off, Selma—"

His daughter went into the kitchen. The woman raised herself. "Well—yes or no? Are we coming up to you tonight or not?"

Neubauer looked at his boots. They were covered with ashes. A hundred and thirty thousand marks' worth of ashes. "There'd be gossip if we suddenly did that now. Not that it isn't permitted— but we haven't done it so far. They'd say I'm making use of advantages I have over others who have to stay down here. And at the moment it's more dangerous up there than here. The camp will be the next target to be bombed. We have essential war industry up there."

Some of this was true; but the real reason for his refusal was that Neubauer wanted to remain alone. Up there he had his private life, as he called it. Newspapers, cognac, and off and on a woman who weighed fifty pounds less than Selma—someone who listened when he talked and who admired him as a thinker, man and sensitive cavalier. A harmless pleasure that was necessary after the struggle for existence.

"Let them say what they like!" declared Selma. "It's your business to look after your family!"

"We can talk about that later. I must be off to the Party Headquarters. Have to see what has been decided there. Perhaps they've already made preparations to evacuate people to the villages. Certainly all those who have lost their apartments. But perhaps you can also—"

"No perhaps! If I stay in the town I'll run around and scream, scream—"

Freya brought the beer. It was not cold. Neubauer tasted it, controlled himself and got up.

"Yes or no?" asked Selma.

"I'll come back. Then we'll talk about it. First I must know the regulations."

"Yes or no?"

Neubauer watched Freya nod behind her mother's back and signal to him to agree for the moment.

"All right—yes," he said, sulkily.

Selma Neubauer opened her mouth. The tension escaped from her like gas from a balloon. She let herself fall forward onto the sofa which belonged to the 18th century *fauteuil*. All of a sudden she was nothing but a heap of soft flesh shaken by sobs. "I don't want to die—I don't want to—with all our beautiful things—not now—"

Above her disheveled hair the shepherds and shepherdesses of the Gobelin covering looked gaily and indifferently into the void, with the ironic smile of the 18th century.

Neubauer stared at her, disgusted. She had it easy; she screamed and howled—but who gave a damn about what he was going through? He had to swallow everything. Be confident; a rock in the sea. A hundred and thirty thousand marks. Not once had she asked about it.

"Watch her carefully," he said curtly to Freya, and left.

In the garden behind the house stood the two Russian prisoners. Although it was dark, they were still working. A few days ago Neubauer had given orders to this effect. He wanted a piece of ground dug up fast. He wanted to plant tulips in it. Tulips and some parsley, marjoram, basil and other kitchen herbs. He loved herbs in salads and sauces. That had been a few days ago. It seemed ages. Now he could plant burned cigars there. Molten lead from the newspaper office.

The prisoners bent over their spades when they saw Neubauer approach. "What is there to goggle at?" he asked. The pent-up rage suddenly broke through.

The elder of the two answered something in Russian.

"Goggle, I said. You're still goggling. Bolshevik swine! Impertinent as well! Delighted that the private property of honest citizens is being destroyed, what?"

The Russian didn't answer.

"Go ahead, work, you lazy dogs!"

The Russians didn't understand. They stared at him and tried to find out what he meant. Neubauer raised his leg and gave one of them a kick in the belly. The man fell over and slowly got up again. He raised himself by his spade and then held the spade in his hand. Neubauer saw his eyes and the hands holding the shovel. He felt fear like the stab of a knife in his stomach and seized his revolver. "Bastard! Rebelling, eh?"

He hit him between the eyes with his revolver butt.

The Russian fell down and didn't get up again. Neubauer breathed heavily. "I could have shot you," he snorted. "Rebellion! Just about to strike with the spade! Ought to be shot! One is too decent, that's it. Anyone else would have shot him!" He looked at the guard who stood stiffly by. "Shot him, that's what anyone else would have done. You saw him about to lift the spade?"

"Yes, Herr *Obersturmbannführer*."

"Well, all right. Get on, pour a can of water over his head."

Neubauer looked at the second Russian. The man stooped low over his spade. His face was blank. From the neighboring plot a dog barked like mad. Washing fluttered over there in the wind. Neubauer felt that his mouth was dry. He left the garden. His hands were trembling. What's happening? he thought. Afraid? I'm not afraid. Not I! Not of a stupid Russian. Of what then? What's wrong with me? Nothing's wrong! I'm just too decent, that's all. Weber would have clubbed that scoundrel slowly to death. Dietz would have shot him on the spot. Not I. I'm too sentimental, that's my trouble. That's my trouble with everything. With Selma, too.

The car stood outside. Neubauer straightened himself. "To the new Party Headquarters, Alfred. Are the streets leading there free?"

"Only if we drive round the town."

"All right, drive round the town."

The car turned. Neubauer saw the chauffeur's face. "Anything the matter, Alfred?"

"My mother has been killed."

Neubauer fidgeted uncomfortably. That, too! A hundred and thirty thousand marks, Selma's screaming, and now he had to offer comfort. "My condolences, Alfred," he said curtly and in military style in order to be done with it. "Swine! Murderers of women and children."

"We bombed them, too." Alfred stared at the road before him. "First. I was there. In Warsaw, Rotterdam and Coventry. Before I was wounded and discharged."

Neubauer stared at him in astonishment. What on earth was wrong today? First Selma and now the chauffeur. Was everything falling to pieces? "That was different, Alfred. Something completely different. Those were strategical necessities. But this is pure murder."

Alfred didn't answer. He thought of his mother, of Warsaw, of Rotterdam and Coventry and the fat German Air-Marshal, and took the corner furiously.

"One must not think like that, Alfred. That's almost high treason! Understandable, of course, in the moment of your grief, but forbidden. I don't want to have heard you say it. Orders are orders, that's enough for our conscience. Remorse is un-German. Wrong thinking, too. The Führer surely knows what he's doing. We follow him. That's all there is to it. He'll pay these mass murderers out all right! Two- and threefold! With our secret weapons! We'll force them to their knees! We're already bombing England day and night with our V.1. With all the new inventions we have we'll reduce the whole island to ashes. At the last moment! And America as well! They'll have to pay! Two- and threefold! Two- and threefold!" repeated Neubauer and grew confident and almost began to believe what he was saying.

He took a cigar from a leather case and bit off the end. He wanted to go on talking. He suddenly felt a great need for it—but seeing Alfred's compressed lips he remained silent. Who ever gives a damn for me? he thought. Everyone is preoccupied with himself. I should drive to my garden out of town. The rabbits, soft and fluffy, with red eyes in the dusk. Always, even as a boy, he had wanted to own rabbits. His father hadn't allowed it. Now he had some. The smell of hay and fur and fresh leaves. The security of boyhood memories. Forgotten dreams. Sometimes one was damned alone. A hundred and thirty thousand marks. As a boy the most he had owned had been seventy-five pfennigs. Two days later they had been stolen from him.

Fire after fire sprang up. It was the old town which burned like tinder. It consisted almost exclusively of wooden houses. The river reflected the flames as though it too were on fire.

Those Veterans who could walk crouched in a dark cluster outside the barrack. In the red darkness they could see that the machine-gun positions were still empty. The sky was overcast; the soft gray layer of clouds had a pink sheen like the feathers of flamingos. The fire sparkled even in the eyes of the dead lying piled up behind them.

A barely perceptible scraping roused 509's attention. Lewinsky's face raised itself from the ground. 509 breathed deeply and got up. He had been waiting for this moment since he had been able to crawl again. He could have remained sitting, but he stood up; he wanted to show Lewinsky that he was able to walk and not a cripple.

"Everything all right again?" asked Lewinsky.

"Sure. To finish us off is not so easy."

Lewinsky nodded. "Is there any place we can talk?"

They walked to the other side of the pile of corpses. Lewinsky glanced quickly around. "The guards haven't returned to your place yet—"

"There isn't much to guard here. Here nobody ever escapes."

"That's what I thought. And there's no control at night?"

"As good as never."

"What's it like in the daytime? Do the SS often come to the barrack?"

"Almost never. They're afraid of lice, dysentery and typhus."

"And your block leader?"

"He comes only for the roll call. Otherwise he doesn't bother about us much."

"What's his name?"

"Bolte. Squad leader."

Lewinsky nodded. "The block seniors don't sleep here in the barrack, what? Only the room seniors. What's yours like?"

"You talked to him the other day. Berger. We couldn't have a better one."

"Is that the doctor now working in the crematorium?"

"Yes. You're well informed."

"We made enquiries about it. Who's your block senior?"

"Handke. A green one. Kicked one of us to death a few days ago."

"Sharp?"

"No. Brutish. But he doesn't know much about us. Is also afraid of getting infected with something. Knows only a few of us. The faces change too fast. The block leader knows even less. The control lies with the room senior. One can do all kinds of things here. That's what you wanted to know, isn't it?"

"Yes, that's what I wanted to know. You understood me." Lewinsky glanced slightly surprised at the red triangle on 509's smock. He hadn't expected as much. "Communist?" he asked.

509 shook his head.

"Social Democrat?"

"No."

"What then? You must be something."

509 looked up. The skin round his eyes was still discolored from the bruises. As a result the eyes seemed brighter; they shone almost transparently in the light of the fire, as though they didn't belong to the dark, demolished face. "Just a human being—if that satisfies you."

"What?"

"Never mind. Nothing."

For a moment Lewinsky was taken aback. "Oh, I see, an idealist," he said then with a trace of good-natured contempt. "Well, that's okay so far as I'm concerned. As long as we can trust you."

"You can do that. You can trust our group. Those sitting over there. They have been here longest." 509 smirked. "Veterans."

"And the others?"

"They're equally safe. Mussulmen. As safe as the dead. Just able to fight for grub and the possibility of dying lying down. No more strength left for treason."

Lewinsky looked at 509. "Then one could hide someone with you for a while, what? It wouldn't attract attention? At least not for a few days?"

"No. If he isn't too fat."

Lewinsky ignored the irony. He moved closer. "There's something in the air. In various barracks the red block seniors have been replaced by green ones. There's some talk about night-and-fog transports. You know what that means—"

"Yes. Transports to the extermination camps."

"Correct. There are also rumors about mass liquidations. People arriving from other camps brought the news. We must take precautions. Organize our defenses. The SS won't pull out so easily. Till now we hadn't thought of you in this connection—"

"You thought we'd kick off here like half-dead fish, eh?"

"Yes. But not any more. We can use you. To make important people disappear for a while when it gets hot over there."

"Is the lazaret no longer safe?"

Lewinsky glanced up again. "So you know that, too?"

"Yes, I know that also."

"Were you with us in the Movement over there?"

"That makes no difference," said 509. "How are things now?"

"The lazaret," answered Lewinsky in a different tone, "is no longer what it was. We still have some of our people in it; but they've been watching us closely for some time."

"How about the spotted fever and typhoid wing?"

"We've still got them. But they're not enough. We need other opportunities to hide people. In our own barracks we can manage it only for a few days. We've always got to reckon, too, with surprise check-ups by the SS at night."

"I understand," said 509. "You want a place like this where everything's in a muddle and constantly changing and there aren't many check-ups."

"Exactly. And where a few people we can trust are in control."

"You can have that with us."

I'm advertising the Small camp like a bakery, thought 509 and said, "What was that about Berger you wanted to know?"

"His job at the crematorium. We haven't anyone there. He could keep us informed."

"He can do that. He pulls teeth in the crematorium and signs death certificates or something like that. He's been there two months. His predecessor was deported with the cremation gang on a night-and-fog transport during the last change-over. Then, for some time, there was a tooth-plumber who died. After that they fetched Berger."

Lewinsky nodded. "In that case he has another two or three months. That'll be enough to begin with."

"Yes. That'll be enough." 509 raised his blue and green face. He knew that those who belonged to the crematorium service were replaced every four or five months and shipped off to be gassed in an extermination camp. This was the simplest way of disposing of witnesses who had seen too much. So at best Berger probably hadn't more than three months to live. But three months were long. A lot could happen. Especially with the help of the labor camp.

"And what can we expect from you, Lewinsky?" asked 509.

"The same as we from you."

"That's not so important for us. For the time being we haven't anyone to hide. Grub's what we need. Grub."

Lewinsky was silent for a while. "We can't supply the whole of your barrack," he said then. "You know that?"

"There's no question of that. We are a dozen men. The Mussulmen can't be saved anyhow."

"We've much too little ourselves. Otherwise new ones wouldn't come here every day."

"I know that, too. I'm not talking about filling our bellies; we just don't want to die of starvation."

"We need what we can save for those we're already hiding. After all, we don't get any rations for them. But we'll do what we can for you. Is that enough?"

509 thought that it was enough and also as good as nothing. A promise—but he couldn't demand anything until his barrack had rendered a return service.

"It's enough," he said.

"Okay. Now let's talk to Berger. He can be your contact man. He's the one who can enter our camp. That's the simplest way. You can take charge of the others. The fewer who know about me the better. Always just a single contact man between one group and another. And one to replace. Old principle which you know, eh?" Lewinsky looked sharply at 509.

"Which I know," answered 509.

Lewinsky crawled away through the red darkness, behind the barracks, the latrines and towards the exit. 509 leaned back. He was suddenly very tired. He felt as though he had talked and thought hard for days. He had concentrated everything on this meeting with Lewinsky. Now his head was swimming. The town below glowed like a gigantic furnace. He crept over to Berger.

"Ephraim," he said to Berger after some time. "I believe we're out of it."

Ahasver had crawled up. "Did you talk to him?"

"Yes, old man. They're going to help us. And we them."

"We them?"

"Yes," said 509, raising himself up again. His head was no longer swimming. "We'll help them, too. Nothing is for nothing."

Something like a senseless pride was in his voice. They wouldn't receive any gifts; they would give something in return. They were still of some use. They could even help the Big camp. A sharp wind could have blown them over in their physical wretchedness, they were that weak—but at this moment they didn't feel it.

"We are out of it," said 509. "We have contact again. We are no longer cut off. The quarantine is broken."

It was as though he had said: We are no longer condemned to death; we have a slight chance. It was the whole vast difference between despair and hope.

"From now on we must always think about it," he said. "We must eat it. Like bread. Like meat. It's coming to an end. It's certain. We'll get out. Earlier it would have killed us. It was too far away. There were too many disappointments. That is over. Now it is here. Now it must help us. We must eat it with our brains. It's like meat."

"Didn't he bring any news?" asked Lebenthal. "A piece of newspaper or something?"

"No. Everything's forbidden. But they've built a secret radio. From scraps and stolen parts. In a few days it'll be working. It's possible that they'll hide it here. Then we'll know what's happening."

509 took two pieces of bread from his pocket; Lewinsky had left them with him. He gave them to Berger. "Here, Ephraim. Divide them. He'll bring more."

Each man took his piece. They ate slowly. Far below them glowed the town. Behind them lay the dead. The small group crouched silently together and ate the bread, and it tasted different from any bread they had eaten before. It was like a strange communion that distinguished them from the others in the barrack. From the Mussulmen. They had taken up the fight. They had found comrades. They had a goal. They looked at the fields and the mountains and the town and the night—and at that moment none of them saw the barbed wire and the machine-gun towers.

CHAPTER TEN

Neubauer again picked up the paper that lay on his writing desk. Simple for those brothers, he thought. One of those elastic regulations out of which anything could be made—reads harmless enough but is meant quite differently. A list should be made of the more important political prisoners—and it was added: provided there are still some left in the camps. That was the twist. The hint was clear enough. To grasp it, this morning's conference with Dietz had not even been necessary. It was easy for Dietz to talk. Do away with the dangerous elements, he had declared—in these hard times we can't afford to have notorious enemies of the Fatherland in our midst and feed them as well. Talking was always easy; but later someone had to do something about it. That was another matter. One should have such things in writing, with all details. Dietz hadn't provided anything written—and this damned inquiry here was no real order; it left one with the whole responsibility.

Neubauer shoved the paper aside and pulled out a cigar. Cigars were also getting scarce. He still had four boxes; after that there remained only the Deutsche Wacht, and not even too many of them. Almost everything had been burned. One should have taken better precautions while there was still plenty—but who'd have thought it would ever come to this?

Weber entered. After a brief hesitation Neubauer pushed the box toward him. "Help yourself," he said with false affability. "Rarities. Genuine Partagas."

"Thanks. I smoke only cigarettes."

"Of course. I always forget that. All right, then, you smoke your coffin nails."

Weber suppressed a grin. The old boy must be in trouble; he was being hospitable. He pulled a flat gold case out of his pocket and tapped a cigarette into shape. In 1933 the case had belonged to the legal councilor, Aaron Weizenblut. It had been a lucky find. The monogram had fitted—Anton Weber. It was the only booty he had acquired in all these years; he didn't need a great deal and cared little for possessions.

"A regulation has just come in," said Neubauer. "Here, just read through it."

Weber picked up the paper. He read slowly and for a long time. Neubauer grew impatient. "The rest is unimportant," he said. "I'm only concerned with the passage about the political prisoners. How many, roughly, do we still have?"

Weber laid the paper back on the desk. It slid across the polished surface towards a small glass vase of violets.

"I don't know the figures so exactly offhand," he answered. "Must be about half the prisoners. Maybe a few more or less. All those with red triangles. Not counting the foreigners, of course. The other half are criminals, a number of homos, Jehovah's Witnesses, and the like."

Neubauer glanced up. He wasn't sure whether Weber was playing dumb on purpose; Weber's face betrayed nothing. "I don't mean that. The men with the red triangles are not all political. Not in the sense of this regulation."

"Of course not. The red triangle is only a vague, general classification. Among them are Jews, Catholics, Democrats, Social Democrats, Communists and who knows what."

Neubauer knew this, too. After ten years Weber didn't need to enlighten him on that. He had again an uncertain feeling that his camp leader was making fun of him. "How about the really political ones?" he asked, without giving himself away.

"Mostly Communists."

"That we can establish exactly, can't we?"

"Fairly exactly. It's in the files."

"Do we still have important political people here, apart from them?"

"I can have that investigated. There may be a number of newspaper people, Social Democrats and Democrats."

Neubauer blew out the smoke of his Partagas. Strange how quickly a cigar had a calming and optimistic effect on one! "Good," he said affably. "Let's first of all get these facts straight. Have the lists combed through. We can always decide afterwards how many people we want to have for our report. Don't you think so?"

"Certainly."

"There's not such a hurry. We have about two weeks. That's quite a nice span of time to settle things in, eh?"

"Certainly."

"Besides, one can antedate here and there; things that are bound to happen anyhow, I mean. There's no longer any point in entering the names of people who will very soon have to be booked as dead. Superfluous work. Only leads to useless inquiries."

"Certainly."

"I guess we won't have too many of these people, in any case—I mean, so many that it'll become conspicuous—"

"We don't need to have them," said Weber calmly.

He knew what Neubauer meant and Neubauer knew that Weber understood him.

"Inconspicuously, of course," he said. "We must arrange it as inconspicuously as possible. I know I can rely on you in this respect—"

He got up and with a straightened-out paper clip bored carefully into the end of his cigar. He had bitten it off too hastily just now, and it wouldn't pull any more. One should never bite the end off good cigars; simply break it off cautiously or cut it with a sharp penknife.

"How's work coming along? Have we enough to do?"

"The copper foundry has been put pretty well out of action by the bombing. We're letting the people clear up there. Almost all the other gangs are working as before."

"Clear up? Good idea." The cigar was pulling again. "Dietz was talking to me about it today. Cleaning of streets, breaking up of bombed houses, the town needs hundreds of men. It's an emergency and after all we do have the cheapest labor. Dietz was in favor of it. So am I. No reason against it, is there?"

"No."

Neubauer stood by the window and looked out. "There's also a request come in about the food supplies. We're expected to economize. How can this be done?"

"Hand out less food," answered Weber laconically.

"That's possible only up to a certain point. If the people collapse they can't work any more."

"We can save on the Small camp. It's full of useless mouths. Who dies no longer eats."

Neubauer nodded. "All the same, you know my motto: Always humane, as long as possible. Of course when it's no longer possible—"

They both now stood near the window, smoking. They talked calmly and objectively like two honorable cattle dealers in a slaughterhouse. Outside, prisoners were working in the flower beds that surrounded the Commandant's house. "I'm having a border of iris and narcissus planted," said Neubauer. "Yellow and blue—a beautiful combination of colors."

"Yes," answered Weber without enthusiasm.

Neubauer laughed. "Doesn't seem to interest you much, eh?"

"Not enormously. I like bowling."

"That's very pleasant, too." Neubauer went on watching the workmen for a while. "By the way, what about the camp band? Those fellows have a damn lazy life."

"They play at the marching in and out and twice a week in the afternoons."

"In the afternoons the labor gangs don't get anything out of it. Couldn't you see to it that in the evenings after roll call they have another hour of music? That's good for the men. Diverts them. Especially when we have to economize on the food."

"I'll see to it."

"Well, it seems we have discussed everything and understand each other."

Neubauer walked back to his desk. He opened a drawer and took out a small case.

"Here's a surprise for you, Weber. Arrived today. Thought it might give you pleasure."

Weber opened the case. It contained a War Service Cross. To his astonishment Neubauer noticed that Weber was blushing. This was the last thing he had expected. "Here's the confirmation," he explained. "You should have had it long ago. After all, in a sense we are at the front here, too. Not another word." He offered Weber his hand. "Hard times. We must see things through."

Weber left. Neubauer shook his head. The little trick with the medal had worked better than he had anticipated. Somewhere everyone had his weak spot. For a while he stood pondering before the great colored map of Europe which hung on the wall opposite the picture of Hitler. The little flags on it were no longer up-to-date. They were still placed far inside Russia. Neubauer had left them there out of a kind of superstition that perhaps one day they might become valid again. He sighed, walked back to the desk, raised the glass vase of violets and sniffed the sweet scent. A vague thought passed through him. That's what we are, the best of us, he thought, almost moved. Room for everything in our soul. Iron discipline at the moment of historical necessity and at the same time deepest sentiment. The Führer with his love of children. Goering the friend of animals. He sniffed the flowers once more. A hundred and thirty thousand marks lost and yet already on top again. Can't be gotten down! Already an eye for the beautiful again! The idea of the camp band had been a good one. Selma and Freya were coming up this evening. It would make an excellent impression on them.

He sat down at his typewriter and his two fat fingers tapped out the order for the band. This was for his private files. In addition there was the regulation to exempt weak prisoners from work. It was meant differently, but this was how he intended to interpret it. What Weber did was his business. He'd be sure to do something about it; the War Service Cross had arrived just in time. The private files contained quite a number of proofs of Neubauer's leniency and solicitude—among them, of course, the usual incriminating material against senior officers and Party members. Those under fire could never take too much care to provide sufficient protection.

Satisfied, Neubauer closed the blue portfolio and grabbed the telephone. His lawyer had given him an excellent tip: to buy bombed lots. They were cheap. Unbombed ones, too. This way one could make up for one's own losses. Lots retained their value, even if they were bombed a hundred times. One had to take advantage of the current panic.

The clearing gang was returning from the copper foundry. They had been working hard for twelve hours. A part of the great hall had collapsed and various sections were badly damaged. There had been few picks and shovels at their disposal and most prisoners had been compelled to work with their bare hands. Their hands were torn and bleeding. All were dead-tired and hungry. At noon they had been given a thin soup with unknown weeds swimming in it. This the management of the copper foundry had generously provided. Its only advantage had been that it was warm. In return the engineers and overseers of the foundry had driven them like slaves. They were civilians; but some of them hadn't been much better than the SS.

Lewinsky marched in the center of the column. Beside him walked Willy Werner. At the formation of the gang both had managed to get into the same group. Single numbers had not been called up; just collective groups of four hundred men. The clearing up was a hard job. Few people had volunteered, and so it had been easy for Lewinsky and Werner to get into it. They knew why they wanted to go. They had done it several times before.

The four hundred men marched slowly. Sixteen of them had collapsed at work. Of these, twelve could still walk if supported; the other four were carried—two on a rough stretcher, the others by the arms and feet.

The road to the camp was long; the prisoners were led around the town. The SS avoided letting them march through the streets. They didn't wish the men to be seen; nor did they want the prisoners to see too much of the destruction.

They approached a small birch grove. The barks shimmered silken in the failing light. The SS guards and the kapos distributed themselves along the column. The SS held their rifles at the ready. The prisoners stumbled forward. Birds chirped in the branches. A breath of green lay over the twigs. Snowdrops and primroses flowered in the ditches. Water gurgled. No one noticed it. Everyone was too tired. Then came fields and freshly ploughed land and the guards gathered together again.

Lewinsky walked close beside Werner. He was excited. "Where did you put it?" he asked, without moving his lips.

Werner made a slight movement and pressed his arm against his ribs.

"Who found it?"

"Muenzer. In the same place."

"The same make?"

Werner nodded.

"Have we all the parts now?"

"Yes. Muenzer can fit them together in the camp."

"I found a handful of bullets. Couldn't see if they fit. Had to hide them quick. Hope they'll fit."

"We'll be able to use them all right."

"Did anyone else get anything?"

"Muenzer has some revolver parts."

"Were they in the same place as yesterday?"

"Yes."

"Someone must have put them there."

"Of course. Someone from outside."

"One of the workers."

"Yes. That's now the third time there's been something. No accident."

"Could it have been one of our people clearing up in the munition works?"

"No. They didn't come over. We'd know it, too. Must be someone from outside."

The camp's underground movement had been trying to get arms for a long time. They were expecting a final battle with the SS and wanted at least not to be completely defenseless. It had been almost impossible to establish connections; but since the bombing started the clearing gang had suddenly found weapons and parts of weapons in certain places. They were hidden under rubble and must have been placed there by workers so as to be found in the confusion of devastation. It was because of these discoveries that the clearing gang suddenly had more volunteers than usual. They were all reliable people.

The prisoners passed a meadow fenced in by barbed wire. Two brown-and-white cows came up to the wires and sniffed. One of them mooed. Their peaceful eyes gleamed. Almost none of the prisoners looked at them; it would only have made them hungrier than they were already.

"D'you think they'll search us today before we break ranks?"

"Why? They didn't yesterday. Our gang wasn't anywhere near the munitions factory. Those who've been clearing up outside are not usually searched."

"One never knows. If we have to throw these things away—"

Werner glanced up at the sky. It radiated pink and gold and blue. "It'll be getting dark by the time we arrive. We'll have to wait and see what happens. Have you got your bullets well wrapped?"

"Yes. In a rag."

"Okay. If anything happens, pass them behind you to Goldstein. He'll pass them on to Muenzer. He to Remne. One of them will throw them away. If we're out of luck and the SS is on all sides, let them drop in the center of the group if necessary. Don't throw them to the side. Then they can't pick on any particular person. I hope the tree-felling gang arrives at the same time as us. Muller and Ludwig there are in the know. At the marching-in, their group will pretend to get an order wrong when we're being searched and will move over to us and pick the things up."

After making a curve the road approached the town again in a long straight line. Allotment gardens with wooden summerhouses skirted the road. People in their shirt sleeves were working in them. Only a few looked up. The prisoners were familiar to them. The smell of freshly dug earth wafted over from the gardens. A rooster began to crow. Signs for motorists stood on the side of the road: CAUTION—CURVE. TWENTY-SEVEN KILOMETERS TO HOLZFELDE.

"What's that over there?" Werner asked suddenly. "Is it the tree-felling gang already?"

Way in front of them on the road they saw a dark mass of people. It was so far away they couldn't recognize what it was. "Probably," said Lewinsky. "They're ahead of us. Maybe we'll catch up with them yet."

He turned round. Behind him staggered Goldstein. He had put his arms around the shoulders of two men and dragged himself along. "Come," said Lewinsky to those holding him up. "We'll relieve you. Later, outside the camp, you can take him again."

He took Goldstein from one side and Werner supported him from the other. "My damned heart," gasped Goldstein. "Forty years old, and the heart gone. Too idiotic!"

"Why did you come along?" asked Lewinsky. "You could have been transferred to the shoe department."

A grin spread wearily over Goldstein's gray face. "Wanted to see for once what it's like outside the camp. Fresh air. Was a mistake."

"You'll get over it," said Werner. "Just let yourself hang on our shoulders. We can easily carry you."

The sky lost its last brilliance and turned paler. Blue shadows tumbled down from the hill. "Listen," whispered Goldstein. "Shove what you have on you among my things. If they do search, they'll search you and maybe the stretchers, too. But they won't check up on us slackers. We simply caved in. And so they'll let us pass."

"If they do search, they'll search everyone," said Werner.

"No, not us who slacked. And there are also a few more who collapsed on the road. Stick the things into my shirt."

Werner exchanged a glance with Lewinsky. "Don't worry, Goldstein. We'll get through all right."

"No, give them to me."

Neither of them answered.

"It doesn't matter much if I'm caught. For you it's different."

"Rot!"

"It has nothing to do with self-sacrifice or talking big," said Goldstein with a distorted smile. "It's just more practical. I won't last much longer anyhow."

"We'll see about all that in time," answered Werner. "We've still almost an hour to go. When we get to the camp you'll move back into your former line. If anything happens we'll give you the things. You'll pass them on immediately to Muenzer. To Muenzer, you understand?"

"Yes."

A woman on a bicycle passed by. She was fat and wore spectacles and had a cardboard box in front of her on the handle bars. She looked aside. She did not want to see the prisoners.

Lewinsky glanced up and then stared ahead. "Look," he said. "Over there. That isn't the tree-felling gang."

The black mass in front of them had come closer. The labor gang wasn't catching up with them, but the others were coming toward them. Now they could also see that it was a long line of people who were not marching in an orderly column.

"A new batch?" asked someone behind Lewinsky. "Or is it a transport?"

"No. There aren't any SS with them. And they're not marching in the direction of the camp. These are civilians."

"Civilians?"

"You can see that for yourself. They're wearing hats. And there are women among them. Children, too. Lots of children."

Now they could be seen clearly. The two columns were fast approaching one another. "Pull into the right!" shouted the SS. "Hard to the right! The right outer line into the ditch! Get on!"

The guards ran along the column of prisoners. "Right! Move! To the right! Keep the left of the road clear! Anyone falling out of line will be shot!"

"These are bombed-out people," Werner said suddenly under his breath. "They're from the town. Refugees."

"Refugees?"

"Refugees," repeated Werner.

"I believe you're right!" Lewinsky screwed up his eyes. "These are actually refugees. But German refugees."

The word ran in whispers through the column. Refugees! German refugees! *Des réfugiés allemands.* It seemed unbelievable, but it was true: after years of victories in Europe and driving people before them, they now had to flee in their own country.

There were women and children and older men. They carried packages, bags and suitcases. Some had small pushcarts on which they had loaded their luggage. They walked out of step and sullenly behind one another.

The two columns were now quite close. It grew suddenly very quiet. All that could be heard was the scraping of feet on the highway. And without a word being said the prisoners' column suddenly began to change. They had not communicated with one another by so much as a glance; but it was as though someone had shouted a soundless order over the heads of these dead-tired, emaciated, half-starved men, as though a spark had inflamed their blood, roused their brain and pulled their nerves and muscles together. The stumbling column began to march. Feet were lifted, heads raised higher, faces became harder and there was life in the eyes.

"Let me go," said Goldstein.

"Nonsense!"

"Let me go! Just till these have passed!"

They let him go. He reeled, clenched his teeth and recovered. Lewinsky and Werner pressed their shoulders against his, but they didn't need to hold him up. He walked, pressed close between them, alone, his head thrown back, breathing heavily, but he walked alone.

The shuffling of the prisoners had now changed into something like a regular step. A division of Belgians and French and a small group of Poles was among them. They, too, marched with them.

The columns had reached one another. The Germans were on their way to outlying villages. They had no train connections because the railroad station was destroyed, and they therefore had to walk. A few civilians with SA arm bands directed the column. The women were tired. A few children cried. The men stared ahead of them.

"This is how we fled from Warsaw," whispered a Pole behind Lewinsky.

"And we from Liége," answered a Belgian.

"And we from Paris."

"No, it was worse. Much worse. They chased us very differently."

They had hardly any feeling of revenge. Nor hatred, either. Women and children were everywhere the same, and as a rule it was more often the innocent than the guilty who were hit by disaster. Among this tired crowd there were no doubt many who had neither consciously intended evil nor indeed done anything to justify their fate. It wasn't this the prisoners felt. It was something quite different. It had nothing to do with the individual person; nor had it much to do with the town; nor even much with the country or the nation. It was rather something like the feeling of an enormous impersonal justice that sprang up the moment the two columns passed one another. A world crime had been committed and almost succeeded; the laws of humanity had been overthrown and almost trampled to death; the law of life had been spat upon, whipped and shot to pieces; robbery had been made legal, murder worthy of reward, terror had become law—and now, suddenly, in this breathless moment, four hundred victims of arbitrary power felt it was enough —that a voice had spoken and that the pendulum of time was swinging back. They sensed that it was not only countries and nations that would be saved; it was the law of life itself. It was that for which many names existed—and one of them, the oldest and simplest, was God. And that meant: Man.

The refugee column had now passed the prisoners' column. For a few minutes it had looked as though the refugees were the prisoners, and the prisoners free. Two open vans drawn by gray horses and filled with luggage formed the rear of the column. The SS ran nervously up and down the prisoners' column on the lookout for some kind of sign, some word. Nothing happened. The column continued silently to march on, and soon the feet began shuffling again, the tiredness returned and once more Goldstein had to place his arms around the shoulders of Lewinsky and Werner—and yet, when the black-red barriers of the camp entrance appeared, with its iron gate adorned by the old Prussian motto *To Each His Own,* everyone suddenly saw these words, which for years had been a terrible mockery, with new eyes.

The camp band was waiting at the gate. It played the Fridericus Rex March. Behind it stood a number of SS-men and the second camp leader. The prisoners began to march.
"Legs high! Eyes right!"
The tree-felling gang had not yet arrived.
"Halt! Number!"
They numbered off. Lewinsky and Werner watched the second camp leader. He rocked from the knees and yelled: "Body inspection! First group, step out!"
With cautious movements the wrapped weapon parts were slipped backwards into Goldstein's hands. Lewinsky suddenly felt the sweat pouring down his body.
SS Squad Leader Guenther Steinbrenner, keeping watch like a sheep dog, had noticed a movement somewhere. Striking out with his fists, he forced his way through to Goldstein. Werner compressed his lips. If the things had not reached Muenzer or Remne by now, all was lost.
Before Steinbrenner got to him, Goldstein fell down. Steinbrenner gave him a kick in the ribs. "Get up, you dirty cur!"
Goldstein made an effort. He got to his knees, raised himself, moaned, suddenly foamed at the mouth and collapsed.
Steinbrenner saw the gray face and the rolling eyes. He gave Goldstein another kick and deliberated whether he should hold a burning match under his nose in order to bring him to. But then he remembered that a short while ago he had boxed a dead man's ears and made a fool of himself in the eyes of his comrades; that sort of thing mustn't be allowed to happen a second time. He stepped back, growling.
"What?" the second camp leader asked the gang leader in a bored tone. "Aren't these the ones from the munitions factory?"
"No. This is only the clearing gang."
"Oh, I see. Then where are the others?"
"Just coming up the hill," said the gang leader.

"Well, all right. Then make room. These blockheads here don't have to be inspected. Buzz off!"

"First group, to the rear! On the double!" ordered the gang leader. "Attention! Left turn! March!"

Goldstein got up. He staggered, but he succeeded in staying with the group.

"Did you throw it away?" asked Werner almost soundlessly as Goldstein's head was close to his.

"No."

Werner's face relaxed. "Certain?"

"Yes."

They marched in. The SS no longer paid any attention to them. Behind them stood the column from the munitions factory. They were being thoroughly searched.

"Who has it?" asked Werner. "Remne?"

"I have," Goldstein said.

They marched to the roll-call ground and took up positions.

"What would have happened if you hadn't got up again?" asked Lewinsky. "How could we have taken it from you without anyone seeing?"

"I'd have gotten up in any case."

"How?"

Goldstein smiled. "I wanted to be an actor once."

"You faked that?"

"Not all of it. The last part."

"The foaming at the mouth, too?"

"Those are school tricks."

"All the same, you should have handed it on. Why not? Why did you keep it?"

"I explained that to you before."

"Look out," whispered Werner. "SS coming."

They stood at attention.

CHAPTER ELEVEN

The transport arrived in the afternoon. About fifteen hundred men dragged themselves up the hill. Among them were fewer invalids than might have been expected. Whoever had broken down on the long road had been promptly shot.

It was a long time before the men were admitted. The accompanying SS who handed them over tried to smuggle in a few dozen dead whom they had forgotten to deduct. The bureaucracy of the camp, however, was on its guard; they had every single body presented to them, living or dead, and accepted only those who had passed the entrance gate alive. This caused an incident from which the SS derived great pleasure. While the transport was standing before the gate, a few more people had caved in. Their comrades tried to drag them along, but the SS gave the order to double march and they had to leave a number of invalids to their fate. About two dozen lay there, strewn over the last two hundred yards of the road. They cawed and gasped and squeaked like wounded birds or just lay there with frightened, wide-open eyes, too weak to scream. They knew what to expect if they remained behind; during the march they had heard hundreds of their comrades die from a bullet in the neck.

The SS were quick to see the joke. "Look at them begging to get into the concentration camp!" shouted Steinbrenner.

"Go on! Go on!" yelled the SS-men who had delivered the transport.

The prisoners tried to crawl. "Tortoise race!" exulted Steinbrenner. "I'm backing the baldhead in the center!"

On widespread hands and knees the baldhead crept forward over the glistening asphalt like an exhausted frog. He passed another prisoner whose arms kept doubling up and who continued painfully to raise himself without moving any further. Every crawling man held his head stretched out in a peculiar way—pressing towards the gate of rescue and at the same time listening in dread for the sound of bullets behind him.

"Go on, forward, baldhead!"

The SS formed a double line. Suddenly two shots rang out in the rear. They had been fired by an SS squad leader belonging to the escort. Grinning, he stuck his revolver back in its holster. He had only fired into the air.

The shots, however, had struck mortal fear into the prisoners. They thought the two furthest in the rear had been shot. In their panic they made less headway than before. One man gave up; he stretched out his arms and folded his hands. His lips prayed and great beads of sweat broke out on his forehead. A second one lay down, quiet and resigned, his face in his hands. He lay down to die and then didn't move any more.

"Sixty seconds to go!" shouted Steinbrenner. "One minute! In one minute the gate to paradise will be closed! Whoever is not in by then has to stay outside!"

He glanced at his wrist watch and moved the gate as though about to close it. A moan from the human insects answered. The SS squad leader of the escort fired another shot. The crawling became more desperate. Only the man with his face in his hands didn't move. He had given up.

"Hurrah!" shouted Steinbrenner. "My baldhead has made it!"

He gave the man an encouraging kick in the behind. At the same time a few others had passed through the gate, but more than half of them were still outside.

"Thirty seconds to go!" shouted Steinbrenner in the tone of a radio time-announcer.

The rustling and scraping and wailing increased. Two men lay helplessly on the road striking out with their arms as though about to swim. They no longer had the strength to get up. One of them cried in a high falsetto.

"Squeaking like a mouse," declared Steinbrenner who kept looking at his watch. "Fifteen seconds to go!"

There followed another shot. This time it had not been fired into the air. The man who had laid his face in his hands jerked convulsively and then seemed to stretch out and sink deeper into the road. His blood formed a black pool around his head—like a dark halo. The praying prisoner beside him tried to jump up, but he managed to get only onto one knee and slipped sideways so that he landed on his back. He had his eyes rigidly closed and moved his arms and legs as though still about to run away yet unaware that he was treading air like an infant kicking in the cradle. A salvo of laughter accompanied his efforts.

"How are you going to take this one, Robert?" one of the SS-men asked the squad leader who had shot the first man. "From behind, through the chest or through the nose?"

Robert walked slowly round the kicking man. For a moment he stood thoughtfully behind him; then he shot him obliquely through the head from the side. The kicking man arched himself, his boots thudded heavily a few times on the road, and he sank back. Slowly he pulled one leg up, stretched it out, pulled it up again, stretched it—

"That wasn't such a good shot, Robert."

"Oh yes, it was," answered Robert indifferently without looking at his critic. "Those are just nerve reflexes."

"All over!" declared Steinbrenner. "Your time is up! Close the gate!"

The guards actually began slowly to close the gates. Shrieks of terror rose up. "No jostling here, gentlemen!" shouted Steinbrenner with shining eyes. "One at a time, please! And there are still people who say we're not popular here!"

Three of the men could get no further. They lay several yards apart on the road. Robert calmly finished off two of them with a shot in the neck; the third one, however, followed him with his head. He was half sitting, and as Robert stepped behind him he turned round and looked at him as though by so doing he could prevent his firing. Robert tried it twice; each time with a supreme effort the other one managed to turn round far enough to look at Robert. Finally Robert shrugged his shoulders. "As you like," he said, and shot him in the face.

He put his weapon away. "That makes exactly forty."

"Finished off forty?" asked Steinbrenner, who had approached.

Robert nodded. "On this transport."

"You're one hell of a guy!" Steinbrenner stared at him full of admiration and envy as at someone who had just set up a sports record. Robert was only a few years older than he. "Tops, that's what that is!"

An older squad leader came over. "You and your banging away!" he grumbled. "Now there'll be another fuss over the papers belonging to those you've just bumped off. They're carrying on about it here just as if we'd brought along a crowd of princes."

Three hours after the transport had lined up for registration, thirty-six men had collapsed. Four were dead. The transport had had no water since the morning. While the SS were occupied elsewhere, two prisoners from Block Six had tried to smuggle in a pail of water. They had been caught and were now hanging with twisted limbs on the crosses near the crematorium.

The registration continued. Two hours later seven men were dead and more than fifty lying around. Then, after six o'clock, things went faster; twelve were dead and more than eighty lying about on the ground. At seven there were a hundred and twenty and the number of dead could no longer be established. The unconscious men moved as little as the dead.

At eight, the registration of those who could still stand came to an end. It had turned dark and the sky was a mass of cirrus clouds. The labor gangs moved in. They had worked overtime so that the transport could be dealt with first. Once more the clearing gang had found weapons. It was the fifth time, always in the same place. This time there had also been a note: *We are thinking of you.* They had known for some while that those who hid the weapons for them by night were workers in the munitions factory.

"Just look at the confusion," whispered Werner. "We'll get through."

Lewinsky pressed a small flat package against his ribs. "Pity we haven't more. Two days from now we won't have another chance. The clearing up will be over by then."

"Make them march in!" commanded Weber. "Roll call will be later."

"Damn it," muttered Goldstein, "if only we'd brought a cannon with us! What incredible luck!"

They marched toward the barracks. "The new ones into the disinfecting chamber!" declared Weber. "We're not going to have any typhus or itch brought in here. Where's the chamber kapo?"

The kapo reported. "These people's clothes must be disinfected and deloused," said Weber. "Have we enough outfits for changing?"

"Yes, Herr Storm Leader. Two thousand more arrived a month ago."

"Of course." Weber remembered. The clothes had been sent from Auschwitz. Extermination camps always had enough clothing to hand on to other camps. "Get on! Into the tubs with the men!"

The command rang out: "Undress! Into the baths! Clothing to the rear, personal belongings in front of you!"

A swaying passed down the dark lines. The command could really mean to bathe; but again it could mean to be gassed. In extermination camps one was led naked into the gas chambers under the pretext of being given a bath. From the spray heads in the ceilings, however, flowed not water but the fatal gas.

"What'll we do?" whispered the prisoner Sulzbacher to his neighbor Rosen. "Collapse?"

They undressed. They knew, as so often before, that they had to make a life-and-death decision in a few seconds. They didn't know the camp; if it was an extermination camp with gas chambers, then it would be better to fake a collapse. This gave one a slight chance of living longer because as a rule unconscious people were not immediately dragged along. With luck, this chance could turn into survival; even in extermination camps not everyone was killed. If, on the other hand, it was not a gas chamber camp, then a collapse was dangerous; one could be promptly syringed to death as useless.

Rosen glanced over at the unconscious ones. He noticed that no attempt was being made to bring them round. He concluded they were not going to be gassed; otherwise they would have taken along as many as possible. "No," he whispered. "Not yet—"

The lines which hitherto had been dark now shimmered dirty white. The prisoners stood naked; each one of them was a human being but this they had almost forgotten.

The transport had been chased through a vast tub of strong disinfectant. In the clothing chamber each man had been thrown a few garments. Now the lines stood once more on the roll-call ground.

They dressed hastily. They were, so far as one could call it that, happy; they had not landed in an extermination camp. The garments they had received didn't fit. For underwear Sulzbacher had been thrown a pair of women's woolen panties with red braid trimming; Rosen a priest's surplice. All the clothing had belonged to people now dead. The surplice had a bullet hole surrounded by a yellowish, frayed bloodstain. It hadn't been properly washed. A number of the men had been given sharp-edged wooden shoes which came from a defunct concentration camp in Holland. For feet not used to them and bleeding from the road they were instruments of torture.

The distribution to the blocks was about to begin. At this moment the town's sirens started. Everyone glanced at the camp leader.

"Keep going!" shouted Weber through the noise.

The SS and kapos ran nervously to and fro. The lines of prisoners stood there quietly; only the faces were slightly raised and shimmered pale in the moonlight.

"Heads down!" shouted Weber.

The SS and the kapos ran along the lines, repeating the command. In between they stared skyward themselves. Their voices were drowned in the noise. They made use of their truncheons.

Hands in his pockets, Weber walked up and down the edge of the ground. He gave no further orders. Neubauer came dashing from his house through the gate.

"What's going on here, Weber? Why aren't the people in the barracks?"

"The distribution isn't finished yet," answered Weber phlegmatically.

"Doesn't matter. They can't remain here. On this open ground they could be taken for troops."

The howling of the sirens was changing.

"Too late," said Weber. "In motion they are even more visible."

He stood still and looked at Neubauer. Neubauer noticed it; he knew Weber expected him to run for the shelter. Annoyed, he too stood still. "Damned lunacy to send those men here!" he inveighed. "First we're supposed to comb our own men through, and then they saddle us with a whole new transport! Crazy! Why haven't the scum been sent to an extermination camp?"

"The extermination camps probably lie too far to the east."

Neubauer glanced up. "What d'you mean by that?"

"Too far to the east. The highways and railways have to be kept clear for other purposes."

Once more Neubauer was suddenly aware of the cold grip of fear round his stomach. "Sure," he said, to calm himself. "To send troops to the front. We'll let them have it all right."

Weber didn't answer. Neubauer looked at him crossly. "Make the men lie down," he said. "Then they'll look less like a formation."

"Very good." Weber strolled a few steps forward. "Lie down!" he commanded.

"Lie down!" repeated the SS.

The lines collapsed. Weber returned. Neubauer had wanted to go to his house; but there was something in Weber's attitude he didn't like. He remained standing. Another of those ungrateful creatures, he thought. Hardly had one gotten him the War Service Cross than he became insolent again. Little wonder! After all, what had he to lose? Those few bits of tin on that ridiculous hero's chest, that's all, the hireling!

The attack didn't come. After some time the All Clear sounded. Neubauer turned around. "As little light as possible. Go a bit faster with the distribution to the blocks. One can't see much in the dark anyway. The rest can be dealt with tomorrow by the block seniors and the office."

"Very good."

Neubauer stood still. He watched the transport march off. The men rose with difficulty. Some had gone to sleep from exhaustion and had to be shaken awake by their comrades. Others lay there too worn out to walk.

"The dead to the crematorium yard. Take the unconscious ones along, too."

"Very good."

The file formed up and began to move down the road to the barracks.

"Bruno! Bruno!"

Neubauer whirled round. His wife was approaching from the entrance gate across the ground. She was almost hysterical. "Bruno! Where are you? Has anything happened? Have you—?"

She saw him and stopped. She was followed by her daughter.

"What are you doing here?" asked Neubauer furiously, but under his breath, for Weber was within earshot. "How did you get in here?"

"The guard. He knows us, after all! You never came back, so I thought something must have happened to you. All these people—"
Selma glanced round her as though just waking up. "Didn't I tell you to stay in my private quarters?" asked Neubauer still under his breath. "Didn't I forbid you both to come in here?"

"Father," said Freya. "Mother was out of her mind with fear. Those huge sirens, so near—"

The transport turned into the main road. It passed close by the three of them. "What is that?" whispered Selma.

"That? Nothing! A transport that arrived today."

"But—"

"No but! What are you doing here anyhow? Out with you!" Neubauer pushed his wife and daughter aside. "On with you! Go ahead!"

"The way they look!" Selma stared at the faces that were just passing through a shaft of moonlight.

"Look? They're prisoners! Traitors to the Fatherland! What should they look like? Fat bankers?"

"And those others they're carrying there, those—"

"Now I've had enough!" snorted Neubauer. "That's the last straw! Squeamish talk! Those people arrived here today. Hasn't anything to do with us what they look like. On the contrary! They've come here to be fattened up. Isn't that so, Weber?"

"Yes, Herr *Obersturmbannführer.*" Weber cast a slightly amused glance at Freya and moved on.

"There you have it. And now out with you! Strictly forbidden to be here. This isn't a zoo!"

He pushed the women on. He was afraid Selma might say something dangerous. One had to watch out on all sides. No one was reliable, not even Weber. Confounded nuisance that Selma and Freya had to come up right after the transport had arrived! He had forgotten to tell them to stay in town. Actually, Selma wouldn't have stayed anyway once the alarm had started. The devil only knew why she was so nervous. A stately woman as a rule, but when a siren went off, just like an anemic flapper.

"That guard I'm going to take severely to task! To let you in here! Unheard of! Next thing he'll be letting anyone in!"

Freya turned round. "There won't be many who'll want to."

For an instant Neubauer stopped breathing. What was this? Freya? His own flesh and blood? Revolution! The apple of his eye. He looked into Freya's calm face. She couldn't have meant it like that. No, she had meant it quite harmlessly. All of a sudden he laughed. "No, I'm not so sure of that! Those here, this transport, they've been begging to be allowed to stay here. Begged! Cried!

What d'you think they'll look like in two or three weeks? Unrecognizable! This is the best camp in all Germany. Famous for it. A sanatorium."

Two hundred men of the transport were still left in front of the Small camp. They were the weakest. They held each other up. Sulzbacher and Rosen were among them. The blocks stood in line outside. They knew that Weber himself was supervising the distribution. This was why Berger had sent 509 and Bucher to fetch the food; he wanted to prevent the camp leader from seeing them; but they had been sent back from the kitchen. Food was to be handed out only after the transport had moved in.

There was no light anywhere. Only Weber and SS Squad Leader Schulte had flashlights which they kept switching on and off. The block seniors reported. "Stick the rest in here," said Weber to the second camp senior.

The camp senior divided the men up. Schulte was supervising. Weber strolled on. "Why are there so many fewer here than over there?" he asked on coming to Section D of Barrack 22.

Block Senior Handke stood at attention. "The room here is smaller than the other sections, Herr Storm Leader."

Weber turned on his flashlight. The light wandered over the rigid faces. 509 and Bucher were standing in the rear row. The circle of light passed over 509, blinded him, passed on and returned. "I'm sure I know you! Where from?"

"I've been in the camp a long time, Herr Storm Leader."

The circle of light moved down to his number. "About time you kicked off!"

"He's one of those who recently had to go to the office, Herr Storm Leader," reported Handke.

"I see." The circle of light wandered back again to the number, and then passed on. "Just make a note of that number, Schulte."

"Very good," declared Squad Leader Schulte in a fresh and youthful voice. "How many men are supposed to go in here?"

"Twenty. No, thirty; have to squeeze together."

Schulte and the camp senior counted and made notes. From the dark the Veterans' eyes followed Schulte's pencil. They couldn't see whether he took down 509's number. Weber hadn't mentioned it to him again and now the flashlight was switched off. "Finished?" asked Weber.

"Yes."

"The rest of the writing business can be done by the office tomorrow. On with you, over there! And drop dead! Otherwise we'll lend you some assistance."

Square and confident, Weber walked back down the camp road. The squad leaders followed him. For a while Handke still hung around.

"Food carriers out!" he growled then.

"Stay here," Berger whispered to 509 and Bucher. "Let a couple of others go. Better for you not to run under Weber's nose again."

"Did Schulte take down my number?"

"I didn't see it."

"No," said Lebenthal. "I was standing in front and watched. He forgot it in his hurry."

For a while the thirty newcomers stood almost motionless in the windy dark. "Is there room in the barracks?" asked Sulzbacher at last.

"Water," said a man hoarsely beside him. "Water! For Christ's sake, give us some water."

Someone appeared with a tin pail half filled with water. The newcomers fell upon it and upset it; they had nothing to drink with but their hollow hands. They threw themselves on the ground and tried to scoop up the water. They moaned. Their lips were black and dirty. They licked the ground.

Berger had observed that Sulzbacher and Rosen had not joined in the tussle. "We have a water pipe near the latrine," he said. "It only trickles; but in time you'll get enough to drink. Take a pail and get some."

One of the newcomers bared his teeth. "So that you can wolf our food in the meantime, eh?"

"I'll go," said Rosen, and took the pail.

"Me, too." Sulzbacher seized the other end of the handle.

"You stay here," said Berger. "Bucher can go along and show him where it is."

The two went off. "I'm the room senior here," said Berger to the newcomers. "We keep order here. I advise you to co-operate. Otherwise you'll have a short life."

No one answered. But Berger wasn't sure that anyone had even listened.

"Is there room in the barracks?" Sulzbacher asked again after a while.

"No. We'll have to take turns at sleeping. Some will have to stay outside."

"Will there be anything to eat? We've been marching all day on nothing."

"The food carriers have gone to the kitchen." Berger didn't express his belief that there wouldn't be any food for the newcomers.

"My name is Sulzbacher. Is this an extermination camp?"

"No."

"Sure?"

"Yes."

"Oh, thank God! You haven't any gas chambers?"

"No."

"Thank God," repeated Sulzbacher.

"You talk as though you were in a hotel," said Ahasver. "Just wait. Where are you from?"

"We've been five days on the road. On foot. We were three thousand. Our camp was disbanded. Whoever couldn't keep going was shot."

"Where are you from?"

"From Lohme."

A number of the newcomers were still lying on the ground. "Water!" squawked one. "Where's the man with the water? Drinking himself full—the swine!"

"Wouldn't you do the same?" asked Lebenthal.

The man stared at him from vacant eyes. "Water," he said, calmer. "Water, please."

"You came from Lohme?" asked Ahasver.

"Yes."

"Did you know a Martin Schimmel there?"

"No."

"Or Moritz Gewurz? One with a bashed-in nose and no hair." Sulzbacher reflected wearily. "No."

"Or maybe Gedalje Gold? He had only one ear," said Ahasver hopefully. "That's something you notice. He was in Block 12."

"Twelve?"

"Yes. Four years ago."

"Oh, God!" Sulzbacher turned away. The question was too idiotic. Four years! Why not a hundred?

"Let him alone, old man," said 509. "He's tired."

"They were friends of mine," murmured Ahasver. "One inquires after friends."

Bucher and Rosen arrived with the pail. Rosen was bleeding. His surplice was torn at the shoulder; his jacket was open. "The new ones are fighting over the water," said Bucher. "Mahner saved us. He organized things over there. Now they're standing in line to get water. We'll have to do the same thing here or they'll upset the pail again." The newcomers had gotten up. "Stand in line!" called Berger. "Every man will get some. We've something for all. Those not in line won't get any!"

All obeyed except two who rushed forward. They beat them down with sticks. Then Ahasver and 509 fetched the mugs and they all drank, one after the other. "Let's see if we can get some more," said Bucher to Rosen and Sulzbacher. "It won't be so dangerous now."

"We were three thousand," said Sulzbacher mechanically and senselessly.

The food carriers returned. They had gotten nothing for the newcomers. At once a row started. The men began beating each other up in front of Sections A and B. The room senior there was helpless. He had almost only Mussulmen, and the newcomers were shrewder and not yet so resigned.

"We've got to give them something," said Berger quietly to 509.

"At most soup. No bread. We need it more than they do. We're weaker."

"That's why we've got to give them something. Otherwise they'll take it. You can see it over there."

"Yes, but only soup. The bread we need ourselves. Let's talk to the one called Sulzbacher."

They fetched him. "Listen," said Berger. "We didn't get anything for you this evening. But we'll share our soup with you."

"Thanks," said Sulzbacher.

"What?"

"Thanks."

They stared at him in astonishment. It wasn't usual to thank in the camp. "Can you help us with it?" asked Berger. "If not, your crowd'll knock everything over again, and this time there won't be anything more to be had. Is there someone else reliable?"

"Rosen. And the two next to him."

The Veterans and the four newcomers went to meet the food carriers and crowded round them. Berger had previously seen to it that all the others were standing in line. Not till then did they bring up the food.

They gathered together and began dividing it up. The newcomers had no bowls. They had to eat their share standing up and then return the bowls. Rosen saw to it that no one came twice. Several of the old inmates grumbled. "You'll get the soup back tomorrow," said Berger. "It's only lent." Then he turned to Sulzbacher. "We need the bread ourselves. Our men are weaker than yours. Maybe they'll hand something out to you tomorrow morning."

"Yes. Thanks for the soup. We'll give it back tomorrow. How are we going to sleep?"

"We'll clear a few of our bunks. You'll have to sleep sitting up. Even then there won't be room for everyone."

"And you?"

"We'll stay outside. Later on we'll wake you up and change over."

Sulzbacher shook his head. "You won't get them out once they're asleep."

A few of the newcomers were already asleep, their mouths open, in front of the barrack. "Leave them there," said Berger, and looked around. "Where are the others?"

"They've already found room for themselves," said 509. "We won't get them out again in the dark. We'll have to leave it this way tonight."

Berger glanced up at the sky. "Maybe it won't be too cold. We can sit close together along the wall. We have three blankets."

"Tomorrow this'll have to be changed," declared 509. "We don't use force in this section."

They crouched together. Almost all the Veterans were outside; even Ahasver, Karel and the sheep dog. Rosen and Sulzbacher and about ten more of the newcomers squatted with them.

"I'm sorry," said Sulzbacher.

"Nonsense. You're not responsible for each other."

"I'll keep watch," said Karel to Berger. "There are at least six of ours who'll die tonight. They're lying below to the right, near the door. When they're dead we can carry them out and then take turns at sleeping in their bunks."

"How can you tell in the dark if they're dead?"

"That's easy. I bend down close over their faces. You can soon tell when they stop breathing."

"By the time we get them outside, there'll already be others from inside in their place," said 509.

"That's what I mean," answered Karel eagerly. "I'll come and report. And then, while we're taking out one of the dead, someone else can lie down right away in his place."

"All right, Karel," said Berger. "You keep watch."

It grew colder. From the barracks came moans and shrieks of terror uttered in sleep. "My God," said Sulzbacher to 509. "What incredible luck! We thought we were coming to an extermination camp. If only they don't send us on!"

509 did not answer. Luck, he thought. But it was true.

"How were things with you?" asked Ahasver after some time.

"They shot everyone who couldn't keep going. We were three thousand—"

"We know that. You've told us several times already."

"Yes," Sulzbacher answered helplessly.

"What did you see on the way?" asked 509. "What do things in Germany look like?"

Sulzbacher thought for a moment. "The night before last we had enough water," he said then. "Sometimes people gave us something. Sometimes not. We were too many."

"One night a man brought us four bottles of beer," said Rosen.

"I don't mean that," said 509 impatiently. "What were the towns like? Destroyed?"

"We didn't come through towns. Always round the outside."

"Didn't you see anything at all, then?"

Sulzbacher looked at 509. "One sees little when one can hardly walk and they're shooting from behind. We didn't see any trains."

"Why was your camp broken up?"

"The front line was coming closer."

"What d'you know about that? Do speak up! Where is Lohme? How far from the Rhine? Far?"

Sulzbacher tried to keep his eyes open. "Yes—rather far—fifty—seventy—kilometers—tomorrow—" Then his head fell forward. "Tomorrow—now I must sleep—"

"It's about seventy kilometers," said Ahasver. "I've been there."

"Seventy? And from here?" 509 began to count. "Two hundred—two hundred and fifty—"

Ahasver shrugged his shoulders. "509," he said quietly. "You're always thinking about kilometers. Has it ever occurred to you that they can do the same with us as with those there? Break up the camp—send us away—and where to? What will happen to us then? We can no longer march."

"Whoever can't march will be shot—" Rosen had wakened with a jolt and was already asleep again.

Everyone was silent. They hadn't thought that far yet. Like a heavy threat, it suddenly hung over them. 509 stared at the silver clouds moving across the sky. Then he stared at the roads in the valley shimmering in the half-light. We shouldn't have shared our soup, he thought for a moment. We must be able to march. But after all, what good would it have done? Good at most for a few minutes of marching. The new ones had been driven on for days. "Maybe here they won't shoot those who lag behind," he said.

"No," said Ahasver with gloomy sarcasm. "They'll feed them on meat and provide them with new clothes and wave farewell to them."

509 looked at him. Ahasver was perfectly calm. There wasn't much left that could frighten him.

"Here comes Lebenthal," said Berger.

Lebenthal sat down beside them. "Did you hear anything more over there, Leo?" asked 509.

Leo nodded. "They want to get rid of as many of the transport people as possible. Lewinsky heard it from the red-haired clerk in the office. How they plan to get rid of them he didn't exactly know. But it should be soon; then they can write off the dead as having died as a result of the transport."

One of the newcomers leapt up in his sleep and screamed. Then he sank back again and snored, his mouth wide open.

"Are they going to finish off only the transport people?"

"That's all Lewinsky knew. But he sends us word to watch out."

"Yes, we must watch out." 509 fell silent for a moment. "It means that we should keep our traps shut. That's what he wants to say. Or isn't it?"

"Of course. What else?"

"If we warn the new ones, they'll be careful," declared Meyer. "And if the SS want to do away with a certain number and can't find them, they'll take the rest from us."

"Correct." 509 looked at Sulzbacher, whose head lay heavily against Berger's shoulder. "Well, what'll we do? Keep our traps shut?"

It was a difficult decision. Meyer was right. Should they do any sifting and not find enough new ones, it was perfectly possible that the quota would be filled up with people from the Small camp; all the more so since the new ones were not so run down as the others.

They were silent for a long time. "They don't concern us," said Meyer at last. "We've got to fend for ourselves first."

Berger rubbed his inflamed eyes. 509 tugged at his jacket. Ahasver turned round toward Meyer. The pale light glittered in his eyes. "If they don't concern us," he said slowly, "then we won't concern anyone, either."

Berger raised his head. "You're right."

Ahasver leaned calmly against the wall and didn't answer. His old emaciated skull with the deep-sunk eyes seemed to be seeing something no one else saw. "We'll tell these two here about it," declared Berger. "They can warn the others. We can't do any more. After all, we don't know what's going to happen."

Karel came over from the barracks. "One is dead."

509 stood up. "Come, we'll carry him out." He turned to Ahasver. "And then you stay in and go to sleep, old man."

CHAPTER TWELVE

The blocks stood lined up on the roll-call ground of the Small camp. Squad Leader Niemann rocked comfortably to and fro from his knees. He was a man of about thirty, with a narrow face, small protruding ears and a receding chin. His hair was sand-colored and he wore rimless glasses. Without his uniform one would have taken him for a typical little office clerk. This was what he had actually been before he had joined the SS and become a man.

"Attention!" Niemann had a high, rather squeaky voice. "New transport, step out! On the double!"

"Look out!" muttered 509 to Sulzbacher. "Look out!"

A double line formed up in front of Niemann. "Sick and invalids out to the right!" he commanded.

The line stirred, but no one stepped to the side. The men were suspicious; they had experienced similar things before.

"On! Come on! Anyone wanting to report to the medic or have his wounds dressed, out to the right!"

Hesitatingly, several prisoners stepped to the side. Niemann walked over to them. "What's wrong with you?" he asked the first one.

"Sore feet and a broken toe, Herr Squad Leader."

"And you?"

"Double rupture of the groin, Herr Squad Leader."

Niemann went on questioning. Then he sent two men back. This was a trick to deceive the prisoners and make them feel safe. It worked. Immediately a number of new ones reported. Niemann nodded casually. "Heart cases step forward! Men who are unfit for hard work but can still darn stockings and cut up shoes."

Again several men reported. Niemann had now collected about thirty men and realized he wouldn't get any more. "You others seem to be in excellent shape!" he barked angrily. "We'll just make sure of that! Right turn! On the double!"

The double line ran round the roll-call ground. Panting heavily, they ran past the other inmates who were standing at attention and each knew that he, too, was in danger. It was possible that should one of them collapse, Niemann wouldn't hesitate to seize him as an addition. Besides, no one could be sure he wouldn't deal with the old ones separately.

The runners passed by for the sixth time. They were already stumbling; but they had understood they were not being made to run in order to discover whether they were unfit for heavy work. They were running for their lives. Their faces dripped with sweat, and in their eyes was the desperate, knowing fear of death which no animal, only man, can feel.

Now those who had reported first also realized what was happening. They became alarmed. Two of them tried to join the line of the runners. Niemann saw it. "Back with you! Over there!"

They didn't listen to him. Deaf from fear, they started to run. They wore wooden shoes which they immediately lost. With bare, bleeding feet they ran on; they had not been given any socks the night before. Niemann didn't take his eyes off them. For a while they ran along with the others. Then, gradually, when a greedy hope that they had escaped began to show in their disfigured faces, Niemann calmly walked a few steps ahead and as they stumbled close past him, he tripped them up. They fell and tried to get up. With two kicks he knocked them down again. They tried to crawl. "Get up!" he shouted in his squeaky tenor. "Over there!" They obeyed.

All this time Niemann's back had been turned to Barrack 22. The fatal merry-go-round had continued to run. Four more men had collapsed. They lay on the ground. Two were unconscious. One of them wore a Hussar's uniform which he had been given the previous evening; the other one a woman's chemise with cheap lace under a kind of shortened caftan. The chamber kapo had used his sense of humor in distributing the garments from Auschwitz. There were still a few dozen other men dressed as though for a carnival.

509 had noticed Rosen stumble on, half doubled up, and then remain behind. He knew that in a few seconds he would be completely exhausted and collapse. It doesn't concern me, he thought, it doesn't. I won't do anything stupid. Each man must fend for himself. Once more the lines passed close to the barracks. 509 saw that Rosen was now the last. Quickly he looked at Niemann, who still had his back turned to the barracks, and then he glanced further round. None of the barrack seniors took any notice of him. Everyone had his eyes on the two whom Niemann had tripped up. Handke, craning his neck, had even taken a step forward. 509 seized Rosen by the arm as he staggered past, pulled him close and pushed him back through the line.

"Quick! Get through! Into the barrack! Hide!"

He heard Rosen panting behind him and out of the corner of his eye saw something like a movement, then he heard the panting no more. Niemann had seen nothing. He still hadn't turned around. Handke hadn't noticed anything, either. 509 knew that the door to the barrack stood open. He hoped Rosen had understood him. And he hoped that Rosen, should he be caught in spite of everything, would not betray him. He must know that he would be lost anyhow. The newcomers had not been counted by Niemann, so he now had a chance. 509 felt that his knees trembled and that his throat was going dry. The blood suddenly roared in his ears.

He glanced cautiously towards Berger. Motionless, Berger was watching the running crowd in which more and more people broke down. His strained face showed that he had seen everything. Then 509 heard Lebenthal whisper behind him. "He's inside." The trembling in his knees grew stronger. He had to lean against Bucher.

The wooden shoes which had been given to a number of newcomers lay strewn all over the place. Unaccustomed to wearing them, the men had lost them. Only two continued desperately to clatter on in them. Niemann wiped his glasses; they had grown dim. It was a result of the warmth he felt while watching the terror of death among the prisoners as they collapsed, dragged themselves up again, collapsed, dragged themselves up and staggered on. It was a warmth in the stomach and behind the eyes. He had felt it for the first time in 1934 when he had killed his first Jew. He hadn't actually intended to do it; but then it had come over him. He had always been a depressed, scared person and at first he had almost been afraid to fall upon the Jew. But when he saw him crawling before him on the ground, begging for his life, he had suddenly felt himself becoming someone else, stronger, more powerful; he had felt his blood, the horizon had widened, the demolished bourgeois four-room apartment of the small Jewish clothes dealer with its green reps furniture had changed into the Asiatic desert of Ghengis Khan; the clerk Niemann had suddenly become master over life and death, power had been there, omnipotence, a wild intoxication that spread in him and rose higher until the first blow on the softly yielding skull with its sparse, dyed hair came all by itself.... "Division, halt!"

The prisoners could hardly believe it. They had expected to be forced to keep on running till they died. Like an eclipse of the sun the barracks, the ground and the people whirled around before them. They held onto one another. Niemann put on his clean glasses again. He was suddenly in a hurry. "Bring the corpses over here!"

They stared at him. So far there hadn't been any corpses. "The ones who collapsed," he corrected himself. "Those who broke down."

They staggered over and seized the prone men by their arms and legs. A whole pile of them lay to one side. They had dropped there, one on to of the other. Amidst the confusion 509 saw Sulzbacher.

He was standing, protected by others in front of him, kicking a man on the ground in the shin and pulling him by the hair and ears. Then he bent down and hauled him to his knees. Unconscious, the man fell back. Sulzbacher kicked him again, placed his hands under his arms and tried to lift him up. He didn't succeed. Now he beat desperately with his fists at the unconscious man until a kapo pushed him aside. Sulzbacher forced his way back again. The kapo gave him a kick. He thought Sulzbacher had a grudge against the unconscious man and wanted to vent his rage upon him. "You damned bastard!" he growled. "Let him alone. He'll kick off anyhow."

The kapo Strohschneider appeared with the flat truck on which the corpses were usually driven away through the gate in the barbed wire. The engine rattled like a machine gun. Strohschneider drove up to the pile. Those who had broken down were loaded on. A few still made efforts to escape. They had regained consciousness. But now Niemann was on the lookout; he let no one get away. "Anyone not belonging here—fall out!" he shouted. "Those who reported sick, load on the rest!"

The men dashed off into the barracks as fast as they could. The unconscious ones were loaded on. Then Strohschneider stepped on the gas. He drove so slowly that those who had reported sick could follow on foot. Niemann walked at their side. "Your troubles have now come to an end," he told his victims in a changed, almost friendly voice.

"Where are they being taken to?" asked one of the newcomers in Barrack 22.

"Probably to Block 46."

"What happens there?"

"I don't know," answered 509. He didn't want to mention what was common knowledge in the camp—that Niemann kept a can of gas and a few syringes for injections in one room of the experimental Block 46, and that none of the prisoners would return. In the evening Strohschneider would take them to the crematorium.

"Why did you give that man such a beating?" 509 asked Sulzbacher.

Sulzbacher looked at him and didn't answer. He choked, as

though he had to swallow a wad of cotton, and then went away. "It was his brother," said Rosen.

Sulzbacher vomited, but out of his mouth came nothing but a trickle of greenish gastric juice.

"Well, I'll be damned! Still here? Looks like they forgot about you, what?"

Handke stood in front of 509 and slowly looked him over from head to foot. It was at the time of the evening roll call. The blocks had lined up outside. "You were supposed to have been booked. Must go and inquire about it."

He swayed to and fro on his heels and stared at 509 from light-blue, protruding eyes. 509 stood very still. "What?" asked Handke.

509 didn't answer. It would have been madness to irritate the block senior in any way. Silence was always best. All he could hope for was that Handke would once more forget the incident or didn't mean it seriously. Handke grinned. His teeth were yellow and spotted. "What?" he repeated.

"The number was taken down at the time," said Berger quietly.

"So?" Handke turned toward him. "Are you sure of that?"

"Yes. Squad Leader Schulte made a note of it. I saw it."

"In the dark? Well, in that case everything's fine." Handke was still swaying. "Then it's okay for me to go and inquire about it. Won't do any harm then, what?"

No one answered. "You can feed first," Handke declared affably. "Supper. No point in asking the block leader about you. I'll go straight to the proper place, you bastard." He looked around. "Attention!" he snorted then.

Bolte arrived. As usual he was in a hurry. For two hours he had been losing at poker and had just struck a lucky streak. With a bored expression he glanced over the dead and went off as soon as he could. Handke stayed. He sent the food carriers to the kitchen and strolled over to the barbed-wire fence separating the women's barracks from the Small camp. There he stood still and looked over.

"Let's go into the barrack," said Berger. "Someone can stay outside and watch him."

"I will," declared Sulzbacher.

"Let us know when he goes away. Immediately!"

The Veterans squatted in the barrack. It was better not to be seen by Handke. "What shall we do?" asked Berger, worried. "Think that swine really means business?"

"Maybe he'll forget it again. It looks as though he were stir-crazy. If only we had some schnapps to make him tight!"

"Schnapps!" Lebenthal spat out. "Impossible! Utterly impossible!"

"Maybe he was only joking," said 509. He didn't quite believe it; but such things had frequently occurred in the camp. The SS were masters at keeping people in a permanent state of fear. More than one hadn't been able to stand it. Some had run into the barbed wire; in other cases, the heart had finally given out.

Rosen moved closer. "I have some money," he whispered to 509. "Take it. I had it hidden and brought it in. Here, forty marks. Give it to him. That's how we did it in the other place."

He thrust the bills into his hand. 509 fingered them and took them almost without realizing what he was doing. "It won't help," he said. "He'll pocket it and still do as he likes."

"Then promise him more."

"Where shall we get any more?"

"Lebenthal has some," declared Berger. "Haven't you, Leo?"

"Yes, I have some. But once we whet his appetite for money he'll come every day and demand more, till we've nothing left. Then we'd soon be back where we are now. Except that the money would be gone."

Everyone was silent. No one found Lebenthal's statement brutal. It was matter of fact, nothing else. The question was whether it was worth sacrificing all Lebenthal's chances for trading, simply to gain a few days' reprieve for 509. The Veterans would get less food, possibly so much less that some or all of them would be bound to perish. None would have hesitated to give up everything if by so doing 509 could really have been saved; but this seemed unlikely if Handke meant business. In this, Lebenthal was right. To prolong the life of a single man for a mere two or three days wasn't worth risking the lives of a dozen. This was the camp's unwritten, merciless law by which they had so far survived. They all knew it; but in this case they didn't yet want to admit it. They were searching for a way out.

"We ought to kill the bastard," Bucher said hopelessly at last.

"What with?" asked Ahasver. "He's ten times as strong as we are."

"If we all together with our food bowls—"

Bucher fell silent. He knew it was idiotic. A dozen people would be hanged if they succeeded. "Is he still standing there?" asked Berger.

"Yes. On the same spot."

"Maybe he'll forget it."

"Then he wouldn't be waiting. He said he'd wait till after we've eaten."

A deadly silence hung in the darkness. "At least you can give him the forty marks," said Rosen to 509 after some time. "They belong to you personally. I'm giving them to you. I to you personally. It has nothing to do with anyone else."

"Correct," declared Lebenthal. "That's correct."

509 stared out through the door. He saw the dark figure of Handke standing against the gray sky. Some time ago, there had been something similar—a dark head against the sky and a great danger. He didn't remember exactly when. He looked out through the door again and wondered why he was so undecided. A dim vague resistance had formed in him. It was a resistance against attempting to bribe Handke. He had never known anything like this before; there had always been only utter fear.

"Go over to him," said Rosen. "Give him the money and promise him more."

509 hesitated. He didn't understand himself. He knew bribery wouldn't be much use if Handke were really determined to ruin him. He had seen many such cases in the camp; they had taken from the men what they possessed and later finished them off so they couldn't talk. But a day of life was a day of life—and in the meanwhile many things could happen.

"Here come the food carriers," reported Karel.

"Listen," Berger whispered to 509, "try it. Give him the money. If he comes back later wanting more, we'll threaten to denounce him for corruption. We have a dozen witnesses. That's a lot. We'll all declare we saw it. Then he won't risk anything. It's the only thing we can do."

"He's coming," whispered Sulzbacher from outside.

Handke had turned around. He came walking slowly toward Section D. "Where are you, you bastard?" he asked.

509 stepped forward. It was pointless to go on hiding. "Here."

"All right. I'm going now. Say good-by and make your will. They'll fetch you later. With drums and trumpets."

He grinned. The remark about the will he considered an excellent joke. The one about the drums and trumpets, too. Berger nudged 509. 509 took a further step forward. "May I talk to you for a moment?"

"You to me? Ridiculous!"

Handke walked toward the exit. 509 followed him. "I have some money," he said to Handke's back.

"Money? So? How much?" Handke walked on. He didn't turn round.

"Twenty marks." 509 had meant to say forty; but the strange inner resistance prevented him. He felt it like a kind of obstinacy; he offered half the money for his life.

"Twenty marks and two pfennigs! Push off, man!"

Handke walked faster. 509 managed to catch up with him. "Twenty marks is better than nothing."

"Shit!"

There was no longer any point in offering forty now. 509 was aware of having made a mistake that could never be repaired. He should have offered it all. His stomach suddenly dropped into an abyss. The resistance he had felt before was gone.

"I have still more money," he said quickly.

"Well, I'll be damned!" Handke stood still. "A capitalist! A croak-capitalist! How much more have you got, then?"

509 took a breath. "Five thousand Swiss francs!"

"What?"

"Five thousand Swiss francs. They're in a bank safe in Zurich."

Handke laughed. "And you expect me to believe that, you wretched rag?"

"I wasn't always a wretched rag."

For a while Handke stared at 509. "I'll transfer half of the money to you," said 509 hastily. "A simple transference is all that's necessary, and it's yours. Two thousand five hundred Swiss francs." He looked into the hard expressionless face before him. "The war's going to be over soon. Money in Switzerland will come in handy then." He waited. Handke still wasn't answering. "When the war has been lost," 509 added slowly.

Handke raised his head. "So," he said in a low voice. "You're already counting on that, what? Worked it all neatly out, eh? You can bet your life we'll spoil that for you all right! Got yourself in a fine mess—now the political department has you, too—illegal foreign currency abroad! And this on top of the other. Man, I wouldn't want to have your head on my shoulders!"

"To have two thousand five hundred francs or not to have them is not the same—"

"Nor is it for you. Go to hell!" Handke suddenly bellowed, and shoved 509 so hard in the chest that he collapsed.

509 got up slowly. Berger approached. Handke had disappeared in the dark. 509 knew there was no longer any point in running after him.

"What's happened?" asked Berger quickly.

"He didn't take it."

Berger didn't answer. He looked at 509. 509 saw that Berger had a stick in his hand. "I even offered him much more," he said. "He didn't want it." He gazed around, bewildered. "I must have done something wrong. I don't know what."

"What on earth has he got against you?"

"He never could stand me." 509 wiped his brow. "It's all the same now. I even offered him money in Switzerland. Francs. Two thousand five hundred. He didn't want it."

They arrived at the barrack. They didn't need to say anything; the others already knew what was up. All of them stood where they had been standing before; no one moved away—but it was as if an empty space had already formed around 509, an invisible uncrossable ring, isolating him; the loneliness of death.

"Damn it!" said Rosen.

509 looked at him. That morning he had saved him. It was

strange that he had been able to do that, and that now he was already some place from which he could no longer stretch out a hand. "Give me the watch," he said to Lebenthal.

"Come into the barrack," said Berger. "We must think it over."

"No. Now there's nothing to do but wait. Give me the watch. And leave me alone—"

He sat alone. The hands of the watch gleamed greenish in the darkness. Thirty minutes of time, he thought. Ten minutes to the administration buildings; ten minutes for the report and the orders; ten minutes back. A half circle of the big hand—that was now his life.

Maybe it was more, he suddenly thought. If Handke had made the report about the Swiss money, the political department would interfere. They would try to get hold of the money and let him live until they got it. When he had mentioned it to Handke he hadn't thought of that—only of the greediness of the block senior. It was a chance. But he wasn't sure whether Handke would report it. Maybe he had reported merely that Weber wanted to see 509.

Bucher came silently through the dark. "Here's still a cigarette left," he said hesitatingly. "Berger wants you to come in and smoke it."

Cigarette. Correct, the Veterans had one left. One of those Lewinsky had produced after the days in the bunker. The bunker—now he knew who the dark figure against the sky had been, whom Handke had reminded him of, and where he had seen it. It had been Weber. Weber, with whom everything had started.

"Come," said Bucher.

509 shook his head. The cigarette. The condemned man's last breakfast. The condemned man's cigarette. How long did it take to smoke a cigarette? Five minutes? Ten, if one smoked slow? A third of his time. Too much. He had other things to do. But what? There was nothing to be done. His mouth was suddenly dry with lust for the tobacco. He didn't want it. If he smoked he admitted he was lost.

"Go away!" he whispered, furious. "Go away with your filthy cigarette!"

He remembered a similar lust. This time he didn't have to think for long. It had been Neubauer's cigar at the time when Weber had beaten up Bucher and himself. Weber, again. As usual. As years ago—

He didn't want to think of Weber. Not now. He looked at the watch. Five minutes had passed. He looked at the sky. The night was humid and very mild. It was a night in which everything grew. A night of roots and buds. Spring. The first spring of hope. It had been a ragged, desperate hope, only the shadow of a hope; a strange faint echo out of dead years, but even this had been enormous and had made one giddy and changed everything. He shouldn't have told Handke the war was lost, something thought in him.

Too late. He had done it. The sky seemed to grow darker, dustier, more charred, lower, a boundless lid lowering itself, full of threats. 509 breathed with difficulty. He longed to crawl away, stick his head in a corner, hide it in the earth, save it, tear his heart out, hide it, so that it would continue to beat if—

Fourteen minutes. A murmuring behind him, monotonous, singing. Ahasver, he thought. Ahasver praying. He heard it and it seemed to take hours before he could remember what it was. It was the same murmuring and singing he had often heard—the prayer for the dead, Kaddish. Ahasver was already saying Kaddish over him. "I'm not dead yet, old man," he said to the rear. "Nowhere near. Stop your praying—"

Someone answered. It was Bucher. "He's not praying," he said.

509 didn't hear it any more. He suddenly felt it coming. He had learned to know many fears in his life; he knew the gray mollusk-like fear of endless captivity; he knew the sharp tearing fear immediately before torture; he knew the deep fleeting fear of one's own despair—he knew them all and he had conquered them, he knew them, but he also knew about the other, the last one, and he knew it was here now—the fear of fears, the great fear of death. He hadn't had it for years and he had thought that it never would come back, that he couldn't feel it any more, that it had been absorbed by the misery, by the continual proximity of death, and by the final indifference. Not even when he had gone to the office with Bucher had he known it—but now he felt its icy drops in his vertebrae, and he

realized that it had happened because he had known hope again; he felt it and it was ice and emptiness and falling apart and soundless scream. He held his hands propped against the ground and stared straight ahead. This was no longer a sky; this sucking deadly menace there over him! Where was the life beneath? Where was the sweet sound of growth? Where were the buds? Where the echo, the gentle echo of hope? Flickering, extinguishing in bitter agonies, the last miserable spark hissed in the intestines and, leaden, froze the world in plunging fear.

The murmuring. What had happened to the murmuring? There was even no murmuring any more. Very slowly 509 raised his hand. He hesitated before opening it as though it held a diamond that could have changed into coal. Releasing his fingers, he still waited the length of several breaths before looking at the two pale lines encircling his fate.

Thirty-five minutes. Thirty-five! Five minutes more than the thirty on which he had counted. Five more; five terribly precious, important minutes. But it was possible that it had taken five minutes more to get the report to the political department—or Handke had allowed himself more time.

Another seven minutes. 509 sat still. He breathed and he was aware again that he was breathing. There was still nothing to be heard. No steps, no clanking, no shouts. The sky was there again and receded. It was no longer black oppression and funeral clouds. Wind filtered through.

Twenty minutes. Thirty. Someone sighed behind him. The brighter sky. Further away. The echo again, a most remote heartbeat, the tiny drum of the pulse, and more: the echo within the echo, hands that again were hands, the spark—not extinguished—glimmering again and stronger than before. One degree stronger. One degree that had been added by the fear. Feebly the left hand let the watch drop.

"Maybe—" whispered Lebenthal behind 509 and fell silent, frightened and superstitious.

Time suddenly meant nothing any longer. It melted away. Melted away in all directions. Time—water flowing away somewhere downhill. It was no surprise when Berger picked up the watch and said, "One hour, ten minutes. Nothing will happen any more today. Maybe never, 509. Maybe he has thought it over."

"Yes," said Rosen.

509 turned round. "Leo, aren't the girls coming tonight?"

Lebenthal stared at him. "You're thinking of that now?"

"Yes."

Of what else? thought 509. Of anything that takes me away from that fear, which has turned my bones into gelatine. "We have money," he said. "I offered Handke only twenty marks."

"You offered him only twenty marks?" asked Lebenthal, incredulous.

"Yes. Twenty or forty comes to the same. If he wants to, he'll take it, that's all, and it doesn't make any difference whether it's twenty or forty."

"And if he comes tomorrow?"

"If he comes, he'll get twenty marks. If he reported me, the SS will come. Then I'll not need the money at all."

"He hasn't reported you," said Rosen. "Certainly not. He'll take the money."

Lebenthal had composed himself. "Keep your money," he declared. "I've enough for tonight." He saw 509 making a gesture. "I don't want it," he said, vehemently. "I have enough. Leave me alone."

509 rose up slowly. While sitting down he had had the feeling that he would never be able to get up again and that his bones had really turned into gelatine. He moved his arms, his legs. Berger followed him. They were silent for a while. "Ephraim," said 509 then. "Do you think we'll ever rid ourselves of the fear?"

"Was it so bad?"

"As bad as possible. Worse than ever."

"It was worse because you are more alive," said Berger.

"Do you believe that?"

"Yes. We have all changed."

"Maybe. But in our lives shall we ever rid ourselves of the fear?"

"That I don't know. Of this one, yes. It was a sensible fear. One with reason. The other, the perpetual one, the concentration camp fear—that I don't know. It doesn't much matter, either. At the moment we must think only of tomorrow. Of tomorrow and of Handke."

"That's just what I don't want to think of," said 509.

CHAPTER THIRTEEN

Berger was on his way to the crematorium. Beside him marched a group of six men. He knew one of them. He was a lawyer called Mosse. In 1932 he had participated in a murder trial of two Nazis as a representative of the plaintiff. The Nazis had been acquitted and immediately after the seizure of power Mosse had been thrown into a concentration camp. Berger hadn't seen him since he had been in the Small camp. He recognized him because he wore spectacles with only one lens. Mosse didn't need a second one; he had only one eye. In 1933 the other one had been burned out as a receipt for the trial.

Mosse walked on the outside. "Where to?" Berger asked him without moving his lips.

"Crematorium. Work."

The group marched past. Berger now realized that he knew

another of the men; Brede, a secretary of the Social Democratic Party. It struck him that all six men were political prisoners. They were followed by a kapo wearing the criminals' green triangle. He was whistling to himself. Berger remembered it as a song-hit from an old operetta. Automatically the words came to his mind: *Adieu, you little tinkle-fairy, fare well till we meet again.*

He followed the group with his eyes. Tinkle-fairy, he thought, irritated. They must have meant a telephone girl. Why did this suddenly come to his mind? Why did he still remember this barrel-organ tune and even its idiotic words? So many more important things had been long since forgotten.

He walked slowly and breathed the fresh morning. Each time he took this walk through the labor camp it seemed to him almost like a walk through a park. Five more minutes before reaching the wall surrounding the crematorium. Five minutes of wind and early day.

He watched the group with Mosse and Brede disappear through the gate. It seemed strange that new men had been ordered to work in the crematorium. The crematorium gang consisted of a special group of prisoners sharing the same quarters. They were better fed than the others and also enjoyed various favors. In return they were usually relieved after a few months and sent off to be gassed. The present gang, however, had been there only two months; and it was rare that outsiders were ordered to join them. Berger was almost the only one. At first he had been sent there just for a few days, to help out, and then, after the death of his predecessor, he had continued to work there. He did not receive better food nor did he share quarters with the actual cremating gang. This was why he hoped not to be sent off with the others in two to three months. But this was only a hope.

He walked through the gate and saw the six men now standing in line in the yard. They stood not far from the gallows which had been erected in the center. They all tried not to look at the scaffolds. Mosse's face had changed. His one eye stared anxiously through the lens at Berger. Brede held his head low.

The kapo turned around and noticed Berger. "What are you doing here?"

"Ordered to the crematorium. Tooth control."

"The tooth-plumber? Then make yourself scarce! You others, stand still!"

The six men stood as still as they could. Berger walked close past them. He heard Mosse whisper something, but he couldn't catch it. Nor could he risk stopping; the kapo was watching him. Strange, he thought, that so small a gang should be led by a kapo—instead of a foreman.

The crematorium cellar had on one side a large slanting shaft leading to the outside. The corpses piled up in the yard were thrown into this shaft down which they slid into the cellar. There, if not yet naked, they were stripped, listed and searched for gold.

It was here that Berger worked. His job was to write out death certificates and pull the gold teeth from the dead. The man who had done it before, a dental technician from Zwickau, had died of blood poisoning.

The kapo who supervised the cellar was called Dreyer. He entered several minutes later. "Start!" he said crossly and settled himself at a small table on which lay the lists.

Apart from Berger, four other men belonging to the crematorium gang were present. They took up positions close to the shaft. The first corpse slid down like an enormous bug. The four men dragged it across the concrete floor to the center of the room. The body was already rigid. They undressed it quickly, stripping off the jacket with the number and badges. One of the prisoners held down the right arm, which was sticking out, long enough for the sleeve to be pulled off. Then he let go and the arm snapped back like a branch. The trousers were easier to strip off.

The kapo noted down the number of the dead. "Ring?" he asked.

"No. No ring."

"Teeth?"

He turned the flashlight into the half-open mouth on which a thin streak of blood had dried.

"Gold filling on the right," said Berger.

"Okay. Out with it."

With the pliers Berger knelt down beside the head which was held fast by a prisoner. The others were already stripping the next corpse, calling out the number and throwing the clothes aside upon those of the first one. With a clatter like dry firewood, more and more dead now slid down the shaft. They fell on top of one another and became entangled. One of the dead came down feet first and remained standing upright. He leaned against the shaft, his eyes wide-open, mouth twisted askew. The hands were bent into half-fists, and a medal hung on a chain from his open shirt. He stood like this for a while. Other corpses fell clattering over him. Among them was a woman with longish hair. She must have come from the exchange camp. She came headfirst and her hair fell over his face. Finally, as though growing tired of so much death on his shoulders, he slipped sideways and toppled over. The woman fell on top of him. Dreyer saw it, grinned, and licked his upper lip on which a large pimple grew.

Meanwhile Berger had broken out the tooth. It was laid in one of two boxes. The second one was for rings. Dreyer booked the filling.

"Attention!" one of the prisoners suddenly called. The five men stood at attention. SS Squad Leader Schulte had entered. "Keep going!"

Schulte sat down astride a chair that stood near the table with the lists. He looked at the pile of corpses. "They're eight men out there throwing them in," he said. "Far too many. Get four of them down; they can lend a hand here. You there—" he pointed at one of the prisoners.

Berger pulled the wedding ring from a corpse's finger. This was usually easy; the fingers were thin. The ring was laid in the second box and Dreyer booked it. The corpse had no teeth. Schulte yawned.

The regulation was that the corpses should be dissected, the cause of death determined and listed in the files; but no one paid any attention to this. The camp doctor seldom came, never looked at the dead, and invariably the same causes of death were entered; usually heart failure. Westhof, too, had died of heart failure.

The naked bodies which had been booked were laid down close to an elevator. Upstairs in the cremation room this elevator was pulled up by two men whenever new supplies for the ovens were required.

The man who had gone out returned with four others. They were from the group that Berger had seen. Mosse and Brede were among them. "Forward, over there!" said Schulte. "Help strip them and book the clothes. Camp clothing in one heap. Civilian garments on another, shoes separate. Forward!"

Schulte was a man of twenty-three, blond, with gray eyes and clear regular features. He had been a member of the Hitler Youth even before the seizure of power and that was where he had been educated. He had learned that there were superhumans and subhumans, and he firmly believed it. He knew the racial theories and the Party dogmas and they were his Bible. He was a good son, but he would have denounced his father had he been against the Party. To him the Party was infallible; he knew nothing else. The inmates of the camp were enemies of the Party and the State, and consequently stood outside the concepts of pity and humaneness. They were lower than animals. Killing them was like killing vermin. Schulte had a completely calm conscience. He slept well and the only thing he regretted was not being at the front. The camp had claimed him on account of a heart ailment. He was a reliable friend, loved music and poetry and considered torture an indispensable method of extracting information from prisoners, since all enemies of the Party were liars. In his life he had killed six people on command—two of them slowly in order to obtain the names of accomplices—and had never given it a moment's thought. He was in love with the daughter of a provincial court councilor and wrote her charming, rather romantic letters. In his free time he liked to sing. He had a pleasant tenor voice.

The last naked corpses were piled up beside the elevator. Mosse and Brede lugged them along. Mosse's face was relaxed. He smiled at Berger. The fear he had felt outside had been unfounded. He had believed he would end up on the gallows. Now he worked according to what had been told them. Things were all right. He was saved. He worked fast to show his good will.

The door opened and Weber entered.

"Attention!"

Every prisoner stood at attention. Weber stepped up to the table in shiny, elegant boots. He loved good boots; they were almost his only passion. Carefully he knocked the ash off the cigarette he had lighted against the stench of corpses. "Through?" he asked Schulte.

"Yes, Herr Storm Leader. This minute. Everything booked and registered."

Weber looked into the boxes containing the gold. He picked up the medal which had been worn by the standing corpse. "What's this?"

"A St. Christophorus, Herr Storm Leader," declared Schulte eagerly. "A good-luck medal."

Weber grinned. Schulte hadn't noticed he had cracked a joke. "Fine," said Weber and put the medal back. "Where are the four from upstairs?"

The four men stepped forward. The door opened again and SS Squad Leader Guenther Steinbrenner came in with the two who had remained outside. "Stand over there with the four," said Weber. "Out with the others! Upstairs!"

The prisoners from the crematorium gang quickly disappeared. Berger followed them. Weber looked at the six who had stayed behind. "Not here," he said. "Stand over there, under the hooks!"

On the traverse wall of the room, opposite the shaft, four strong hooks were fixed. They were about two feet above the heads of the prisoners who stood underneath. In the corner to the right stood a three-legged stool; beside it in a chest lay ropes tied into short nooses with hooks on their ends.

With his left boot Weber gave the stool a push so that it slid in front of the first prisoner. "Up with you!" The man trembled and stepped onto the stool. Weber looked at the chest with the short ropes. "Now then, Guenther," he said to Steinbrenner, "the show can start. Let's see what you can do."

Berger pretended to be helping to load two corpses onto iron stretchers. As a rule he was not given this kind of work; he was far too weak for it. But when the dismissed prisoners came upstairs the foreman had yelled at them all to make themselves useful, so the simplest way out had been to pretend to be carrying out the order.

One of the corpses on the stretchers was the woman with the loose hair; the other a man who looked as though he were made of dirty wax. Berger raised the woman's shoulders and pushed her hair under them so that, while shoving her into the furnace it would not be set on fire by the blazing wind, fly back and burn his and the others' hands. It was strange that it hadn't been cut off; at one time this had been done regularly and the hair collected. Now it was probably no longer worth while, since there were only a few women left in the camp.

"Ready," he said to the others.

They opened the furnace doors. The blazing heat flared out. They shoved and the flat iron stretchers rolled into the furnace. "Shut the doors!" someone called. "Shut the doors!"

Two of the prisoners slammed the heavy doors to, but one of them flew open again. Berger could see the woman arch herself as though waking up. For a moment the burning hair surrounded her head like a wild yellow-white halo, then the door, on whose corner a small piece of bone had been caught, slammed to for the second and last time.

"What was that?" asked one of the prisoners, frightened. Up to now he had only stripped corpses. "Was she still alive?"

"No. That was the heat," answered Berger, choking. The hot wind had dried out his throat. Even his eyes seemed to be burned. "They always move."

"Sometimes they dance," said a powerful man who belonged to the cremation gang and was passing by. "What are you doing up here, you cellar ghosts?"

"We were sent up."

The man laughed. "What for? To be put in the furnace, too?"

"There are some new people downstairs," said Berger.

The man stopped laughing. "What? New ones? What for?"

"I don't know. Six new ones."

The man stared at Berger. His eyes shone very white in the black face. "That can't be! We've only been here two months. They can't relieve us yet. They've no right to! Is it really true?"

"Yes. They said so themselves."

"Find out! Can't you find out for certain?"

"I'll try," said Berger. "Have you a piece of bread? Or anything else to eat? I'll let you know."

The man took a piece of bread from his pocket and broke it in two. He gave the smaller piece to Berger. "Here. But find out. We must know!"

"Yes." Berger stepped back. Someone tapped him on the shoulder from behind. It was the green kapo who had led Mosse, Brede and the four others to the crematorium. "Are you the tooth-plumber?"

"Yes."

"There's one more tooth to be pulled downstairs. You're to come down."

The kapo was very pale. He sweated and leaned against the wall. Berger glanced at the man who had given him the bread, and winked. The man followed him to the exit. "It's already solved," said Berger. "They weren't the relief. They're dead. I must go down."

"Sure?"

"Yes. Otherwise I wouldn't have to go down."

"Thank God." The man breathed with relief. "Give me back that bread," he said then.

"No." Berger stuck his hand in his pocket and held onto the bread.

"Fathead! I only wanted to give you the bigger piece instead! The thing is well worth it."

They exchanged the bread and Berger went back into the cellar. Steinbrenner and Weber had gone. Only Schulte and Dreyer were still there. From the four hooks on the wall four men were hanging. One of them was Mosse. He had been hanged wearing his spectacles. Brede and the last one of the six were already lying on the ground.

"Take that one down," said Schulte calmly. "He has a gold crown in front."

Berger tried to lift the man. He couldn't do it. Only when Dreyer helped him did he manage, and the man fell to the ground like a doll filled with sawdust. "Is he the one?" asked Schulte.

"Yes."

The dead man had a gold canine tooth. Berger pulled it out and put it in the box. Dreyer made a note of it.

"Have any of the others got anything?" asked Schulte.

Berger examined the two dead men on the floor. The kapo switched on his flashlight. "These here have nothing. One of them has a cement and silver amalgam filling."

"We can't use that. How about those still hanging?"

Berger tried in vain to lift Mosse. "Stop that!" declared Schulte impatiently. "It's easier to see it while they're hanging."

Berger pushed aside the swollen tongue in the wide-open mouth. The one protruding eye behind the spectacle glass was right in front of him. Through the strong lens it seemed even bigger and more distorted. The lid over the empty eye-socket stood half open. Some fluid had oozed out. The cheek was moist from it. The kapo stood beside Berger; Schulte immediately behind him. Berger felt Schulte's breath on his neck. It smelt of peppermint drops. "Nothing," said Schulte. "Next one."

The next one was easier to examine; he had no front teeth. They had been knocked out. Two useless silver amalgam fillings in the right jaw. Schulte's breath was again on Berger's neck. The breath of an eager Nazi innocently doing his duty, surrendering himself to the task of finding gold fillings, indifferent to the accusation of a mouth murdered just a minute ago. Berger suddenly realized he wouldn't be able to stand the feel of this panting boyish breath much longer. As though he were searching for bird's eggs in a nest, he thought.

"All right, nothing," said Schulte, disappointed. He seized the lists and the boxes of gold and pointed at the six dead.

"Have them carried up and the room thoroughly scrubbed."

Upright and young, he walked out. Berger started to strip Brede. It was simple. He could do it alone. These dead were still soft. Brede wore a net shirt and civilian pants. Dreyer lit a cigarette. He knew Schulte wouldn't come back again.

"He forgot the spectacles," said Berger.

"What?"

Berger pointed at Mosse. Dreyer came close. Berger took the spectacles off the dead face. Steinbrenner had considered it a joke to hang Mosse with his spectacles on.

"The one lens is still intact," said the kapo. "But what can a single lens be used for? At most as a burning glass for children."

"The spectacle frame is good."

Dreyer bent further forward. "Nickel," he said contemptuously. "Cheap nickel."

"No," said Berger. "White gold."

"What?"

"White gold."

The kapo took the spectacles. "White gold? Are you sure?"

"Absolutely. The frame is dirty. When it's washed with soap, you'll see for yourself."

Dreyer weighed Mosse's spectacles on the flat of his palm. "That's worth something."

"Yes."

"We must enter it."

"The lists are gone," said Berger and looked at the kapo. "Squad Leader Schulte has taken them away."

"That doesn't matter. I can go after him."

"Yes," said Berger, and went on looking at Dreyer. "Squad Leader Schulte didn't notice the spectacles. Or maybe he thought they had no value. Maybe they haven't. I could be wrong; maybe they're nickel after all."

Dreyer looked up. "They could have been thrown away," said Berger. "With those useless things over there. A pair of broken nickel spectacles."

Dreyer laid the frame on the table. "Just clear up here first."

"I can't do that alone. The bodies are too heavy."

"Then go and get a couple of men from upstairs."

Berger left and returned with two prisoners. They took Mosse down. The dammed-up air escaped with a rattling sound from the lungs as the noose round the neck was loosened. The hooks on the walls were just high enough to prevent the hanged men from reaching the ground with their feet. Dying this way took considerably more time. On a normal gallows the neck was usually broken by the fall. This the Thousand Year Reich had changed. The gallows were arranged for slow suffocation. The aim was not simply to kill, but to kill slowly and very painfully. One of the first cultural achievements of the Nazis had been to abolish the guillotine and reintroduce the hatchet instead. As a result, condemned men often jumped around the execution yard with heads half chopped off, when the hangman had failed to do his job properly.

Mosse now lay naked on the ground. His fingernails were broken off. White chalk dust stuck under them. In his fight for breath he had clawed them into the wall. Hundreds of hanged men before him had scratched holes there.

Berger laid Mosse's clothes and shoes on the separate heaps. He glanced at Dreyer's table. The spectacles were no longer there. Neither were they on the little heap of paper, dirty letters and useless rags which had been taken from the pockets of the dead.

Dreyer was busying himself round the table. He didn't look up.

"What's that?" asked Ruth Holland.
Bucher listened. "A bird singing. It must be a thrush."
"A thrush?"
"Yes. No other bird sings so early in the year. It's a thrush. I remember it from the old days."

They were crouching on either side of the barbed-wire fence that separated the women's barracks from the Small camp. They weren't conspicuous. By now the Small camp was so crowded that people were lying and sitting about all over the place. The guards, moreover, had left the watchtowers because their time was up. They hadn't waited to be relieved. Nowadays this happened sometimes in the Small camp. It was forbidden, but discipline was no longer what it used to be.

The sun was setting. Its reflection hung red in the windows of the town. A whole street which had not been destroyed glittered as though there were fire in the houses. The river reflected the unquiet sky.

"Where is it singing?"
"Over there. Where the trees are."

Ruth Holland stared out through the barbed wire at what lay over there: a meadow, fields, a few trees, a farmhouse with a thatched roof, and further away on a hill, a low white house and garden.

Bucher looked at her. The sun made her emaciated face appear more gentle. He took a crust of bread from his pocket. "Here, Ruth—Berger gave it to me for you. He got it today. An extra piece for us."

He threw the crust adroitly through the barbed wire. Her face twitched. The crust lay beside her. For a while she didn't answer. "It's yours," she said finally with an effort.

"No. I've already had a piece."

She swallowed. "You're just saying that."

"No, I swear I'm not." He watched her fingers close quickly over the crust. "Eat it slowly," he said. "Then you get more out of it."

She nodded and was already chewing. "I've got to eat it slowly. I've just lost one more tooth. They simply fall out. It doesn't hurt. That's six now."

"So long as it doesn't hurt, it doesn't matter. We had someone here whose whole jaw had festered. He groaned until he died."

"I soon won't have any teeth left."

"You can get false ones put in. Lebenthal has a denture."

"I don't want a denture."

"Why not? Lots of people have them. It really doesn't matter, Ruth."

"They won't give me a denture."

"Not here. But later you can have one made. There are wonderful dentures. Much better ones than Lebenthal's. His is an old one. He's had it twenty years. Now there are new ones, he says, which one doesn't notice in the least. They fit tight and are far more beautiful than real teeth."

Ruth had eaten her piece of bread. She turned her dim eyes toward Bucher. "Josef, do you really believe we'll ever get out of here?"

"I'm sure. Absolutely sure. 509 believes it, too. We all believe it now."

"And then what?"

"Then—" Bucher had not yet thought far beyond it. "Then we are free," he said, without quite being able to imagine it.

"We'll have to hide again. They'll hunt us again. As they have hunted us before."

"They won't hunt us any more."

She looked at him for a long time. "And you believe that?"

"Yes."

She shook her head. "Maybe they'll leave us in peace for a while. But then they'll hunt us again. They don't know any better."

The thrush began to sing anew. It sounded clear and very sweet and unbearable.

"They won't hunt us any more," said Bucher. "We'll be together. We will walk out of the camp. The barbed wire will be torn down. We will walk across that road there. No one will fire at us. No one will send us back. We will walk across the fields, into a house, like the white house over there, and sit down on chairs."

"Chairs—"

"Yes. Real chairs. There will be a table and china plates and an open fire."

"And people to chase us out."

"They won't chase us out. There will be a bed with blankets and clean sheets. And bread and milk and meat."

Bucher watched her face grow distorted. "You must believe it, Ruth," he said, helplessly.

She sobbed without tears. The sobbing was only in her eyes. They veiled over as something indefinable welled up in them. "It's so hard to believe, Josef."

"You must believe it," he repeated. "Lewinsky has brought more news. The Americans and British are already far across the Rhine. They're coming. They're going to liberate us. Soon."

The evening light suddenly changed. The sun had reached the mountain line. The town fell into a blue darkness. The windows grew dim. The river became still. Everything became still. The thrush, too, had ceased to sing. Only the sky began now to glow. The clouds turned into ships of mother-of-pearl, broad beams struck them like winds of light and they sailed into the red gate of the evening. The last glow fell full on the white house on the hill, and while the rest of the land grew dim it was the last that still shimmered and it seemed closer and further away than ever before.

They saw the bird only when it had come quite close. They saw a small black ball with wings. They saw it outlined against the mighty sky, it flew high and then suddenly dived down, they saw it and both of them meant to do something and didn't do it; one moment, just before it approached the ground, the whole silhouette was there, the small head with the yellow beak, the outspread wings and the round breast with the melodies, and then came the slight crackling and the spark from the electrically charged wire, very small and pale and fatal against the sunset, and nothing was left but the charred remains with a tiny claw hanging down on the lowest wire and a scrap of wing which had touched the ground and beckoned death toward it.

"That was the thrush, Josef—"

"No, Ruth," Bucher said quickly. "That was another bird. That wasn't a thrush. And if it were, it wasn't the one that sang—surely not, Ruth—not ours—"

"You thought I forgot all about you, what?" asked Handke.

"No."

"It was too late yesterday. But we have time. Time enough to report you. Tomorrow, for instance—the whole day."

He stood in front of 509. "You millionaire! You Swiss millionaire! They'll beat the money out of your kidneys, franc by franc."

"No one need beat the money out of me," said 509. "It can be had in a simpler way. I'll sign a paper and it's no longer mine." He looked steadily at Handke. "Two thousand five hundred francs. A lot of money."

"Five thousand," answered Handke. "For the Gestapo. D'you imagine they'll share it?"

"No. Five thousand for the Gestapo," 509 confirmed.

"And the whipping block and the cross and the bunker and Breuer with his special treatment and then the gallows."

"That's not yet certain."

Handke laughed. "What else? Maybe a letter of acknowledgment? For being in possession of illegal money?"

"Not that, either." 509 still looked at Handke. He was surprised not to feel any more fear although he knew he was in Handke's hands. But stronger than anything he suddenly felt something else: hatred. Not the dim blind petty hatred of the camp, the trivial puny hatred bred by the despair of a starved creature because of some advantage or disadvantage—no, he felt a cold clear intelligent hatred, and he felt it so intensely that he lowered his eyes, for he thought Handke would recognize it.

"What else then, you sly ape?"

509 smelt Handke's breath. This was new, too; in the past the stench of the Small camp had not permitted any individual smell.

509 was also aware that he didn't smell Handke because his smell was stronger than the stench of decay all round him—but because he hated Handke.

"Have you gone dumb with fear?" Handke kicked 509 in the shin.

509 didn't budge. "I don't think I'll be tortured," he said calmly and looked again at Handke. "It wouldn't be very practical. I could die away under the hands of the SS. I'm very weak and can hardly stand anything any more. This, at the moment, is an advantage. The Gestapo will prefer to wait with all that till they've laid hands on the money. Until then they'll need me. I'm the only one who has the power to dispose of it. In Switzerland the Gestapo has no power. Until they've got the money, I'm safe. And that will take a little time. Before then lots of things can happen."

Handke pondered. In the half-dark 509 watched his thoughts at work in his flat face. He saw the face clearly. He felt as though behind his eyes searchlights had been fixed, lighting it up. The face itself remained the same; but each detail of it seemed to be magnified.

"So? You've thought all this out for yourself, what?" the block senior finally uttered.

"I haven't thought anything out. It just is like that."

"And what about Weber? He also wanted to talk to you. He won't wait."

"Oh yes," answered 509 calmly. "Herr Storm Leader Weber will have to wait. The Gestapo will see to that. It's more important for them to get Swiss francs."

Handke's protruding pale-blue eyes seemed to rotate. His mouth chewed. "You've become very sly," he said finally. "At one time you could hardly shit! Just recently all you people here have become as sprightly as rams, you stinkers! That'll all be spoiled for you! Just you wait! You'll all be chased through the chimney yet!" He tapped 509 on the chest. "Where are the twenty marks?" he hissed then. "Out with them! Make it snappy!"

509 pulled the bill out of his pocket. For a second he had felt the desire not to do it, but he realized immediately that it would have been suicide. Handke tore the money out of his hand. "For this, you can go on shitting for another day!" he declared, and blew out his

chest. "I'll let you live one day longer for this, you worm! One day, until tomorrow."

"One day," said 509.

Lewinsky meditated. "I don't believe he'll do it," he said then. "After all, what's he going to get out of it?"

509 shrugged his shoulders. "Nothing. He's always unpredictable when he's had something to drink. Or when he's stir-crazy."

"He must be gotten out of the way." Lewinsky reflected again. "At the moment we can't do much against him. There's danger in the air. The SS is combing the lists for names. We let whomever we can disappear into the lazaret. Soon we'll have to smuggle a few people over here, too. That's still possible, or not?"

"Yes. If you provide the food for them."

"That goes without saying. But there's something else. We've got to be prepared for raids and check-ups now in our place. Could you hide a few things so they're certain not to be found?"

"How big?"

"As big as—" Lewinsky looked round. They were crouching in the dark behind the barrack. Nothing could be seen but the stumbling line of Mussulmen on their way to the latrine. "As big as a revolver, for instance—"

509 took a quick breath. "A revolver?"

"Yes."

509 remained silent for a moment. "There's a hole in the ground under my bunk," he then said, fast and under his breath. "The boards next to it are loose. More than one revolver could be hidden in there. Easily. They don't check up here. It's quite safe."

He didn't realize he was talking like someone trying to persuade another, instead of someone who is being persuaded to take a risk. "Have you got it on you?" he asked.

"Yes."

"Give it to me."

Lewinsky glanced round again. "You know what that means?"

"Yes, yes," answered 509 impatiently.

"It was difficult to get it. We had to risk a great deal."

"Yes, Lewinsky. I'll take care of it all right. Just give it to me."

Lewinsky delved into his jacket and pushed the weapon into 509's hand. 509 fingered it. It was heavier than he had expected. "What's it wrapped in?" he asked.

"A greasy rag. Is the hole under your bunk dry?"

"Yes," said 509. It wasn't true; but he didn't want to hand back the weapon. "Is there any ammunition with it?" he asked.

"Yes. Not much; a few bullets. It's loaded, too."

509 stuck the revolver inside his shirt and buttoned the jacket over it. He felt it next to his heart and was aware of a sudden shudder passing over his skin.

"I'm going now," said Lewinsky. "Take great care of it. Hide it immediately." He talked of the weapon as though of an important person. "Next time I come I'll bring someone with me. Have you really got room?"

He looked around the roll-call ground on which in the dark lay darker figures. "We have room," answered 509. "For your men we'll always have room."

"Fine. When Handke returns give him some more money. Have you got some?"

"I still have some left. For one day."

"I'll see that we collect some. I'll give it to Lebenthal. Is that all right?"

"Yes."

Lewinsky disappeared in the shadow of the next barrack. From there on he stumbled, bent over like a Mussulman, toward the latrine. 509 remained sitting for a while. He leaned his back hard against the barrack wall. With his right hand he pressed the revolver against his body. He resisted the temptation to take it out, unwrap the rag and touch the metal; he just held it tight. He felt the lines of the barrel and the butt and he felt them as though a dark, heavy power emanated from them. It was the first time in many years that he held something pressed against his body with which he could defend himself. He was suddenly no longer completely helpless. He was no longer completely at their mercy. He knew it was an illusion and that he mustn't use the weapon; but it was sufficient that he had it on him. It was sufficient to change something in him. The small tool of death was like a dynamo of life. From it resistance poured into him. He thought of Handke. He thought of the hatred he had felt for him. Handke had received the money; but he had been weaker than 509. He thought of Rosen; he had been able to save him. Then he thought of Weber. He thought of him a long time and of the first period in the camp. He hadn't done it for years. He had banished all memories from within him; also those of the time prior to the camp. Even his name he had no longer wanted to hear. He had ceased to be a human being and had no longer wanted to be one; it would have broken him. He had become a number and had called himself and let himself be called by a number. Silently he sat in the night and breathed and held the weapon tight, and the memories came, and it seemed as though he were simultaneously eating and drinking something he couldn't see and which was like a strong medicine.

He heard the guards being relieved. Carefully he got up. He reeled for several seconds as though he had been drinking wine. Then he walked slowly round the barrack.

Someone was crouching beside the door. "509," he whispered. It was Rosen.

509 started, as though waking from a deep, endless dream. He looked down. "My name is Koller," he said absent-mindedly. "Friedrich Koller."

"Yes," answered Rosen, uncomprehendingly.

CHAPTER FOURTEEN

"I want a priest," wailed Ammers.

He had been wailing it all afternoon. They had tried to argue him out of it, but it hadn't been of any use. It had suddenly come over him.

"What kind of a priest?" asked Lebenthal.

"A Catholic. Why do you ask, you Jew?"

"Look, look!" Lebenthal shook his head. "An anti-Semite! That's just what we needed here!"

"There are enough of them in the camp," said 509.

"It's you who are to blame!" inveighed Ammers. "For everything! Without you Jews we wouldn't be here!"

"What? How d'you figure that one?"

"Because then there wouldn't be any camps. I want a priest."

"You ought to be ashamed of yourself, Ammers," said Bucher angrily.

"I don't need to be ashamed. I'm sick! Get a priest."

509 looked at the blue lips and the sunken eyes. "There are no priests in the camp, Ammers."

"They must have one. It's my right. I'm dying."

"I don't believe you'll ever die," declared Lebenthal, annoyed. "You've been promising us that for weeks."

"I'm dying because you damned Jews have wolfed up my share. And now you don't even want to get me a priest. I want to confess. What do you know about such things? Why must I be in a Jew barrack? I've a right to be in an Aryan one."

"Not here. Only in the labor camp. Here all are equal."

Ammers wheezed and turned his head away. On the wooden wall above his matted hair was an inscription in blue pencil: EUGEN MAYER 1941 TYPHUS. AVENGE—

"How are things with him?" 509 asked Berger.

"He ought to be dead long ago, but today I believe is really his last day."

"It looks like it. He's already getting everything mixed up."

"He's not getting anything mixed up," declared Lebenthal. "He knows what he's saying."

"I hope not," said Bucher.

509 looked at him. "He was different once, Josef," he said calmly. "But he has been smashed to pieces. There's nothing left of what he was before. This is another man who has grown together from the bits and pieces. And even the pieces were not sound. I've seen it."

"A priest," wailed Ammers again. "I must confess! I don't want to go into everlasting damnation."

509 sat down on the edge of the bunk. Beside Ammers lay a man from the new transport who had high fever and breathed flat and fast.

"You can do that without a priest, Ammers," said 509. "After all, what have you done? Here there are no sins. Not for us. We're atoning for everything here all the time. Repent for what you have to repent. If no confession is possible, that's good enough. That's what the catechism says."

For a moment Ammers ceased wheezing. "Are you a Catholic too?" he asked.

"Yes," said 509. It was not true.

"Then you know what it is! I must have a priest! I must confess and be given Holy Communion! I don't want to burn in eternity." Ammers was trembling. His eyes were torn wide-open. His face was no bigger than two fists and his eyes were far too large for it; as a result there was something of a bat about him. "If you're a Catholic, then you know how it is. Like the crematorium; but one is never entirely burned and never dies. D'you want this to happen to me?"

509 glanced at the door. It was open. In it, like a picture, stood the serene evening sky. Then he looked back at the emaciated head in which burned the picture of Hell. "For us here it's different, Ammers," he said finally. "We have a favored position over there. We've already had one slice of Hell down here."

Ammers moved his head restlessly. "Don't blaspheme," he whispered. Then he raised himself with difficulty, stared about him, and suddenly broke out: "You! All of you! You're healthy! And I've got to croak! Just now! Yes, laugh! Laugh! I've heard everything you've been saying! You want to get out! You will get out! And I? I! Into the crematorium! Into the fire! The eyes into the fire! And forever! Boo-hoo! Boo-hoo—"

He howled like a moon-struck dog. His body was stretched taut and he howled. His mouth was a black hole out of which came a hoarse howl.

Sulzbacher got up. "I'm going," he said. "I'm going to ask for a priest."

"Where?" asked Lebenthal.

"Anywhere. In the office. From the guards."

"Don't be crazy. There are no priests here. The SS won't stand for it. They'll throw you in the bunker."

"That doesn't matter."

Lebenthal stared at Sulzbacher. "Berger, 509," he said then. "Did you hear that?"

Sulzbacher's face was very pale. His jawbones stood out sharply. He didn't look at anyone. "It won't be any use," said Berger to him. "It's forbidden. Nor do we know any priest among the prisoners. Do you imagine we wouldn't have fetched him already?"

"I'm going," answered Sulzbacher.

"Suicide!" Lebenthal tugged at his hair. "And for an anti-Semite as well!"

Sulzbacher's jaws were working. "All right, for an anti-Semite."

"*Meschugge!* One more *Meschugge!*"

"All right, *Meschugge,* I'm going."

"Bucher, Berger, Rosen," said 509 calmly.

Bucher was already standing behind Sulzbacher with a stick. He banged him on the head. Though the blow wasn't hard, it was enough to make Sulzbacher reel. Then they all dragged him down and rolled on top of him. "Give me the sheep dog's straps, Ahasver," said Berger.

They tied Sulzbacher's hands and feet and let him go.

"If you yell, we'll have to stuff something in your mouth," said 509.

"You don't understand me—"

"Yes, we do. You stay like this till your fit's over. We've lost enough people this way already."

They rolled him into a corner and didn't take any more notice of him. Rosen raised himself. "He's still confused," he murmured, as though he ought to ask forgiveness for him. "You must try to understand. His brother that time—"

Ammers had grown hoarse. He could only just whisper. "Where is he? Where—the priest—"

By now they had all had enough. "Is there really no priest or sexton or acolyte in the barracks?" asked Bucher. "Anyone to make him quiet."

"There used to be four in Barrack 17. One has been set free; two are dead; and the other is in the bunker," said Lebenthal. "Breuer beats him up every morning with a chain. He calls it 'reading the Mass with him.'"

"Please," Ammers continued whispering. "For Christ's sake, a—"

"I believe there's a man in Section B who knows Latin," said Ahasver. "I once heard about it. Couldn't we get him?"

"What's his name?"

"I'm not sure. Dellbruck or Hellbruck or something like that. The room senior is bound to know it."

509 got up. "That's Mahner. We can ask him."

He walked over with Berger.

"It may be Hellwig," said Mahner. "That's the one who speaks languages. He's a bit mad. He recites off and on. He's in A."

"That'll be him."

They walked to Section A. There, Mahner talked to the room senior, a tall thin man with a pear-shaped head. The pear-head shrugged his shoulders. Mahner walked into the labyrinth of bunks, legs, arms and moaning and called out the name.

A few minutes later he returned. A suspicious-looking man followed him. "That's him," said Mahner to 509. "Let's go out. One can't hear a word in here."

509 explained the situation to Hellwig. "Do you speak Latin?" he asked.

"Yes." Hellwig's face twitched nervously. "D'you realize they'll be stealing my food bowl now?"

"Why?"

"They steal here. Yesterday my spoon disappeared while I was sitting on the latrine. I had hidden it under my bunk. Now I've left my food bowl inside."

"Then get it."

Hellwig disappeared without a word. "He won't come back," said Mahner.

They waited. It turned darker. Shadows were creeping out of shadows; darkness out of the darkness of the barracks. Then Hellwig appeared. He held the food bowl pressed to his chest.

"I don't know how much Ammers understands," said 509. "Certainly not more than *Ego te absolvo*. That might have stayed in his memory. If you say that to him and anything else that occurs to you—"

Hellwig's long legs doubled up while walking. "Virgil?" he asked. "Horace?"

"Don't you know anything ecclesiastical?"

"*Credo in unum Deum—*"

"Very good."

"Or *Credo quia absurdum est—*"

509 glanced up. He looked into two strangely restless eyes. "We all do that," he said.

Hellwig stood still. He pointed with a knobby forefinger at 509 as though he wanted to spear him. "This is a sacrilege, you know that. But I'm going to do it. He doesn't need me. There is a repentance and an absolution of sin without confession."

"Maybe he can't repent without someone being present."

"I'm doing it only to help him. In the meantime they're stealing my portion of soup."

"Mahner will keep your soup for you," said 509. "But give me your food bowl. I'll look after it for you while you're inside."

"Why?"

"He might be more likely to believe in you without a food bowl."

"Good."

They walked through the door. Now the front of the barrack was almost in darkness too. Ammers could be heard whispering. "Here," said 509. "We've found one, Ammers."

Ammers fell silent. "Really?" he then asked clearly. "Is he here?"

"Yes."

Hellwig bent down. "Glory be to Jesus Christ."

"For ever and ever, Amen," whispered Ammers with the voice of a surprised child.

They began murmuring. 509 and the others walked out. Outside, the late evening lay very still over the forests on the horizon. 509 sat down with his back to the barrack wall. It had still kept some warmth from the sun. Bucher came and sat down beside him. "Strange," he said. "Sometimes hundreds die and one doesn't feel anything, and then a single man dies, one who doesn't even concern us much—and it seems as though it were a thousand."

509 nodded. "Imagination cannot count. And feeling does not grow stronger through numbers. It can never count beyond one. One—but that's enough if one feels it."

Hellwig came out of the barrack. He came through the door stooping, and for a moment it was as though he carried the stinking darkness as a shepherd carries a black sheep on his shoulders, in order to take it away and wash it in the pure evening. Then he straightened himself and was once more a prisoner.

"Was it a sacrilege?" asked 509.

"No. I didn't perform any clerical act. I helped him only with the repentance."

"I wish we had something for you. A cigarette or a piece of bread." 509 handed the food bowl back to Hellwig. "But we haven't anything ourselves. All we can offer you is Ammers' soup if he dies before supper. We'll still get his portion tonight."

"I don't need anything. Nor do I want anything. It would be a dirty trick to take anything for that."

Only then did 509 notice that there were tears in Hellwig's eyes. He looked at him in utter amazement. "Is he calm?" he asked.

"Yes. At noon today he stole a piece of bread belonging to you. He wanted me to tell you."

"I knew that."

"He'd like you to come in. He wants to apologize to you all."

"For God's sake, why that?"

"He wants to—especially to one called Lebenthal."

"Do you hear, Leo?" asked 509.

"He wants to make his deal with God before it's too late. That's what it is," declared Lebenthal, unforgiving.

"I don't think so." Hellwig took his food bowl under his arm. "Funny, I once really wanted to be a priest," he said. "Then I ran away. Don't understand it any more now. Wish I'd done it." He let his strange eyes flutter over the sitting men. "One suffers less if one believes in something."

"Yes. But there are a lot of things one can believe in. Not only God."

"Certainly." Hellwig suddenly answered with the politeness of someone standing in a salon holding a discussion. He held his head slightly askew as though listening for something. "It was a kind of emergency confession," he said then. "Private baptisms have always existed. Emergency confessions—" His face twitched. "A question for the theologians—good evening, gentlemen."

Like a giant spider, he stalked toward his section. The others gazed after him, dumbfounded. It was the farewell greeting that had dumbfounded them. Gentlemen! They hadn't heard anything like that since they'd been in the camp. "Go to Ammers, Leo," said Berger, after a while. "After all, why not?"

Lebenthal hesitated. "Go on," repeated Berger. "Otherwise he'll start yelling again. The rest of us will now unstrap Sulzbacher."

The dusk had turned into a light darkness. A church bell was ringing up from the town. In the furrows of the fields lay deep blue and violet shadows.

They were sitting in a small group in front of the barrack. Inside, Ammers was still dying. Sulzbacher had recovered. He sat ashamed beside Rosen.

Lebenthal suddenly raised himself. "What's that there?"

He stared through the barbed wire at the fields. Something there flitted back and forth, stopped, and flitted on.

"A hare," said Karel, the boy from Czechoslovakia.

"Bunk! How d'you know what a hare looks like?"

"There used to be some at home. I saw lots when I was young. I mean, at the time when I was free," said Karel. For him his youth had stopped when he came to the camp. At the time when his parents had been gassed.

"It actually is a hare." Bucher screwed up his eyes. "Or a rabbit. No, it's too big for that."

"Merciful God!" said Lebenthal. "A live hare!"

Now they all saw it. For a moment it sat upright and its long ears stood up. Then it loped on.

"Imagine if it came in here!" Lebenthal's denture rattled. He was thinking of Bethke's fake hare, the dachshund, for which he had given up Lohmann's gold tooth. "We could swap it. We wouldn't eat it ourselves. We'd swap it for two, no two and a half times as much offal-meat."

"We wouldn't swap it. We'd eat it ourselves," said Meyerhof.

"Really? And who'd roast it? Or would you rather eat it raw? If you gave it to someone to roast, you'd never get it back," declared Lebenthal heatedly. "Funny what some people know without having left the barrack for weeks."

Meyerhof was one of the wonders of Barrack 22. He had been

lying around for three weeks on the point of death with pneumonia and dysentery. He had been so weak that he hadn't been able to speak. Berger had given him up. Then, in a few days, he had suddenly recovered. He had risen from the dead. For this reason Ahasver had called him Lazarus Meyerhof. Today he was outside again for the first time. Berger had forbidden it; but he had crawled out all the same. He wore Lebenthal's coat, the dead Buchsbaum's sweater and a Hussar tunic which someone had been given as a jacket. The bullet-pierced surplice which Rosen had received as underwear was wrapped around his neck as a scarf. Every Veteran had contributed towards fitting him out for his first excursion; each of them considered his recovery a personal triumph.

"If it tried to get in here, it would run into the electric wire. Then it would be roasted on the spot," said Meyerhof hopefully. "One could pull it in here with a dry stick."

They watched the animal with eager attention. It loped through the furrows, stopping off and on to listen. "The SS will shoot it for themselves," declared Berger.

"That's not so easy with a bullet in the dark," answered 509. "The SS are only used to shooting men, in the back and at a few yards' range."

"A hare." Ahasver moved his lips. "What that must taste like!"

"It tastes like a hare," explained Lebenthal. "The best part is the back, it must be larded. Bits of lard are stuck into it, to make it more juicy. With it goes a cream sauce. That's how the Gojim eat it."

"With mashed potatoes," said Meyerhof.

"Nonsense, mashed potatoes. Chestnuts and cranberries."

"Mashed potatoes are better. Chestnuts! They're for Italians."

Lebenthal stared at Meyerhof, annoyed. "Listen—" he began.

Ahasver interrupted him. "What's the good of a hare? I'd rather have a goose than all the hares in the world. A fine stuffed goose—"

"Stuffed with apples—"

"Shut up!" someone shouted from behind. "Are you crazy? That's the way to go off one's head!"

Bent forward, they crouched and followed the hare with eyes sunk deep in their skulls. At a distance of barely a hundred yards a dream meal was leaping about, a furry bundle containing several pounds of meat which could have saved a number of their lives. Meyerhof felt it in all his bones and intestines. For him the animal would have been an assurance against a relapse. "All right, with chestnuts, too, for all I care!" he squawked. His mouth was all of a sudden as dry and dusty as a coal cellar.

The hare raised itself and sniffed. At this moment one of the dozing SS guards must have seen it. "Edgar! Man alive! A long-ear!" he yelled. "At it!"

A few shots rang out. Earth flew up. In long bounds, the hare leapt away. "You see," said 509, "they can only hit prisoners from the closest range. For that they then get a furlough and decorations."

Lebenthal sighed and stared after the hare.

"Is he dead?"

"Yes. At last. He still tried to make us take the new one out of his bunk. The one with the fever. He thought he'd catch something from him. Instead, he gave it to the other. He was wailing and growling again toward the end. The priest didn't quite last out."

509 nodded. "It's difficult to die now. Earlier it was easier. Now it's hard. So near the end."

Berger sat down beside 509. It was after the evening meal. The Small camp had received only a thin soup; a mug each. No bread. "What did Handke want from you?" he asked.

509 opened his hands. "He gave me this. A clean sheet of notepaper and a fountain pen. He wants me to transfer my money in Switzerland to him. Not half of it. Everything. The whole five thousand francs."

"And?"

"In return he promises to let me live for the time being. He even hinted at something like protection."

"Until he gets your signature."

"That's until tomorrow evening. It's already something. There have been times when we haven't had so long."

"It's not enough, 509. We must find something else."

509 shrugged his shoulders. "Maybe it'll work. Maybe he thinks he'll need me in order to get the money."

"It could also be that he thinks the opposite. To get rid of you, so you can't withdraw the signature."

"I can't withdraw it once he's got it."

"He doesn't know that. Maybe you could do it. You gave it to him under pressure."

509 was silent for a while. "Ephraim," he then said calmly. "I don't need to do that. I have no money in Switzerland."

"What?"

"I haven't one franc in Switzerland."

Berger stared for some time at 509. "You invented all that?"

"Yes."

Berger drew the back of his hand across his inflamed eyes. His shoulders twitched.

"What's wrong?" asked 509. "Are you crying?"

"No, I'm laughing. It's idiotic, but I'm laughing."

"Go ahead, laugh. We've had damn little reason to laugh here."

"I laughed thinking of Handke in Zurich. What on earth gave you that idea, 509?"

"I don't know. Many things occur to one when one's life is at stake. The main thing is he swallowed it. He can't even find out until the war's over. He simply has to believe it."

"That's true." Berger's face grew serious again. "That's why I don't trust him. He can get stir-crazy again and do something unexpected. We must take precautions. The best thing is for you to die."

"Die? How? We haven't any lazaret. How could we wangle that? This place is the last stop."

"Via the last stop of all. The crematorium."

509 looked at Berger. He looked at the worried face with the watering eyes and the narrow skull and he felt a wave of warmth. "Do you think that's possible?"

"One can try it."

509 didn't ask how Berger planned to try it. "We can still talk about it," he said. "For the present we have time. Today I'm going to transfer only two thousand five hundred francs to Handke. He'll take the paper and demand the rest. In this way I gain a few days. Then I've still got Rosen's twenty marks."

"And when they're gone?"

"Maybe before then something else will happen. One can think only of the most immediate danger. One at a time. And one after the other. Otherwise one goes nuts." 509 turned the notepaper and fountain pen from side to side. He watched the pale reflections on the pen. "Funny," he said, "I haven't had anything like these in my hand for a long time. Paper and pen. Once I lived by them. Will one ever be able to do that again?"

CHAPTER FIFTEEN

The two hundred men of the new salvage gang had been distributed down the street in a long line. It was the first time they had been employed to clear up inside the town. So far they had been set to work only in the demolished factories of the suburbs.

The SS had occupied the street exits and also stationed squads as guards along the left-hand side. The bombs had fallen mainly on the right-hand side; walls and roofs had crashed across the roadway, rendering almost all traffic impossible.

The prisoners hadn't enough picks and shovels; some of them had to work with their bare hands. The kapos and foremen were nervous; they weren't sure whether to beat and drive the men on or to restrain themselves. Although civilians had been forbidden to use the street, the tenants living in the undamaged houses could not be evicted.

Lewinsky was working alongside Werner. Both had volunteered

for the salvage gang with a number of other political prisoners whose lives were in danger. Although the work here was harder than anywhere else, it enabled them to avoid being seized in the camp by the SS in the daytime; in the evenings, after marching in under cover of night, it was easier to make themselves scarce and go into hiding.

"Did you see the name of the street?" asked Werner under his breath.

"Yes." Lewinsky grinned. The street was called the Hitler Strasse. "Sacred name. Wasn't any use against bombs, though."

They lugged a beam away. The backs of their striped jackets were dark with sweat. At the collecting place they ran into Goldstein. He had joined the gang despite his weak heart, and Werner and Lewinsky had done nothing to prevent him—he was in danger as a political prisoner. His face was gray. He sniffed the air. "It stinks here. Of corpses. Not of fresh ones—some old ones must still be lying here."

"Sure!" They were familiar with it. They knew the smell of corpses. In this respect they all were experts.

They now piled broken-off stones against a wall. The mortar was cleared away in small carts. Behind them, on the other side of the street, was a grocery store. The windows had been blown out; but several posters and cardboard boxes had already been put back in the shop front. A man with a mustache looked out from behind them. He had one of those faces which in 1933 had been seen in large numbers marching behind placards bearing the inscription: DON'T BUY FROM JEWS. His head seemed to be cut off by the rear wall of the shop window—resembling those cheap photographs on fair grounds where the customers' heads perch above the painted uniforms of officers. This head appeared above empty boxes and dusty advertisements; the setting seemed to suit it.

In an undamaged doorway children were playing. Beside them stood a woman in a red blouse who watched the prisoners. Suddenly a few dogs broke out of the doorway and dashed across the street towards the prisoners. They sniffed their shoes and pants and one of them wagged its tail and leapt up at Number 7105. The kapo supervising this section was at a loss what to do. The dog was a civilian dog and not a man; even so, it seemed improper for it to befriend a prisoner, particularly in the presence of the SS. 7105 knew still less what to do. He did the only thing a prisoner can. He behaved as though the animal did not exist. But the dog followed him; it had taken a sudden liking to him. 7105 bent down and worked with intense eagerness. He was worried; the dog could mean his death.

"Get out of here, you lousy cur!" shouted the kapo at last, raising his truncheon. He had made up his mind. It was always better to be tough when the SS were looking on. The dog, however, paid no attention to him; it leapt and danced again around 7105. It was a big liver-and-white German pointer.

The kapo picked up some stones and threw them at it. The first stone struck 7105 on the knee; only the third one caught the dog full in the stomach. The dog howled, leapt aside and barked at the kapo. The kapo picked up the nearest rock. "Go to hell, you monster!"

The dog ducked but didn't run away. It turned swiftly and leapt at the kapo. The man collapsed on a heap of mortar and the dog promptly stood over him, growling. "Help!" howled the kapo, and didn't move. The SS-men laughed.

The woman in the red blouse came running out. She whistled to the dog. "Come here! Here at once! Oh, that dog! Always getting us into trouble!"

She dragged it off and into the doorway. "He ran out," she said fearfully to the nearest SS-man. "Please! I didn't see him! He ran away! He'll get a good hiding for it!"

The SS-man grinned. "He could have taken a chunk out of that silly mug, for all I care!"

The woman smiled feebly. She had thought the kapo belonged to the SS. "Thanks! Many thanks! I'll chain him up at once!"

She dragged the dog away by the collar but suddenly began stroking it. The kapo brushed the chalk dust off his pants. The SS guards were still grinning. "Why didn't you bite it?" shouted one of them to the kapo.

The kapo didn't answer. That was always best. He went on dusting himself for a while. Then he angrily stamped over towards the prisoners. 7105 was busily trying to drag out a toilet from under a heap of stones and mortar. "Get on, you lazy cur!" hissed the kapo, and kicked him in the back of the knee. All the prisoners watched the kapo out of the corners of their eyes. The SS-man who had talked to the woman strolled over. He approached the kapo from behind and gave him a kick with his boot. "Leave that one alone! It's not his fault. Bite the dog instead, you night owl!"

Surprised, the kapo turned round. The rage faded from his face and gave way to a servile grimace. "Of course! I only meant—"

"Get going!" The kapo received another kick in the belly, stood half at attention, and trundled off. The SS-man strolled back.

"Did you see that?" Lewinsky whispered to Werner.

"Signs and wonders! Maybe he did it because of the civilians."

The prisoners continued surreptitiously to watch the other side of the street, and the other side of the street watched them. Although they were separated from one another by only a few yards, the distance was greater than if they had been living on different continents. Most of the prisoners were seeing the town from close quarters for the first time since they had been in camp. Once again they were seeing people going about their daily business. It was like seeing things happening on Mars.

A servant girl in a blue dress with white spots was cleaning the unbroken windows of an apartment. Her sleeves were rolled up and she was singing. In another window stood an old woman with white hair. The sun fell on her face and on the drawn curtains and the pictures in the room. She looked sadly at the prisoners. On the corner of the street was a pharmacy. The pharmacist stood in front of the door and yawned. A woman in a leopard-skin coat walked down the street, close to the houses. She wore green gloves and shoes. The SS on the corner had let her pass. She was young and stepped nimbly over the heaps of rubble. Many of the prisoners hadn't seen a woman for years. They all noticed her but only Lewinsky stared after her.

"Look out!" whispered Werner. "Lend me a hand here."

He was pointing at a piece of material which stuck out from under the rubble. "There's someone buried here."

They shoveled the mortar and stones aside. There emerged from underneath a completely smashed face with a bloody, chalk-smeared beard. Beside it a hand was visible. The man had probably raised it to protect himself when the building collapsed.

The SS-men on the other side of the street were shouting provocative jokes at the daintily tripping girl in the leopard-skin coat. She laughed and made eyes at them. Then the sirens began to howl.

The pharmacist on the corner vanished into his shop. The girl in the leopard-skin coat started and ran back. She stumbled over a rubble heap and fell; her stockings tore and her green gloves were white with chalk dust. The prisoners had straightened themselves. "Stand still! Anyone moving will be shot!" The SS came running from the street corners. "Close ranks! Form fours, double march!"

The prisoners weren't sure which command to obey. A few shots rang out. The SS guards from the street corners finally drove them together into one group. The squad leaders deliberated what they should do. It was only the first warning; but they all kept looking up anxiously. The radiant sky seemed to have become at once brighter and darker.

Now the other side of the street grew more lively. People, unseen before, came out of the houses. Children screamed. The grocer with the mustache dashed out of his shop, and crept like a fat maggot over the ruins. A woman in a plaid shawl carried a parrot in a cage, carefully stretched out before her. The white-haired woman had disappeared. The servant girl, skirts raised high, ran from the door. Lewinsky's eyes followed her. Between the black stockings and the taut blue panties gleamed the white skin of her legs. Suddenly everything was reversed: the peaceful quiet on the side of freedom had all of a sudden vanished; people rushed in terror from their apartments and ran for their lives to the air-raid shelters; whereas on the opposite side the prisoners stood silent and calm in front of the ruined walls and watched them.

One of the squad leaders seemed to notice this. "Whole division about turn!" he commanded. The prisoners now stared at the ruins. The debris glared in the sun. In only one of the bombed houses had a passage to a cellar been cleared. Here could be seen steps, an entrance gate, a dark corridor and a shaft of light from an exit leading from the rear.

SPARK OF LIFE

The squad leaders were undecided. They didn't know where to send the prisoners. No one dreamed of leading them to an air-raid cellar. In any case, the cellars were filled with civilians. On the other hand, the SS themselves were not eager to remain unprotected. Several of them quickly searched the neighboring houses. They found a concrete cellar.

The tone of the sirens changed. The SS made a dash for the cellar. They left only two guards at the front door and two at each of the street entrances. "Kapos, foremen, see that no one budges! Anyone moving will be shot!"

The prisoners' faces grew tense. They stared at the walls in front of them and waited. They had not been given orders to lie down; it was easier for the SS to guard them standing up. They stood there silently, crowded together, surrounded by the kapos and foremen. Suddenly the pointer appeared among them. It had torn itself loose and was searching for 7105. Finding him, it jumped up and tried to lick his face.

For a moment the noise ceased. In the unexpected silence, which was like an airless room and tore at every nerve, suddenly the sounds of a piano could be heard. They rang out loud and clear but were distinctly audible only for a short while. Werner recognized it, however, in the immense concentration of listening, as the choir of the prisoners from *Fidelio*. It couldn't be a radio. The station did not broadcast any music during the air-raid alarm—it could only be a gramophone someone had forgotten to turn off, or else someone playing the piano at an open window.

The noise started again. Werner clung with his full power of concentration to the few bars he had heard. He pressed his jaws together and tried to continue them in his mind. He didn't want to think of bombs and death. If he succeeded in remembering the melody he would be saved. He closed his eyes and felt the hard knots of effort behind his brow. He must not die now. Not in this senseless way. He did not even want to think of it. He must remember the melody; the melody of those prisoners who had been freed. He clenched his fists and tried to go on hearing the sounds of the piano; but they had been drowned in the metallic raging of horror.

The first explosion shook the town. The shrill yelling of the falling bombs cut through the howling of the sirens. The ground shook. A chunk of molding fell slowly off one wall. Several of the prisoners had thrown themselves onto the rubble. Foremen came running. "Get up! Get up!"

Their voices couldn't be heard. They tugged at the men. Goldstein saw the skull of one prisoner, who had thrown himself down, crack and the blood gush forth. The man standing beside him grabbed his stomach and fell forward. They had been wounded not by bomb splinters but by the SS who had fired at them. The shots couldn't be heard.

"The cellar!" shouted Goldstein to Werner through the din. "The cellar there! They won't come after us!"

They stared at the entrance. It seemed to grow bigger. The darkness within was cool safety. It was a black whirlpool which seemed almost impossible to resist. As though hypnotized, the prisoners stared at it. Their lines swayed. Werner held Goldstein back. "No!" He was staring at the cellar himself and shouting through the noise. "No! Not that! We'd all be shot! No! Stand still!"

Goldstein turned his gray face toward him. His eyes lay in it like flat shining pieces of slate. His mouth was twisted with effort. "Not to hide in!" he muttered. "To escape! Run through it! There's an exit in the back!"

It hit Werner like a blow in the stomach. He suddenly began to tremble. It wasn't his hands or his knees that trembled; but his veins deep within him. His blood was quivering. He knew that an escape was highly unlikely to succeed, but the thought alone was temptation enough; to run away, to steal clothes in some house and to vanish in the confusion.

"No!" He thought he was whispering, but he was shouting through the turmoil. "No!" It wasn't meant only for Goldstein; it was for himself. "Not now! Not now!" He knew it was madness; everything they had so far achieved would be endangered by it, comrades would be killed, ten for each of those who attempted escape, a blood bath in this dense crowd; new regulations in the camp—and yet there it yawned and tempted—"No!" shouted Werner and held Goldstein back, and thereby himself.

The sun! thought Lewinsky. This damned sun! It revealed everything mercilessly. Why didn't they shoot the sun? It was as though one were standing naked under enormous spotlights, a sitting target for the planes' telescopic sights. If only a cloud would appear, just for a moment! Streams of sweat poured down his body.

The walls shook. A gigantic concussion thundered nearby, and into the thunder there slowly fell a great segment of wall containing an empty window frame. As it came tumbling over the prisoners it didn't look particularly dangerous. The segment was about fifteen feet wide. Only the one prisoner over whom the empty window frame had fallen was still standing, staring about him in amazement. He couldn't understand why he suddenly found himself standing up to his stomach in rubble and yet alive. Beside him legs, sticking out of the fallen wreckage, jerked up and down a few times and then lay still.

The pressure slowly subsided. At first it was almost unnoticeable, only the clamp around the brain and ears became slightly looser. Then consciousness began to filter through like weak light through a shaft. The din raged as before, yet suddenly everyone knew it was over.

The SS crept out of their cellar. Werner glanced at the wall in front of him. Gradually it turned again into an ordinary sunlit wall through which a passage had been cleared—no longer a glaring block of mockery wherein raged a whirlpool of dark hope. At his feet he saw again the dead face with the beard; and he saw the legs of his buried comrades. Then surprisingly he heard once more the sound of the piano through the subsiding roar of guns. He pressed his lips tight together.

Commands rang out. The surviving prisoner who had stood in the window frame climbed out of the rubble. His right foot was twisted. He raised it and stood on one leg. He didn't dare to let himself fall down. One of the SS-men came running up. "Get going! Dig out those men there!"

The prisoners tore away at the rubble and stones. They worked with hands, picks and shovels. It wasn't long before they had uncovered their comrades. There were four. Three were dead. One was still alive. They lifted him out. Werner looked around for help. He saw the woman with the red blouse come out of the doorway. She had not fled to the air-raid cellar. Carefully she carried a tin bowl of water and a towel. Paying no attention to anything, she carried the water past the SS and put it down beside the wounded man. The SS glanced at one another undecided, but didn't say a word. She washed the face clean.

The wounded man vomited bloody foam. The woman wiped it off. One of the SS-men started laughing. He had an immature, lumpy face with eyelashes so light that the pale eyes appeared naked.

The flak ceased. In the silence the piano could be heard resounding again. Werner now saw where it came from; from a window in the first floor of the grocery store; a pale man in spectacles was sitting there playing the choir of the prisoners on an upright brown piano. The SS grinned. One of them tapped his forehead. Werner wasn't sure whether the man had played for himself in order to get through the bombardment or whether his playing had meant something else. He decided to believe it had been meant as a message. He always chose to believe in the better, provided it entailed no risks. It made life easier.

People came running back. The SS resumed their military attitude. Commands rang out. The prisoners fell into line. The squad leader ordered an SS-man to stay with the dead and wounded; then came the command to double march down the street. The last bomb had struck an air-raid cellar. The prisoners were to dig it out.

The crater stank of acids and sulphur. On its edge a few trees leaned over, their roots exposed. The railing around the public lawn had been wrenched out and pointed up to the sky. The bomb had not struck the cellar directly; it had flattened it out sideways and buried it.

The prisoners worked more than two hours over the entrance. They cleared the staircase step by step. It had been knocked askew. They all worked as fast as they could; they worked as though those buried here were their own comrades.

By the end of another hour they had cleared the entrance. Long before this they had begun to hear screams and whimperings. The cellar must have been getting air from somewhere. As they made the first opening the screaming increased. A head shoved itself through and yelled, and immediately beneath it appeared two hands which scratched in the rubble as though an enormous mole were working its way out.

"Look out!" shouted a foreman. "It can still collapse!"

The hands went on scratching. Then the head was dragged down from within and another appeared, yelling. It, too, was pulled back. The people within were fighting in panic for a place in the light.

"Shove them back! They'll get hurt! First the hole must be made bigger. Shove them back!"

They pushed the faces back with their hands. The faces bit their fingers. With their picks they tore the concrete loose. They worked as though their own lives were at stake. At last the opening was big enough for the first one to crawl through. He was a powerful man. Lewinsky recognized him at once. He was the one with the mustache whom he had seen standing in the grocery store. He had worked himself to the front and shoved and moaned to get through. His stomach got stuck. The yelling within increased; he was darkening the cellar. They dragged at his legs to pull him back. "Help!" he screamed in a high whistling voice. "Help! Help me out! Out of here! Out! I promise to—I'll give you—"

His small black eyes started from their sockets in his round face. "Help! Gentlemen! Please! Gentlemen!" His Hitler mustache quivered. He resembled a trapped seal.

They seized him by the arms and finally pulled him through. He fell, jumped up and ran away without another word. They pressed a board against the entrance and enlarged it. Then they stepped back.

The people scrambled out. Women, children, men—some hastily, pale, sweating, having escaped a grave—others hysterical, sobbing, screaming, cursing—and then slowly and silently came those who had not been seized by the panic.

They ran and climbed past the prisoners. "Gentlemen!" whispered Goldstein. "Did you hear that? Please, gentlemen! The man meant us—"

Lewinsky nodded. "I'll give you—" he repeated the words of the seal. "Nothing," he added; "scrammed like a monkey he did." He looked at Goldstein. "What's wrong with you?"

Goldstein leaned against him. "Damn funny!" He could hardly breathe. "Instead of their setting us free," he panted, "we have freed them!"

He giggled and slowly toppled over sideways. They took hold of him and lowered him slowly onto a mound of earth. Then they waited until the bunker was empty.

They stood there, the prisoners of many years, and watched those who had been prisoners for a few hours hurry past them. Lewinsky remembered that something similar had happened once before—when the prisoners had met the procession of refugees from the town on the road. He saw the servant girl in the blue dress with white spots, crawling out of the entrance. She shook her skirts and smiled at him. A one-legged soldier with crutches followed. He raised himself, put the crutches under his arms and saluted the prisoners before he went on. One of the last to appear was a very old man. His face had long wrinkles like those of a bloodhound. He looked at the prisoners. "Thank you," he said. "There are still some people buried in there." Slowly, fragile and with dignity, he walked up the crooked steps. After he had gone the prisoners went down into the bunker.

They were marching back. They were done in. They carried their dead and wounded. The ones who had been buried alive had died in the meantime. A magnificent sunset colored the sky. Its light filled the air, and so vast was its beauty that it seemed as though time stood still and for one hour there could be neither ruins nor death.

"Nice bunch of heroes we are!" said Goldstein. He had recovered from his attack. "Working our fingers to the bone for those who do nothing for us."

Werner looked at him. "You're not to go out with the clearing gang again. It's madness. It'll kill you, however scarce you make yourself."

"What else can I do? Wait till the SS catch me up there?"

"We've got to find something else for you."

Goldstein smiled wearily. "I'm gradually getting fit for the Small camp, eh?"

Werner showed no surprise. "Why not? It's safe and it might be useful to have one of us in there."

The kapo who had kicked 7105 came up to him. He walked beside him for a while, then pushed something into his hand and fell back again. 7105 looked at it. "A cigarette," he said, surprised.

"They're growing soft," declared Lewinsky. "The ruins are getting on their nerves. They're thinking of the future."

Werner nodded. "Keep that kapo in mind. Maybe we can make use of him."

They dragged themselves along through the soft light. "A town," said Muenzer after a while. "Houses. Free people. Three yards away. It's as though one were no longer so completely cooped up."

7105 raised his skull. "I'd like to know what they think of us."

"What should they think? God knows how much they know about us. And they don't look happy themselves now."

"Now," said 7105.

They began the steep climb to the camp. "I wish I had that dog," said 7105.

"It would make a good roast," answered Muenzer. "I bet it weighs thirty pounds net."

"I didn't mean for eating. Just to have it."

The car couldn't get through. The streets were blocked everywhere. "Drive back, Alfred," said Neubauer. "Wait for me in front of my house."

He got out and tried to continue on foot. He climbed over a collapsed wall which had fallen across the street. The rest of the house was still standing. The wall had been torn off like a curtain and one could see into the apartments and the naked winding staircase. On the first floor a mahogany bedroom had been perfectly preserved. The two beds stood side by side; only one chair was turned over and a mirror was cracked. On the floor above the kitchen, water pipes had been ripped out. Water flowed over the floor and from there in cascades into the open—a thin, glittering waterfall. In the drawing room a red plush sofa stood upright. Pictures in gold frames hung askew against a striped wallpaper. A man stood where the front wall had been torn off. He was bleeding and stared down without moving. Behind him a woman ran to and fro with suitcases into which she tried to cram knickknacks, sofa cushions and soiled linen.

Neubauer felt the rubble moving under his feet. He stepped back. The rubble went on moving. He bent over and scraped away the stones and mortar. Out came a dusty hand and a length of arm, gray, like a tired snake. "Help!" shouted Neubauer. "There's someone still here! Help!"

No one heard him. He looked around. There were no people in the street. "Help!" he cried to the man on the second floor. The man slowly wiped the blood from his face and didn't react.

Neubauer pushed a lump of mortar aside. He saw hair and grabbed it, intending to pull it up. It didn't give. "Alfred!" he shouted and gazed round.

The car was no longer there. "Swine!" he said suddenly in a senseless rage. "When you want them they're never there!"

He went on digging. Sweat poured into the collar of his uniform. He was no longer used to such exertion. Police, he thought. Rescue squads! Where are all those crooks?

A chunk of mortar broke and gave way and under it Neubauer saw something which a short while before had been a face. Now it was a flat gray smeared mess. The nose had been smashed in. The eyes were no longer there; the sockets were filled with chalk dust. The lips had vanished and the mouth was a mass of mortar and loose teeth. The whole face was just a gray oval with hair over it through which blood was oozing.

Neubauer choked and began to throw up. He threw up a luncheon of sauerkraut, hard sausage, potatoes, rice pudding and coffee. It landed near the flat head. He tried to hold on to something but there was nothing there. He turned half round and went on throwing up.

"What's going on here?" someone asked behind him.

A man had approached without his having heard. He carried a shovel. Neubauer pointed at the head in the rubble.

"Someone buried there?"

The head moved slightly. At the same time something began moving in the gray pulp of the face. Neubauer vomited once more. He had eaten a great deal for lunch. "He's suffocating!" cried the man with the shovel, leaping close. He rubbed the face with his hands so as to find and free the nose, and with his fingers poked about where he imagined the mouth to be.

The face suddenly began to bleed more freely. The flat mask was now made more alive by the approaching death. The mouth began to move. The fingers of the hand scratched over the mortar, and the head with the blind eyes quivered. It quivered and then lay still. The man with the shovel raised himself. He wiped his smeared hands on a yellow silk curtain which had tumbled down with a window. "Dead," he said. "Are there any more down there?"

"I don't know."

"Aren't you from this house?"

"No."

The man pointed at the head. "Relative of yours? Acquaintance?"

"No."

The man glanced at the sauerkraut, the sausage, the rice and potatoes, then looked at Neubauer and shrugged his shoulders. He didn't seem to have much respect for a high-ranking SS officer. It had certainly been a copious meal, considering the year of the war. Neubauer felt himself blushing. He turned quickly away and clambered off over the rubble.

It took him almost an hour to reach the Friedrichs Allee. It was undamaged. He walked hopefully along it. If the houses in the next street were not destroyed, then his office building would also be standing, he thought superstitiously. The street was intact. The next two also. He took courage and walked faster. I'll try it once more, he thought. If the first two houses in the next street have not been destroyed, then I too have been spared. It worked. Only the third house was a heap of rubble. Neubauer spat; his throat was dry with dust. Confidently he turned the corner of the Hermann Goering Strasse and stood still.

The bombs had done a thorough job. The upper floors of his office building had completely collapsed. The corner front was missing.

It had been flung over to the other side of the street, into an antique shop. The counterblast had thrown an iron Buddha from there into the middle of the street. The saint sat alone on a chunk of undamaged plaster. He held his hands in his lap and stared, smiling calmly, across the occidental devastation in the direction of the demolished railroad station, as though waiting for an Asiatic ghost train to take him back to the simple laws of the jungle where man killed in order to live rather than lived in order to kill.

For a moment Neubauer had the silly sensation of having been let down by fate in the most infamous manner. The streets he had crossed had all been intact—and now this happened! It was the deep disappointment of a child. He felt like crying. To him, just to him this had to happen! He gazed down the street. Several houses were still standing. Why not those? he thought. Why should this happen just to me, to a decent patriot, a good husband, a responsible father?

He walked around the crater in the street. Every window in the dress shop was blown out. The splinters lay everywhere like ice. They crunched under his feet. He came to the section: LATEST FASHION FOR THE GERMAN WOMAN. One half of the sign hung down. He stooped and entered. There was a smell of burning but he didn't see any fire. The mannequins lay all over the floor. They gave the impression of having been raped by a horde of savages. Several lay on their backs, their dresses blown up, their legs raised; others lay on their bellies, their wax behinds sticking out. One was nude but for her gloves; another stood in a corner, one leg broken off, wearing a hat and a veil over her face. All, in their various positions, were smiling—which made them look gruesomely obscene.

Finished, thought Neubauer. Finished. Gone. What would Selma say now? There was no justice. He went out and waded through the glass and debris round the building. On reaching the corner he saw on the other side a figure which, hearing him, ducked and ran away.

"Stop!" shouted Neubauer. "Stand still! Or I'll shoot!"

The figure stood still. It was a small crumpled man.

"Come here."

The man drew nearer. Neubauer recognized him only as he

stopped in front of him. It was the previous owner of the office building.

"Blank!" he said, surprised. "Is that you?"

"Yes, Herr *Obersturmbannführer.*"

"What are you doing here?"

"Pardon, Herr *Obersturmbannführer.* I—I—"

"Talk sense, man! What are you doing here?"

Seeing the effect his uniform made, Neubauer had quickly recovered his authority and himself.

"I—I—" stuttered Blank. "I've just come over, to—to—"

"What, to—to?"

Blank gestured helplessly towards the rubble.

"To gloat over it, what?"

Blank almost jumped back. "No, no, Herr *Obersturmbannführer.* No, no! Only—it's a pity," he whispered. "Pity."

"Of course it's a pity. Now you can laugh."

"I'm not laughing! I'm not laughing, Herr *Obersturmbannführer!*"

Neubauer eyed him. Blank stood fearful before him, his arms pressed tight to his body. "You got off better than I," said Neubauer bitterly. "Been well paid? Or not?"

"Yes, very well, Herr *Obersturmbannführer.*"

"You received cash, I a rubble heap."

"Yes, Herr *Obersturmbannführer!* Regret—regret immensely. This incident—"

Neubauer stared in front of him. He was now actually convinced that Blank had made an excellent deal. For a moment he wondered whether he couldn't sell the rubble heap back to him for a lot of money. But this was against the principles of the Party. And in any case even the rubble was worth more than he had paid Blank at the time. Not to mention the building ground. Five thousand he had paid him. The annual rents alone had come to twenty thousand. Twenty thousand! Lost!

"What's wrong with you? Why are you fumbling about with your arms?"

"Nothing, Herr *Obersturmbannführer.* I fell down years ago—"

Blank was sweating. Large drops ran down his forehead into his eyes. He blinked more with the right eye than with the left. In the left, which was made of glass, he didn't feel the sweat so much. He feared Neubauer might interpret his trembling as impudence. Things like that had happened before. But at this moment Neubauer wasn't thinking anything of the kind; nor of the fact that Blank had been interrogated by Weber in the camp the day before the sale. He was thinking only of the rubble.

"You've come off better than I. Maybe you didn't quite believe it at the time. But now you would have lost everything. Instead, you have hard cash."

Blank didn't dare to wipe his sweat away. "Yes, Herr *Obersturmbannführer*," he murmured.

Neubauer threw him a searching glance. A thought had crossed his mind. It was a thought that had recurred more and more frequently during recent weeks. It had first occurred to him when the Mellern newspaper building had been destroyed; he had dispelled it, but it had returned again and again like a bothersome fly. Could it possibly happen that the Blanks would one day return? The fellow before him didn't look like it; he was a wreck. But the rubble heaps around him were that, too. They didn't look like victories. Least of all when they belonged to oneself. He thought of Selma with her prophecies of doom. Not to mention the newspaper reports. The Russians were at the gates of Berlin. One couldn't get away from that. The Ruhr was surrounded; that, too, was a fact.

"Listen, Blank," he said cordially. "I've always treated you decently, eh?"

"Exceedingly so! Exceedingly!"

"You've got to admit that, what?"

"Most certainly, Herr *Obersturmbannführer!* Most certainly!"

"Humanely—"

"Very humanely, Herr *Obersturmbannführer.* I'm deeply grateful—"

"Well, then—don't forget that! I've risked quite a number of things for you. What are you doing here anyhow? In town?"

Why haven't you been thrown into a camp long ago? he nearly asked.

"I—I—"

Blank was drenched. He didn't know where this might lead. He only knew from experience that Nazis who were affable invariably had a particularly gruesome joke up their sleeves. This was how Weber had talked before he had squeezed his eye out. He cursed himself for not having been able to resist leaving his hide-out to have a look at his old firm.

Neubauer noticed his confusion. He made use of the opportunity. "The fact that you are free—you are aware to whom you owe that, eh?"

"Yes—thank you—thank you very much, Herr *Obersturmbannführer.*"

Blank did not owe it to Neubauer. He knew it and Neubauer knew it, too. But faced by the smoldering rubble old notions suddenly began to melt. Nothing was certain any longer. One had to take precautions. Crazy as it seemed to Neubauer, one could never be quite sure whether there might not come a day when a Jew like this could be made use of. He pulled a Deutsche Wacht from his pocket.

"Here, take this, Blank. Good stuff. That trouble years ago was harsh necessity. Always bear in mind how I protected you."

Blank did not smoke. After Weber's experiments with burning cigarettes it had taken Blank years not to become hysterical at the smell of tobacco. But he didn't dare to refuse. "Thanks very much. Very kind, Herr *Obersturmbannführer.*"

Cautiously he withdrew, the cigar in his crippled hand. Neubauer looked round. No one had seen him talk to the Jew. That was a good thing. He promptly forgot Blank and started figuring. Then he began to sniff the air. The smell of burning had increased. He walked fast to the other side. The fashion department was now in flames. He ran back, shouting, "Blank! Blank!" And not seeing him, "Fire! Fire!"

No one came. The town was on fire in many places and the fire brigade had long since been incapable of coping with it. Neubauer dashed back to the fashion windows. He leapt in, seized a bale of material and dragged it out. At the second attempt he no longer got through. A lace dress he had grabbed flared up in his hand. The fire shot over the materials and dresses. He just managed to escape.

Paralyzed, he watched the fire from the other side of the street.

It caught the mannequins, shot over them and devoured the dresses, and suddenly—melting, burning—they acquired a strange life. They twisted and arched themselves. Arms were raised and bent, it was a waxen hell—then everything was submerged and the fire closed over it—as over the corpses in the crematorium.

Neubauer retreated from the heat until he ran into the Buddha. Without glancing back he sat down on it, but at once jumped up again. He hadn't realized that the saint's headgear had a bronze point. He stared furiously before him at the bale he had saved; it was a light blue material on which flying birds were printed. He gave it a kick with his boot. Damn it! What was the good of it? He lugged the bale back and threw it into the flames. Might as well all go to the devil! Damn it! He stamped away. He didn't want to see any of it any more! God was no longer on the side of the Germans. Nor Wotan, either. Who then?

Behind a heap of rubble on the other side of the street a pale face slowly raised itself. Max Blank's eyes followed Neubauer. For the first time in many years he smiled. He smiled, while crushing the cigar between his crippled fingers.

CHAPTER SIXTEEN

Once more eight men stood in the yard of the crematorium. All wore the red badge of the political prisoner. Berger knew none of them; but he knew their fate.

The kapo Dreyer was already at his place in the cellar. Berger felt something crumbling within him which had still been secretly counting on a reprieve. Dreyer hadn't been there for three days. This had prevented Berger from doing what he wanted to do. Today there was no longer any way out; he had to risk it.

"Start right here," said Dreyer grumpily. "Otherwise we'll hardly get through. They're croaking like flies in your place nowadays."

The first dead came tumbling down. Three prisoners stripped them and sorted their things. Berger inspected the teeth; then the three others loaded the dead into the elevator.

Half an hour later Schulte arrived. Though he looked fresh and well rested, he kept yawning. Dreyer took notes while now and again Schulte looked over his shoulder.

The cellar was large and well aired, but the stench of corpses soon grew very strong. It clung not only to the naked bodies but also to the clothes. The avalanche of corpses didn't cease; it seemed to bury time beneath it, and when Schulte finally rose and declared he was going to eat, Berger hardly knew whether it was already evening or only noon.

Dreyer folded his papers. "By how many are we ahead of the cremation room?"

"Twenty-two."

"Okay. Time for lunch. Tell them up there to stop throwing people down until I get back."

The other three prisoners walked out at once. Berger dealt with one more corpse. "Out with you. Push off!" growled Dreyer. The pimple on his upper lip had grown into a painful boil.

Berger straightened himself. "We forgot to book this one here."

"What?"

"We forgot to book this one here."

"Nonsense! We booked them all."

"That's not true." Berger kept his voice as calm as he could. "We booked one too few."

"Good God, man!" exploded Dreyer. "Are you crazy! What the hell are you talking about?"

"We must put one more man on the list."

"So?" Dreyer glanced sharply at Berger. "And why must we do that?"

"To make the list correct."

"Don't start sticking your nose into my lists."

"I'm not interested in the other lists. Just in this one here."

"Others? What other lists are there, you carcass?"

"The gold lists."

Dreyer remained silent for a moment. "So? And now what are you really trying to say by all this?" he asked then.

Berger took a deep breath. "I'm trying to say that I don't care whether the gold lists are correct or not."

Dreyer started but controlled himself. "They are correct," he said threateningly.

"Maybe. Maybe not. One only has to compare them."

"Compare them? What with?"

"With my own lists. I've been keeping them ever since I started working here. As a precaution. For myself."

"Look at that! So he also keeps a list, the sneak! And you think they're more likely to believe you than me?"

"I should think that's possible. I don't get any advantages out of my list."

Dreyer eyed Berger from head to foot as though he were seeing him for the first time. "So? You don't get any? I doubt that, too. And to tell me this you've waited for just the right moment, here in the cellar, what? Alone with me—that's just where you've made your mistake, you egghead." He grinned. The boil hurt him. The grin looked as if an angry dog were baring its teeth. "Would you mind telling me what's to stop me bashing in your egghead and leaving you here with the others? Or to jam up your windpipe? Then you yourself will be the one to be missing from your list. Explanations won't be necessary. We are alone here. You just collapsed. Heart failure. One more or less makes no difference here. They won't investigate that. I'll book you all right."

He came closer. He was more than sixty pounds heavier than Berger. Even with the pliers in his hand, Berger didn't stand the slightest chance. He took one step back and stumbled over the dead that lay behind him. Dreyer seized his arm and twisted his wrist. Berger let the pliers drop. "There, that's better," declared Dreyer.

He pulled Berger close with one jerk. His distorted face was right before Berger's eyes. It was red and the boil with its blue rim shone on the lip. Berger didn't say anything; he bent his head back as far as possible and tightened what remained of his neck muscles.

He watched Dreyer's right hand come up. His brain cleared. He knew what he had to do. There was little time left; but fortunately the hand seemed to rise like something in a slow-motion picture. "This case here has been reckoned with," he said quickly. "It has been taken down and signed by witnesses."

The hand did not stop. It came slow but it continued to rise.

"Swindle!" growled Dreyer. "Trying to talk yourself out of it. The whole thing's a swindle! You won't be talking much longer."

"It's no swindle. We've counted on your trying to do away with me." Berger stared into Dreyer's eyes. "It's always the first thing that occurs to imbeciles. It has been taken down and if I don't return this evening it will be handed to the camp leader with the list mentioning the two missing gold rings and one pair of gold spectacles."

Dreyer's eyes blinked. "So?" he said.

"Just so. D'you think I didn't know what I was risking?"

"So, you knew that?"

"Yes. It's all been taken down. Weber, Schulte and Steinbrenner will remember the missing gold spectacles very well. They belonged to a man with one eye. That's the kind of thing one doesn't forget so easily."

The hand stopped rising. It remained motionless, and then fell down. "It wasn't gold," said Dreyer. "You said so yourself."

"It was gold."

"It was worthless. Trash. Not worth the trouble of throwing away."

"You can explain all that later yourself. We have evidence from the friends of the man they belonged to. They were pure white gold."

"Lousy bastard!"

Dreyer gave Berger a shove. Again Berger fell. Trying to steady himself he groped and felt the teeth and the eyes of a corpse under his hand. He fell over it but didn't take his eyes off Dreyer.

Dreyer breathed heavily. "So—and what d'you imagine will happen to your friends? D'you think they'll be rewarded? For being in the know about your trying to smuggle a corpse in here?"

"They are not in the know."

"And who's going to believe that?"

"Who's going to believe you when you explain it to them? All they'll believe is that you invented the story to get me out of the way because of the rings and the spectacles."

Berger had gotten up again. He felt he was suddenly beginning to tremble. He bent over as though to dust his knees. There was nothing to dust; but he couldn't control the trembling in his knees and didn't want Dreyer to see it.

Dreyer didn't notice it. He was picking at his boil. Berger saw that the abscess had burst. Pus was oozing out. "Don't do that," he said quickly.

"What? Why?"

"Don't touch that boil. Cadaverine poisoning is fatal."

Dreyer stared at Berger. "I haven't touched a corpse today."

"But I have. And you touched me. My predecessor died of blood poisoning."

Dreyer jerked his hand away and wiped it on his trousers. "Damn it! What'll happen now? Filthy business. I've already touched it." He glanced at his fingers as though he had leprosy. "Get on! Do something!" he shouted at Berger. "D'you think I want to croak?"

"Certainly not." Berger had pulled himself together. Diverting Dreyer's attention had given him time. "Least of all now, so near the end," he added.

"What?"

"So near the end," repeated Berger.

"What end? Do something, you dog! Put something on it."

Dreyer had turned pale. Berger took down a bottle of iodine that stood on a shelf. He knew that Dreyer was not in danger; he didn't care, anyway. The main thing was that he had diverted his attention. He spread some iodine over the boil. Dreyer shrank back. Berger put the bottle away. "There—now it's disinfected."

Dreyer tried to look at the boil. He squinted down his nose. "Are you sure?"

"Sure."

For a moment Dreyer went on squinting. Then he moved his upper lip like a rabbit. "So? And what actually did you want?" he asked.

Berger realized he had won. "What I said. Alter the particulars of one corpse. That's all."

"And what about Schulte?"

"He wasn't paying attention. Not to the names. In any case, he went out twice."

Dreyer deliberated. "And the clothes? What about them?"

"They'll tally. The numbers, too."

"How? Have you—"

"Yes," said Berger. "I've brought with me the ones we want to swap."

Dreyer glanced at him. "The bunch of you have planned this quite well. Or did you do it on your own?"

"No."

Dreyer stuck his hands in his pockets and walked slowly to and fro. Then he stopped in front of Berger. "And who'll guarantee me your so-called list won't turn up all the same?"

"I will."

Dreyer shrugged his shoulders and spat.

"Until now there's been only this list," said Berger calmly. "The list and the accusation. I could have used it and nothing would have happened to me. At best I'd have been praised. After this—" he pointed at the papers on the table—"I'm implicated in the disappearance of a prisoner."

Dreyer reflected. He carefully moved his upper lip and squinted down his nose.

"For you the risk is considerably smaller," Berger went on. "It's just one more offense added to three or four others. That can hardly make much difference. But I'm incriminating myself for the first time. I'm running a far greater risk. That I consider your guarantee."

Dreyer didn't answer.

"There's still something else to consider," said Berger, continuing to watch him. "The war is as good as lost. German troops have been driven out of France and Russia, far across the frontiers and the Rhine. Against this no propaganda or talk of secret weapons is any use. In a few weeks or months it'll all be over. Then will come the day of reckoning here, too. Why let yourself be caught and punished for others? If it gets known that you helped us you'll be safe."

"Who is this—*us?*"

"There are a lot of us. Everywhere. Not only in the Small camp."

"And supposing I denounce you all? Let out that you exist?"

"What's that got to do with rings and gold spectacles?"

Dreyer raised his head and smiled crookedly. "You've really worked it all out pretty nicely, what?"

Berger remained silent.

"Does the man you're trying to hush up want to bolt?"

"No. We're merely trying to protect him against that." Berger pointed at the hooks on the wall.

"A political one?"

"Yes."

Dreyer screwed up his eyes. "And if there were to be a thorough check-up and he's found, what then?"

"The barracks are overcrowded. They won't find him."

"He could be recognized. If he's a notorious political one."

"He isn't notorious. In any case, we in the Small camp all look alike. There isn't much to recognize."

"Is there a block senior in the know?"

"Yes," lied Berger. "Otherwise it wouldn't be possible."

"Have you connections with the office?"

"We have connections everywhere."

"Is the man's number tattooed in?"

"No."

"And his clothes?"

"I know the ones I want to swap. I've put them aside."

Dreyer glanced at the door. "Then start! Quick! Before someone comes."

He pushed the door ajar and listened. Berger crept about among the dead and examined them. Just then another idea occurred to him. He decided to make a double exchange. In this way Dreyer could be misled and prevented from discovering 509's name.

"Get a move on, damn it!" cursed Dreyer. "Why are you taking so long?"

Berger was lucky with the third corpse; it was from the Small camp and had not been tattooed. Berger stripped off the jacket, took out from under his own jacket 509's coat and pants with the numbers and put them on the corpse. Then, tossing the dead man's garments on the heap of clothing, he pulled out from under it the jacket and pants which he had previously laid aside. He wrapped them around his hips, buckled the belt over them and buttoned his jacket.

"Finished!"

Berger was panting. Black spots danced over the walls in front of his eyes. Dreyer turned around. "Everything under control?"

"Yes."

"Okay. I haven't seen a thing. I don't know anything. I was in the latrine. What happened here is your doing. I know nothing. Understand?"

"Yes."

The elevator full of naked corpses went up, returning empty after a short while.

"I'm going up now to get the three from outside for loading," said Dreyer. "In the meantime, you'll be alone here. Is that clear?"

"Clear," answered Berger.

"And the list?"

"I'll bring it tomorrow. Or I can destroy it."

"Can I rely on that?"

"Absolutely."

Dreyer thought for a while. "You're in it now," he said. "More than I. Or aren't you?"

"Far more."

"And if anything leaks out—"

"I don't talk. I have poison on me. I won't talk."

"You really seem to have just about everything." Dreyer's face showed a kind of reluctant respect. "I didn't know that." Otherwise I'd have been more on my guard, he thought. These blasted three-quarter dead ones! Can't trust even them. "Get the elevator going—" he started to leave.

"I've got something for you," said Berger.

"What?"

Berger took a five-mark bill from his pocket and laid it on the table. Dreyer pocketed it. "Well, at least that's something for the risk."

"Next week you'll get another five—"

"And—what for?"

"Nothing. Just another five marks for this one here."

"Okay." Dreyer started to grin, but stopped immediately; the boil was hurting. "After all, one isn't a monster," he said. "Always glad to help a comrade."

He left. Berger leaned against the wall. He felt giddy. Things had gone better than he expected. But he didn't deceive himself; he knew Dreyer was still pondering how he could do away with him. For the time being the danger had been postponed by the threat of the underground movement and the promise of the five marks. Dreyer would wait for that. Criminals could be relied upon to seize such advantages. This was a lesson the Veterans had learned from Handke. The money had been produced by Lewinsky and his group. They would continue to give assistance. Berger felt for the jacket which was tied round his waist. It was safe. It wasn't visible. He was so thin that even now his own jacket hung loosely about him. His mouth was dry. The corpse with the false number lay in front of him. He dragged another one off the pile and pushed it next to the disguised corpse. At the same moment a new corpse came whizzing down through the opening. The unloaders had started again.

Dreyer appeared with the three prisoners. He cast a glance at Berger. "What are you doing here? Why aren't you outside?" he snarled.

This was for the alibi. It was meant to impress the three others with the fact that Berger had been alone down here.

"I had to pull one more tooth," said Berger.

"Insolence! You're here to do what you're told. Otherwise anything might happen."

Dreyer settled himself ostentatiously at the table with the lists. "Go ahead!" he commanded.

Shortly afterwards Schulte arrived. In his pocket he had a copy of Knigge's *Social Conduct in Society*, which he pulled out and began to read.

The stripping of the dead continued. The third in line was the corpse with 509's jacket. Berger had wangled it so that the other two helpers did the stripping. He heard them call out the number 509. Schulte didn't look up. He was reading from the classic on social etiquette the rules on how to eat crayfish. In May he was expecting an invitation from the parents of his fiancée and wanted to be prepared. Mechanically Dreyer booked the particulars and compared them with the reports from the blocks. The fourth corpse was again a political prisoner. Berger reported it himself. He called the number in a slightly louder voice and noticed that Dreyer looked up. He brought the dead man's belongings to the table. Dreyer glanced at him. Berger winked back. Then he took the pliers and the flashlight and bent over the dead. He had achieved what he wanted. Dreyer was under the impression that the number of the fourth corpse was that of the still living man who had been exchanged, not that of the third one. Thus he knew that Dreyer had been thrown off the scent and could under no condition give the show away.

The door opened. Steinbrenner came in. He was followed by Breuer, the supervisor of the bunker, and Squad Leader Niemann. Steinbrenner smiled at Schulte. "We've been told to relieve you when the dead here have been booked. Weber's orders."

Schulte closed his book. "Have we got that far?" he asked Dreyer.

"There are still four corpses left."

"All right. Finish up."

Steinbrenner was leaning against the wall on which the scratchings of the hanged men were visible. "Take your time. We're in no hurry. And then send down the five men who've been working upstairs. We have a surprise for them."

"Yes," said Breuer. "Today's my birthday."

"Which of you is 509?" asked Goldstein.

"Why?"

"I've been transferred here."

It was evening and Goldstein had arrived in the Small camp with a transport of twelve others. "Lewinsky sent me," he said to Berger.

"Are you in our barrack?"

"No. In Barrack 21. In the hurry nothing else could be done. We can change that later. It was high time I got away. Where's 509?"

"509 no longer exists."

Goldstein looked up. "Dead or hidden?"

Berger hesitated. "You can trust him," said 509 who was squatting beside him. "Lewinsky talked about him last time he was here."

He turned toward Goldstein. "My name is now Flormann. What's the news? We haven't heard from you for a long time."

"Long? Two days—"

"That's long. What's the news? Come nearer. No one can listen in here."

They sat down a short distance from the others. "Last night in Block Six we managed to get some news over our radio. British. There was a lot of interference; but one thing came through clearly: the Russians are bombarding Berlin."

"Berlin?"

"Yes."

"And the Americans and British?"

"There was no other news. There were interferences and we had to be careful. The Ruhr is surrounded and they are a long way over the Rhine, that's certain."

509 stared at the barbed wire beyond which glimmered a strip of sunset under heavy rain clouds. "How slow all this goes—"

"Slow? You call that slow? In one year the German armies have been driven from Russia to Berlin and from Africa to the Ruhr—and you call that slow!"

509 shook his head. "I don't mean that. It's slow for here. For us. Just now! Can't you understand that? I've been here many years—but this seems the slowest spring of all. It's slow because it's so difficult to wait."

"I understand." Goldstein smiled. His teeth shone chalky in his gray face. "I know that. Especially at night. When one can't sleep or get one's breath." His eyes were not part of the smile. They remained expressionless and the color of lead. "Damn slow it is, if you look at it that way."

"Yes, that's what I mean. A few weeks ago we didn't know anything. Now already everything seems slow. Strange, it all changes the moment one has hope! And is waiting. And is afraid one might still be caught."

509 was thinking of Handke. He was not yet out of danger. The plot could have been fool-proof if only Handke had not known 509 personally. In that case 509 would simply have become the corpse as soon as the corpse had been booked as 509. Now, however, he had been officially declared dead and was called Flormann. But he was still in the Small camp. More could not have been achieved. It was

already a great deal that the block senior of Barrack 20, where Flormann had died, had been willing to co-operate. 509 had to take great care not to be seen by Handke. He also had to be careful not to be betrayed by anyone else. There was, moreover, Weber who might recognize him in the event of a surprise check-up.

"Did you come alone?" he asked Goldstein.

"No. Two others were sent along."

"Any more coming?"

"Probably. But not as official transfers. We have at least fifty to sixty people hidden over there."

"How do you manage to hide so many?"

"They change barracks every night. Sleep elsewhere."

"And if the SS order them to report at the gate? Or at the office?"

"Then they don't go."

"What?"

"They don't go," repeated Goldstein. He watched 509 straighten himself in surprise. "The SS have no longer a clear idea of the situation," he declared. "During the last few weeks the confusion has mounted daily. We've done our best to increase it. The men they're looking for have always been sent off with the gangs or simply couldn't be found."

"And the SS? Don't they come and get them?"

Goldstein's teeth gleamed. "They no longer like to do that. Or at most in groups and armed. The only dangerous group is the one with Niemann, Breuer and Steinbrenner in it."

509 remained silent for a while. What he had just heard was too fantastic. "How long has this been going on?" he asked at last.

"For about a week. Things change every day."

"You mean the SS have got the jitters?"

"Yes. They have suddenly realized that we are thousands. And they know the way the war's going."

"You simply don't obey?" 509 still couldn't grasp it.

"We obey, but in our own way. We delay them and sabotage where we can. Even so, the SS catch enough of us. We can't save everyone." Goldstein stood up. "I must try and find somewhere to sleep."

"If you don't find anything, ask Berger."
"Okay."

509 lay beside the pile of dead between the barracks. The pile was higher than usual. The previous evening there had been no bread. This always showed the following day in the number of dead. 509 lay near them because a wet cold wind was blowing. The dead protected him against it.

They protected him, he thought. They protected him even from the crematorium and beyond it. Somewhere in the wet cold wind blew the smoke of Flormann, whose name he now bore; what remained of him were a few charred bones out of which bonemeal would soon be made in the mill. But the name, the most elusive and least significant part of man, had remained, had become a shield for another life which defied extinction. He heard the pile of dead, moaning and shifting. The tissues and juices in them were still at work. A second chemical death was creeping through them, splitting them, gassing them, preparing them for decay; and like a spectral reflex of vanished life, their bellies still moved, swelling and shrinking, the dead mouths expelled air and from the eyes oozed fluid like long-belated tears.

509 moved his shoulders. He wore the Attila-tunic of a Honved Hussar. It was one of the barrack's warmest garments and was worn in turns by those spending the night outside. He contemplated the facings which gleamed dull in the dark. There was a certain irony in it; just now, as he was beginning again to remember his past and himself, when he no longer wanted to be a number, he had to live under the name of a dead man and wear a Hungarian uniform at night.

He shivered and buried his hands in the sleeves. He could have returned to the barrack and slept there several hours in the warm stench; but he didn't want to. He was too restless. He preferred to sit and shiver and stare into the night. He waited and didn't know what it was that could happen in the night that should make him want so much to wait. It was this waiting that drove one crazy, he thought. Waiting hung soundlessly over the camp like a net, gathering into itself all hopes and all fear. I'm waiting, he thought, and

Handke and Weber are pursuing me. Goldstein is waiting and every minute his heart misses a beat. Berger is waiting and isn't sure he won't be finished off with the crematorium gang before we are liberated; and all of us are waiting and are not sure whether we won't be sent at the last moment on death transports and into extermination camps—

"509," Ahasver said from the dark. "Are you there?"

"Yes, here. What is it?"

"The sheep dog is dead."

Ahasver groped closer. "He wasn't sick," said 509.

"No. He just slept away."

"Shall I help you carry him out?"

"That's not necessary. I was outside with him. He's lying over there. I just wanted to tell someone about it."

"Yes, old man."

"Yes, 509."

CHAPTER SEVENTEEN

The transport came as a surprise. The railroad connections into the town from the west had been interrupted for several days. After they had been repaired a number of boxcars had arrived with one of the first trains. They were supposed to continue to an extermination camp. At night, however, the connections had been bombed again. One whole day the train had stood on the tracks; then the inmates were sent to the Mellern camp.

They were exclusively Jews. Jews from all over Europe. There were Polish and Hungarian, Rumanian and Czech, Russian and Greek Jews; Jews from Yugoslavia and Holland and Bulgaria and even some from Luxembourg. They spoke a dozen different languages and most of them didn't understand one another. Even the Yiddish they had in common seemed to differ. They had been two thousand and now they were five hundred. A few hundred lay dead in the train.

Neubauer was beside himself. "Where on earth shall we put them? The camp's overcrowded as it is! And besides, they haven't been officially assigned to us! It has nothing to do with us! This is a crazy mess! There's no order left! What on earth's happening?"

He paced up and down in his office. On top of all his personal worries, now came this, too! His sense of order was outraged. He couldn't understand why so much fuss should be made about people condemned to death. Enraged, he stared out the window. "There they lie, like gypsies, with their rags and tatters in front of the gates! Are we in the Balkans or in Germany? Can you figure out what's going on, Weber?"

Weber was unmoved. "Some authority must have given the orders," he said. "Otherwise they wouldn't have come up here."

"That's just what I mean! Some official down there at the railroad station. Without my having been consulted. Not even informed beforehand. Not to mention the complete lack of organization. That simply doesn't seem to exist any more! Every day new authorities turn up. Those down at the railroad station maintain that the people screamed too much. That it was making a bad impression on the civilian population. What's that got to do with us? Our people don't scream."

He glanced at Weber. Weber was leaning indolently against the door. "Have you talked to Dietz about it yet?" he asked.

"No, not yet. You're right. I'll do it at once."

Neubauer had the call put through and spoke for some time. Then he put down the receiver. He had grown calmer. "Dietz says we're to keep them only overnight. The whole lot in one block. Not to distribute them through the barracks. Not to admit them officially. Just leave them here and guard them. Tomorrow they'll be sent on. By then the railroad will be repaired." He gazed out of the window. "But where shall we put them? We're overcrowded already."

"We can leave them on the roll-call ground."

"We need the roll-call ground tomorrow morning for the working gangs. That'll only create confusion. Besides, those Balkans will make a complete mess of it. We can't have that."

"We can put them on the roll-call ground in front of the Small camp. There they won't be much in the way."

"Is there enough room?"

"Yes. Then we'll just have to pack all our own people into the barracks. Lately a number of them have been sleeping out."

"Why? Are the barracks that overcrowded?"

"That depends on how one looks at it. People can be packed like sardines. Even on top of one another."

"It'll have to be done for one night."

"It shall be done. None of the people in the Small camp will care to get mixed up with the transport crowd." Weber grinned. "They'll shrink from that as from the plague."

A fleeting grin passed over Neubauer's face. It pleased him to hear that his prisoners preferred to stay in the camp. "We must post guards," he said. "Otherwise the new ones will disappear into the barracks. Then there'll be a real mess."

Weber shook his head. "The people in the barracks will be on their guard against that, too. They're afraid enough as it is that we'll send some of them along to make up the quota."

"All right. Appoint a few of our men and enough kapos and camp police as guards. And have the barracks in the Small camp locked up. We can't risk using any searchlights to keep a watch on the transport."

It looked as though a vast horde of great tired birds no longer able to fly were approaching through the twilight. They swayed and stumbled, and when one fell the others trampled over him almost without looking, until those who followed picked him up.

"Barrack doors closed!" commanded the SS squad leader who was locking up the Small camp. "Stay inside! Anyone coming out will be shot!"

The crowd was driven onto the ground between the barracks. It surged to and fro. Some fell, others crouched beside them, forming in the turmoil an island which kept on growing bigger, and soon all were lying on the ground and the evening fell on them like a rain of ashes.

They lay and slept; but their voices were not silent. They kept on fluttering up out of dreams and anguished sleep and sudden awakening, foreign and shrill, and sometimes they joined into a long-drawn wail which rose and fell with the same few sounds and surged against the barracks like a sea of misery against the safe arks of security.

In the barracks they heard it all through the night. It tore at the nerves, and even during the first hours men began to grow wild. They started screaming, and when the crowd outside heard it their wailing also rose and this in turn increased the screaming within. It was like a sinister, medieval, alternating lamentation—until revolver butts thundered against barrack doors, shots resounded and the hollow thump of truncheons could be heard as they fell on bodies, then the sharper sounds as they fell on skulls.

Then it grew calmer. The screaming men in the barracks had been overwhelmed by their comrades; and the crowd outside had been overcome by the sleep of exhaustion rather than by the truncheons. They hardly felt the truncheons any longer. Off and on the lamentation rose again; it grew weaker but never died down entirely.

The Veterans listened for a long time. They listened and shuddered and feared they might be going to share the same fate. In appearance they differed little from the transport people outside—but they felt sheltered in their death barracks, between stench and death, packed together and on top of each other, under the hieroglyphs scratched into the walls by the dying, and in their agony at not being able to go to the latrine—they felt as sheltered as though these barracks were home and security against the strange, boundless suffering outside—and this seemed almost more horrifying than many things they had gone through before.

They were awakened in the morning by many low, foreign voices. It was still dark. The wailing had ceased. Instead, there now came a scratching on the barrack walls. It scratched as though hundreds of rats outside were gnawing to get in. It scratched secretly and not very loud, and then there began a cautious knocking against the door, against the walls, and then a murmuring, low, almost fawning, beseeching, in a foreign singsong, in the broken voices of last despair; they were begging to be admitted.

They were imploring those in the Ark for help against the Flood. They were quieter, already resigned, they no longer screamed; they just begged, they caressed the wood of the walls, they lay in front of the doors and scratched with hands and nails and implored with soft, dim voices in the darkness.

"What are they saying?" asked Bucher.

"They're pleading to be let in in the name of their mothers. In the name of—" Ahasver broke off. He was weeping.

"We can't do it," said Berger.

"Yes, I know."

An hour later came the order to march on. Outside, commands were being shouted. In answer there came a loud wailing, followed by more commands, loud and furious.

"Can you see anything, Bucher?" asked Berger. They were crouching on a top bunk in front of the small window.

"Yes. They're refusing. They don't want to go."

"Get up!" shouted someone outside. "Fall in! Fall in line and number!"

The Jews didn't get up. They remained flat on the ground and glanced with terror-filled eyes at the guards and hid their heads in their arms.

"Get up!" roared Handke. "Up with you! Up, you stinkers! Or shall we give you some encouragement? Get out of here!"

The encouragement had no effect. The five hundred creatures who, because they worshiped God in other ways than their tormentors, had been reduced to something that could no longer be described as human, reacted no more to screams, curses and beatings. They remained prone, they tried to hug the ground, they clawed themselves into it—the wretched, filthy earth of the concentration camp appeared to them most desirable, it was for them paradise and salvation. They knew where they were going to be taken. As long as they had been on the transport and in motion they had apathetically kept on moving. Now, having once stopped and come to rest, they refused as apathetically to move again.

The guards grew bewildered. They had been given orders not to beat the people to death, and this was rather difficult. The command had no other reason than the usual bureaucratic one; the transport had not been assigned to the camp and consequently had to leave it as complete as possible.

More SS-men appeared. From the window of Barrack 20, 509 saw Weber arrive in his shiny elegant boots. He stopped at the entrance to the Small camp and gave an order. The SS raised their rifles and fired close over the bodies lying on the ground. Legs apart, hands on hips, Weber stood near the gate. After the salvos he had expected the Jews to leap up.

They didn't. They were beyond all threats. They wanted to stay where they were. They didn't want to move. Even had they been fired upon, they probably wouldn't have stirred.

Weber's face changed color. "Get them up!" he shouted. "Beat them till they get up! Beat their legs and feet!"

The guards threw themselves upon the crowd. They beat them with truncheons and fists, they trampled on their stomachs and genitals, they tore at the people by their hair and beards and pulled them onto their feet; but the people let themselves drop again as though they had no bones.

Bucher stared out. "Just look at that," whispered Berger. "It's not only the SS who are doing the beating up. Not only green ones, either. Not only criminals. There are other colors among them. Some of our men are there, too! Prisoners like ourselves turned kapos and cops. They're behaving just like their masters." He rubbed his inflamed eyes as though he wanted to squeeze them out of his head. Close beside the barrack stood an old man with a white beard. Blood poured from his mouth and slowly reddened his beard.

"Come away from the window," said Ahasver. "If they see you, they'll take you, too."

"They can't see us."

The window was grimy and dim and from outside no one could see what was going on behind it in the dark room. From the inside, on the other hand, one could see enough.

"You oughtn't to watch that," said Ahasver. "It's a sin unless you're forced to."

"It's no sin," said Bucher. "We don't want ever to forget this, that's why we're watching it."

"Haven't you seen enough of it here in the camp?"

Bucher didn't answer. He was staring out of the window.

Gradually the frenzy outside began to exhaust itself. The guards would have had to drag each one away singly. For that they would have needed a thousand men. Sometimes they managed to get ten or twenty Jews together out onto the road; but not more. As soon as there were more they broke through the men guarding them and dashed back again to the large twitching mass.

"There's Neubauer himself," said Berger.

He had suddenly appeared and was talking to Weber. "They don't want to leave," said Weber, less unperturbed than before. "One could practically beat them to death and still they wouldn't move."

Neubauer blew out dense clouds of cigar smoke. The stench was very high. "Horrible story! Why on earth were they sent here? They could so easily have been finished off where they were, instead of having them sent all over the country to be gassed. I'd like to know the reason for this."

"The reason is that even the filthiest Jew has a body. Five hundred corpses are five hundred corpses. Killing is simple; but it's far more difficult to make corpses disappear. And these were two thousand."

"Nonsense! Nearly every camp has a crematorium like ours."

"That's true. But for these times crematoriums work far too slow. Especially if the camp has to be cleared in a hurry."

Neubauer spat out a piece of tobacco leaf. "All the same I don't understand why the people have to be shipped about all over the place."

"That again is a question of corpses." Weber had recovered his calm. "Our authorities don't like the idea of too many bodies being found. So far only crematoriums have been able to dispose of them in such a way that their number cannot afterwards be established. Unfortunately, for our enormous requirements, they work much too slowly. We've still no really effective means of quickly disposing of large crowds. Mass graves can be opened long afterwards, allowing atrocity stories to be invented. One has seen this in Poland and Russia."

"Why didn't they simply leave this rabble during the retreat—" Neubauer promptly corrected himself, "I mean, during the strategic shortening of the line, where they were? They surely can no longer be used for anything. Should have been left to the Russians or Americans to cope with."

"There'd still remain the same problem of the bodies," answered Weber patiently. "They say the American army has a great number of journalists and photographers. They could take pictures and maintain that the people are undernourished."

Neubauer took the cigar from his mouth and looked sharply at Weber. He wasn't sure whether his camp leader was making fun of him. However often he tried, he had never been able to find this out. As usual Weber's face was noncommittal. "What do you mean?" asked Neubauer. "What are you talking about? Of course they're undernourished."

"I'm talking about the atrocity stories which the democratic press invents about us. The ministry of propaganda is warning us against it every day."

Neubauer kept staring at Weber. I actually don't know him at all, he thought. He has always done what I wanted, but fundamentally I don't know anything about him. I wouldn't be surprised if he suddenly laughed in my face. In mine, and maybe even in that of the Führer himself. A hireling without any real ideology. To him probably nothing is sacred, not even the Party. It just happened to suit him. "You know, Weber—" he began, and then broke off. There was no point in making a fuss. For a moment the sudden fear in his stomach had returned. "Of course the people are undernourished," he said. "But that's not our fault. The enemy forces us into it with his blockade. Or doesn't he?"

Weber raised his head. He didn't trust his ears. Neubauer glanced at him with strained apprehension. "Of course," said Weber, unperturbed. "The enemy with his blockade."

Neubauer nodded. The instant of anguish had passed again. He looked around the roll-call ground. "Frankly speaking," he said almost confidentially, "there's nevertheless a mighty difference between the camps. Our people look considerably better than the ones over there, even these here in the Small camp. Don't you agree?"

"Yes," answered Weber, perplexed.

"It's quite obvious if you compare them. I'm sure we have one of the most humane camps in the whole Reich." Neubauer had a sense of smug relief. "Of course people die. Even quite a number. That's unavoidable at such times. But we are humane. Here, those no longer able to work, don't have to. Where else would you find that, for traitors and enemies of the State?"

"Almost nowhere."

"That's what I think. Undernourished? That's not our fault! I tell you, Weber—" Neubauer suddenly had an idea. "Listen, I know how to get the people out of here. You know how? With food!"

Weber grinned. There were times, after all, when the old man emerged from the clouds of his own wish-dreams. "Excellent idea!" he declared. "When truncheons don't help—food always does. But we haven't any extra rations ready."

"Then for once the camp inmates will have to go without. They'll have to show some comradeship. They'll just get less for the noon meal." Neubauer stretched his shoulders. "Do these people here understand German?"

"A few perhaps."

"Is there an interpreter?"

Weber asked a few of the guards. They dragged three men along. "Translate to your people what the Herr *Obersturmbannführer* is saying!" bellowed Weber.

The three men stood side by side. Neubauer took a step forward. "Men!" he said with dignity. "You have been wrongly informed. You're on your way to a recreation camp."

"Go on!" Weber nudged one of the three. They uttered something in an unintelligible language. No one on the ground stirred.

Neubauer repeated the words. "You're to go to the kitchen now," he added, "to receive coffee and food."

The interpreters repeated it. No one moved. No one believed such talk. They had seen people disappear in a similar manner many a time. Food and baths were dangerous promises.

Neubauer grew annoyed. "Kitchen! March to the kitchen! Food! Coffee! Get food and coffee! Soup!"

With their truncheons the guards threw themselves at the crowd. "Soup! Can't you hear? Food! Soup!" At each word they used their clubs.

"Stop!" shouted Neubauer angrily. "Who gave you orders to beat them up, damn you!"

The guards sprang back. "Get out of here!" yelled Neubauer.

The men with the clubs suddenly turned into prisoners again. Huddled together, they crept along the edge of the ground.

"They're actually battering them into cripples!" snarled Neubauer. "Then we'll have them on our necks for good!"

Weber nodded. "As it is, we've already been sent several truckloads of dead for cremating from the station."

"What happened to them?"

"They're piled up at the crematorium. Just now, when we're short of coal anyway! We need our fuel stock badly enough for our own people!"

"Damn it, how the hell are we going to get these people out of here?"

"They're in a state of panic. They no longer understand what they're told. Maybe they will when they smell it."

"Smell what?"

"Smell the food. Smell or see it."

"You mean if we bring a cauldron up here?"

"Yes. Promises don't work with those people. They must see and smell it."

Neubauer nodded. "Possible. Haven't we got a number of wheeled cauldrons? Have one brought over here. Or two. One with coffee. Is the food ready?"

"Not yet. But there should be a cauldron left over from last night, I think."

The cauldrons were wheeled up. They stopped on the road at a distance of about two hundred yards from the crowd. "Push one of them up into the Small camp," ordered Weber. "And take off the lid. Then, when the people start coming, wheel it slowly back again onto the road."

He turned to Neubauer. "We must get them to move," he said. "Once they have left the roll-call ground it'll be easier to get them out. It's always like this. They want to stay where they've slept because nothing has happened to them there. For them, it means a kind of security. Everything else they're afraid of. But once they're in motion again, they'll keep moving."

He turned to the kapos. "First bring in the coffee," he ordered. "And don't wheel it back. Dish it out! Distribute it over there."

The coffee cauldron was pushed right into the crowd. One of the kapos ladled it out and poured the brew over the head of the nearest man. It was the old man with the white bloodstained beard. The liquid ran over his face, turning the beard brown. This was the third transformation. The old man raised his head and licked up the drops. His clawlike hands fumbled about. The kapo held the ladle with the remains of the coffee to his mouth. "Drink! Coffee!"

The old man opened his mouth. His scraggy neck muscles suddenly began working. His hands closed round the ladle, and he swallowed, swallowed, he was nothing but swallowing and slobbering; his face twitched, he trembled and swallowed.

His neighbor saw it. Then a second and third. They raised themselves, shoved their mouths, their hands, close; pushed one another, fought for the ladle, clung to it, a mass of arms and heads.

"Stop that! Damn it!"

The kapo couldn't get the ladle free. He tugged and kicked, glancing cautiously over his shoulder to where Neubauer was standing. Others had risen in the meantime and were bending over the steaming cauldron. They tried lowering their faces into the coffee and scooping it up with their thin hands. "Coffee! Coffee!"

The kapo noticed that his ladle was free. "Order!" he shouted. "Get into line—one behind the other!"

It had no effect. The crowd could not be kept in check. They didn't hear anything. They smelled what called itself coffee, something warm that could be drunk, and they blindly stormed the cauldron. Weber had been right: where the brain no longer registered, the stomach was still master.

"Now pull the cauldron slowly over there," ordered Weber.

It was impossible. The crowd surrounded it. One of the guards made a surprised face and slowly toppled over. The crowd had pulled his legs from under him. He flung his arms about him like a swimmer and then slipped down.

"Form a wedge!" commanded Weber.

The guards and camp police took up positions. "Get going!" shouted Weber. "Make for the coffee cart! Pull it out!"

The guards broke into the crowd. They flung the people aside. They succeeded in forming a cordon round the cauldron and managed to move it. It was already almost empty. Shoulder to shoulder they pushed it out. The crowd followed. Hands tried to reach over their shoulders and under their arms. They continued pushing the cauldron out.

Someone in the moaning throng suddenly discovered the second cart standing some way off. He made for it, swaying grotesquely. Others followed him. But here Weber had taken precautions. It was surrounded by powerful men and promptly set in motion.

The crowd plunged after it. Only a few remained behind, wiping the sides of the coffee cauldron with their hands and then licking their fingers. About thirty others, unable to stir, remained lying on the ground.

"Drag them with you!" shouted Weber. "And then form a cordon across the road so that they can't come back."

The ground was littered with human filth; but it had been a resting place for one night. This meant a great deal. Weber knew it from experience. He knew that, as water must recede to the lowest level, the crowd would instinctively try to return here once the frenzy of hunger had passed. This he wanted to prevent.

The guards drove on those who had remained behind. They lugged along the dead and the dying. There were only seven dead—the transport consisted of the toughest last five hundred.

At the Small camp's exit to the road several men broke away. The guards with the dead and dying couldn't follow them fast enough. Three of the strongest fled back. They ran towards the barracks and pulled at the doors. That of Barrack 22 gave way. They crept in.

"Halt!" screamed Weber when the guards made efforts to follow. "Everyone come here! We'll get those three later. Watch out! The others are coming back."

The crowd was coming down the road. The food cauldron had been emptied and while the SS were trying to form them into groups for marching off, the people had turned around. Now, however, they were no longer what they had been before. Previously they had been a single block, beyond despair, and this had given them an inert power. Now, through hunger and food and movement, they had been cast back into despair; fear fluttered up in them again and made them wild and weak; they were no longer a solid mass but many single beings, each one with the remainder of his own life, and this made them easy victims. Moreover, they no longer crouched close together. They no longer had any power. They felt hunger and pain again. They began to obey.

A number of them had been cut off further up the road; some more on the way back; the rest were received by Weber and his men. They didn't beat them over the head, only on the body. Slowly groups began to form. Stupefied, they stood four deep, their arms interlocked so as to avoid collapsing. A dying man was hooked in between each couple of stronger men. From afar, for someone not knowing what was going on, it could have looked as though a group of gay drunkards was tottering along arm in arm. Then suddenly some of them began to sing. They stared in front of them and raised their heads and held up the others and sang. They weren't many and the song was thin and incoherent. They walked across the large roll-call ground, past the lined-up labor formations, out through the gate.

"What's that they're singing?" asked Werner.

"A song for the dead."

The three men who had escaped were cowering in Barrack 22. They had forced their way in as far as they could. Two cowered half under one bunk. They had pushed their heads far under it. Their legs stuck out and trembled. The trembling ran over them, stopped for a moment, then began again. White-faced, the third one stared at the prisoners. "Hide me—man—man—" He repeated it over and over again, tapping his breast with his forefinger.

Weber pulled the door open. "Where are they?"

With two guards he stood in the doorway. "Get a move on! Where are they?"

No one answered. "Room senior!" yelled Weber.

Berger stepped forward. "Barrack 22, Section C—" he began to report.

"Shut up! Where are they?"

Berger had no choice. He knew the escaped men were bound to be found in a few moments. He also knew that the barrack must under no condition be searched. They were hiding two political prisoners from the labor camp.

He raised his arm to point into the corner, but one of the guards, glancing past him, forestalled him. "There they are! Under the bunk!"

"Get them out!"

A shuffling started in the crowded room. The two guards pulled the escaped men by their legs, like frogs, from under the bunk. The prisoners' hands clung to the posts. They swung in the air. Weber trod on their hands. There was a crack and their hands gave way. The men were dragged out. They didn't scream. They just uttered a soft high moaning while being dragged over the dirty floor. The third, the one with the white face, got up by himself and followed them. His eyes were large black holes. He looked at the prisoners while passing them by. They averted their eyes.

Legs apart, Weber stood in front of the entrance. "Which of you swines opened the door?"

No one answered. "Step out!"

They stepped out. Handke was already standing outside.

"Block senior!" bellowed Weber. "There was an order for the doors to be closed. Who opened them?"

"The doors are old. The escaped men tore out the lock, Herr Storm Leader."

"Nonsense! How could they?"

Weber bent over the lock. It hung loose in the rotten wood. "Have a new lock put in at once! Should have been done long ago! Why wasn't it done before?"

"The doors here are never locked, Herr Storm Leader. There's no latrine in this barrack."

"Doesn't make any difference! Have it seen to." Weber turned round and walked up the road behind the escaped men, who no longer resisted.

Handke eyed the prisoners. They expected one of his outbursts. But it didn't come. "Fatheads!" he said. "Hurry up and get the filth out of here!" Then he turned to Berger. "I'll bet you wouldn't have liked it much, would you, if the barrack had been thoroughly searched?"

Berger didn't answer. Expressionless, he glanced at Handke. Handke let out a guffaw. "Think I'm dumb, eh? I know more than you think. And I'll get you all yet! All you stuck-up political idiots, understand?"

He stamped out behind Weber. Berger turned around. "What was that?" he asked Goldstein.

Goldstein shrugged his shoulders. "We must warn Lewinsky at once. And try to move those two who are hiding here somewhere else. D'you think it could be done in Block 20?"

"Yes—we'll talk to 509."

CHAPTER EIGHTEEN

In the morning the fog hung close over the camp. The machine-gun towers and the palisades could not be recognized. It seemed for a while as though the concentration camp no longer existed; as though the fog had dissolved the enclosure into a soft, treacherous freedom and one had only to walk on to discover it was no longer there.

Then came the sirens and soon afterwards the first explosions. They came from some soft nowhere and had no direction and no origin. They could just as well have been in the air or beyond the horizon as in the town. They were flung about, as thunder by many muffled storms, and in the gray-white of the woolly infinity they gave the impression of holding no danger.

The inmates of Barrack 22 crouched wearily on the bunks and in the corridors. They had slept little and were wretched from hunger;

there had only been a thin soup the evening before. They paid hardly any attention to the bombardment. This, too, had grown familiar by now, it had become a part of their existence. None of them, however, had been prepared for the howling to increase furiously all of a sudden and to end with a gigantic detonation.

The barrack swayed as in an earthquake. Into the echoing reverberation of the crash sounded the tinkling of broken windowpanes.

"They're bombing us. They're bombing us!" someone cried. "Let me get out! Out of here!"

A panic started. Men tumbled out of their bunks. Others tried to clamber down and hung entangled with those below in a maze of limbs. Feeble arms lashed out, bared teeth gleamed from the skulls, and eyes stared fearfully out of deep sockets. What gave it all a ghostlike quality was that everything seemed to proceed without sound; the raging of the antiaircraft guns and the bombs was now so violent that it completely drowned the screaming within. Open mouths appeared to scream without voices as though fear had made them mute.

A second explosion shook the earth. The panic turned into uproar and flight. Those still able to walk swarmed helter-skelter through the corridors; others, utterly indifferent, lay on their bunks staring at their soundless gesticulating comrades as though they were spectators of a pantomime that no longer concerned them. "Shut the door!" shouted Berger.

It was too late. The door was flung open and the first batch of skeletons stumbled into the fog. Others followed. The Veterans crouched in their corner and only with difficulty kept from being dragged out with the rest. "Stay here!" shouted Berger. "The guards will fire!"

The flight continued. "Lie down!" called Lewinsky. Despite Handke's threats, he had spent the night in Barrack 22. It had still seemed safer to him. The previous day four men whose names began with the letters H and K had been caught in the labor camp by the special SS gang consisting of Steinbrenner, Breuer and Niemann and taken to the crematorium. Fortunately the search had been carried out bureaucratically. Lewinsky had not waited for them to reach the letter L. "Flat on the ground!" he shouted. "They're going to fire!"

"Out! Who wants to be caught in this mousetrap?"

Outside, shots were already crackling into the howling and thunder. "There! It's started! Lie down! Flat! The machine guns are more dangerous than the bombs!"

Lewinsky was mistaken. After the third explosion the machine guns ceased. The guards had quit the towers in a hurry. Lewinsky crept out of the door. "The danger's over!" he shouted into Berger's ear. "The SS have disappeared."

"Shall we stay inside?"

"No! That's no protection. We can get trapped and burn to death."

"Out!" shouted Meyerhof. "If the barbed wire is bombed we can flee!"

"Shut up, idiot! They'd catch you in those clothes and shoot you!"

"Come out."

They hustled out of the door. "Stick together!" shouted Lewinsky. He seized Meyerhof by the front of his jacket. "If you do anything foolish I'll break your neck with my own hands, d'you hear? Damned idiot, d'you think we can risk that kind of thing now?" He shook him. "D'you understand? Or shall I break your neck this minute?"

"Leave him alone," said Berger. "He won't do it. I'll watch him."

They lay beside the barrack, close enough to see the dark walls in the steaming fog. It looked as though they were giving off fumes from an invisible fire. They lay there, the giant hands of many thunders in the back of their necks, hugging the earth and waiting for the next explosion.

It didn't come. Only the flak continued raging. Soon bombs could no longer be heard even from the direction of the town. Instead, it was the crack of rifle shots that sounded clearer through the noise.

"That's here in the camp," said Sulzbacher.

"It's the SS." Lebenthal raised his head. "Maybe the SS quarters have been hit and Weber and Neubauer are dead."

"Too good to be true," said Rosen. "Things like that don't happen. They certainly couldn't have done any precision bombing in that fog. Maybe they hit a few barracks."

"Where's Lewinsky?" asked Lebenthal.

Berger looked around. "I don't know. He was here a few minutes ago. Don't you know where he is, Meyerhof?"

"No."

"Maybe he's gone out to explore."

They went on listening. The tension increased. Once more isolated rifle shots could be heard. "Maybe some men over there have escaped and they're after them."

"I hope not."

They all knew the whole camp would have to line up for roll call and be left standing until the escaped men had been brought back dead or alive. That would mean dozens of dead and a thorough search of all barracks. This was the reason why Lewinsky had shouted at Meyerhof. "Why should they still try to escape now?" asked Ahasver.

"Why not?" retorted Meyerhof. "Each day—"

"Be quiet," interrupted Berger. "You've risen from the dead and that's made you crazy. You think you're Samson. You wouldn't get five hundred yards."

"Maybe Lewinsky himself has bolted. He had reason enough. More than anyone else."

"Ridiculous! He won't bolt."

The flak died down. In the silence commands and running could be heard. "Wouldn't it be better for us to get into the barrack?" asked Lebenthal.

"You're right." Berger got up. "Everyone from Section C back into the room. Goldstein, see to it that your men hide themselves well to the rear. Handke'll be here any minute."

"I'll bet they didn't hit the SS," said Lebenthal. "Those gangsters always get through. Probably a few hundred of us have been torn to pieces."

"Perhaps the Americans are already here," said someone in the fog.

For a moment everyone fell silent. "Shut up!" said Lebenthal then, annoyed. "Don't talk like that!"

"In with you, those who can still crawl. There's bound to be a roll call."

They crept back into the barrack. Again there was a near-panic. Many, especially those who owned a strip of bunkboard, were suddenly afraid that others, faster, might take it from them. They yelled with hoarse, feeble voices, fell down and scrambled forward. The barrack was still overcrowded and there was room for less than a third of them. Some remained outside despite all warnings to get in; they were too exhausted by the excitement even to crawl. The panic had swept them out with the others, but now they could move no longer. The Veterans dragged several of them as far as the barrack; through the fog they saw that two were dead. They were bleeding. Bullets had killed them.

"Look out!" Through the white surging fog they heard steps heavier than those of Mussulmen.

The steps drew closer and stopped in front of the barrack. Lewinsky looked in. "Berger," he whispered, "where's 509?"

"In 20. What's up?"

"Just come out for a moment." Berger went to the door.

"509 needn't be afraid any more," said Lewinsky fast and abruptly. "Handke is dead."

"Dead? From a bomb?"

"No. Dead."

"How did it happen? Did the SS catch him in the fog?"

"Something caught him in the fog. That's enough, or isn't it? The main thing is, he's gone. He was dangerous. The fog was convenient." Lewinsky remained silent for a moment. "You'll see him all right in the crematorium."

"If the shot was from too close, they'll see traces of powder and burns."

"There was no shot. Two other bullies got finished off too in the fog and confusion. Two of the worst. One of them was from our barrack. He squealed on two men."

The All Clear sounded. The fog rose and scattered. It looked as though the explosions had torn it apart. Through it a scrap of blue began to shine, then it turned silver and the sun beyond it filled it with a white glow. Like dark scaffolds, the machine-gun towers began rising out of it.

Someone approached. "Look out," whispered Berger. "Come in, Lewinsky. Hide!"

They closed the door behind them. "It's only one," said Lewinsky. "No danger. For a week now they've given up coming alone. They're in too much of a funk."

The door was cautiously opened. "Is Lewinsky here?" someone asked.

"What d'you want?"

"Come quick. I have it here."

Lewinsky disappeared in the fog.

Berger looked around. "Where's Lebenthal?"

"Went to 20. Wanted to tell 509 about it."

Lewinsky returned. "Did you hear any more about what happened over there?" asked Berger.

"Yes. Come out."

"What was it?"

Lewinsky smiled slowly. His face was wet from the fog and unfolded itself into teeth, eyes and a broad quivering nose. "A part of the SS quarters has collapsed," he said. "Dead and wounded. Don't know yet how many. Barrack 1 has losses. The arms depot and the clothes chamber have been damaged." He glanced cautiously into the fog. "We've got something to hide. Maybe only until tonight. We managed to get hold of something. Our people didn't have much time. Only until the SS returned."

"Give it to me," said Berger.

They stood close together. Lewinsky handed Berger a heavy package. "From the arms depot," he whispered. "Hide it in your corner. I've still got another one. We'll stick it into the hole under 509's bunk. Who's sleeping there now?"

"Ahasver, Karel and Lebenthal."

"Fine." Lewinsky breathed heavily. "They worked fast. They started the moment the bomb had smashed the depot wall. The SS weren't there. Our men had left before they returned. We even got hold of more. We'll hide that in the typhus ward. Distribute the risk, you understand? Werner's principle."

"Won't the SS discover what's missing?"

"Maybe. That's why we're not going to leave anything in the

labor camp. We haven't taken too much and everything's in a hell of a mess. Maybe they won't notice anything. We've tried to set the depot on fire."

"You've worked damn well," said Berger.

Lewinsky nodded. "A lucky day. Come, let's hide it without anyone seeing. No one here suspects anything. It's getting brighter. We couldn't get hold of more because the SS returned too soon. They thought the fences had been destroyed. Shot at everyone crossing their path. Expected a wholesale escape. Now they're calmer. Discovered the barbed wire was intact. Damn lucky the labor gangs had been kept back this morning; danger of escape in the fog. That's how we could let our best men go to work. Now there'll probably soon be a roll call. Come, show me where we can put the things."

An hour later the sun came out. The sky turned soft and blue and the last of the fog disappeared. There lay the fields with the rows of trees fresh and damp and with a shimmer of green, as after a bath.

In the afternoon Block 22 heard that twenty-seven prisoners had been shot during and after the bombardment; twelve had been killed in Barrack 1, twenty-eight injured by splinters. Ten SS-men were dead; among them Birkhauser of the Gestapo. Handke was dead; so were two men from Lewinsky's barrack.

509 came over. "What about the receipt for the Swiss francs that you gave Handke?" asked Berger. "Supposing it's found among his things? What then? What if it falls into the hands of the Gestapo? We didn't think of that!"

"Yes, someone did," said 509. He took a piece of paper out of his pocket. "Lewinsky knew about it. And he thought of it. He managed to get hold of Handke's things. A reliable kapo stole them for him right after Handke's death."

"Lewinsky has been damned efficient today. Tear it up!" Berger heaved a sigh of relief. "I hope we'll at last have some peace now."

"Perhaps. It depends on who's going to be the new block senior."

A flight of swallows appeared suddenly above the camp. For a long time they circled high up in wide spirals, then came down and shot screeching over the barrack. Their blue glistening wings almost touched the roof.

"That's the first time I've seen birds in the camp," said Ahasver.

"They're looking for somewhere to nest," declared Bucher.

"Here?" guffawed Lebenthal.

"They no longer have the church spires."

The smoke above the town had cleared a little. "True enough," said Sulzbacher. "The last spire has collapsed."

"Here!" Shaking his head, Lebenthal glanced up at the swallows which were now circling round the barrack, uttering shrill cries. "And that's what they're coming back from Africa for! Here of all places!"

"There's no place for them in town as long as it's burning."

They all gazed down. "What a sight!" said Rosen.

"There must be a lot of towns burning like that," said Ahasver. "Bigger and more important ones. Think what they must look like!"

"Poor Germany!" said someone crouching nearby.

"What?"

"Poor Germany."

"My God!" said Lebenthal. "Did you hear that?"

"Yes," Berger said. "And it's true."

It turned warm. In the evening the barrack learned that the crematorium had been damaged, too. One of its exterior walls had fallen in and the gallows had been knocked sideways; but the chimney continued smoking full blast.

The sky grew cloudy. The air became more and more sultry. The Small camp received no evening meal. The barracks were quiet. Those who could, lay outside. It seemed to them as though the heavy air ought to yield some nourishment. The clouds, turning denser, more livid, looked like sacks out of which food might fall. Lebenthal returned tired from a patrol around the camp. He reported that only four barracks in the labor camp had received an evening meal. Rumor had it that the commissary had been damaged. There had been no check-ups in the barracks, he said. Apparently the SS hadn't yet discovered the disappearance of the weapons.

It grew continuously warmer. The town lay in a strange sulfurous light. Although the sun had set long ago, the clouds still hung full of the yellow livid light that refused to yield.

"There's a thunderstorm coming," said Berger. He lay pale beside 509.

"I hope so."

Berger looked at him. Sweat ran into his eyes. Very slowly he turned his head, and suddenly blood gushed from his mouth. It seemed so effortless and natural that in the first instant 509 couldn't believe it. Then he raised himself. "What's wrong? Berger! Berger!"

Berger doubled up and then lay still. "Nothing."

"Is that a hemorrhage?"

"No."

"What then?"

"Stomach."

"Stomach?"

Berger nodded. He spat out the blood still in his mouth. "Nothing serious," he whispered.

"Serious enough. What shall we do? Tell me what we can do!"

"Nothing. Let me lie. Lie quiet."

"Shall we carry you in? You can have a bunk to yourself. We'll throw a few others out."

"Just let me lie here."

509 suddenly felt utter despair. He had seen so many people die and had nearly died himself so often that he had believed an individual death could no longer affect him much. But now it hit him as it had the first time. It seemed to him that he was losing the one and only friend of his life. He promptly lost all hope. Berger was already smiling at him again from a face covered with sweat—but 509 had a vision of him lying motionless on the edge of the concrete road.

"Someone must still have something to eat! Or be able to get some medicine! Lebenthal!"

"Nothing to eat," said Berger. He raised one hand and opened his eyes. "Believe me. I'll tell you what I need. And when. Nothing now. Nothing, believe me. It's only the stomach."

He closed his eyes again.

→》》《《←

After the last whistle Lewinsky emerged from the barrack. He squatted beside 509. "Why is it you're not in the Party?" he asked.

509 glanced at Berger. Berger's breathing was regular. "Why d'you want to know that just now?" he retorted.

"It's a pity. I wish you were one of us."

509 knew what Lewinsky meant. In the camp's underground organization the Communists formed an extremely tough, reserved and energetic group. Though they co-operated with the others, they never entirely trusted them and pursued their own special aims. They always protected and promoted their own people first.

"We could use you," said Lewinsky. "What were you actually before? Professionally, I mean?"

"Editor," answered 509 and was himself surprised at how strange it sounded.

"We could make particularly good use of editors."

509 didn't answer. He knew that a discussion with a Communist was as pointless as one with a Nazi. "Have you any idea what sort of block senior we're going to get?" he asked after a short while.

"Yes. Probably one of our own people. In any case, he's sure to be political. We've got a new one in our barrack. He's one of us."

"In that case you'll go back again?"

"In a day or two. That has nothing to do with the block senior."

"Have you heard anything else?"

Lewinsky gave 509 a searching glance. Then he moved closer. "We expect the camp to be taken over in about two weeks."

"What?"

"Yes. In two weeks."

"You mean the liberation?"

"The liberation and our taking over. We've got to take over when the SS pulls out."

"Who's *we?*"

Lewinsky hesitated a moment. "The future camp management," he said then. "There has to be one and it's already being organized. Otherwise there'd be nothing but confusion. We must be prepared to take over at once. The maintenance of the camp must be continued without interruption. That's the most important thing. Maintenance, supplies, administration—thousands of people can't disperse at the same time and run in all directions."

"Certainly not here. Here not everyone can run."

"That has also to be taken into account. Doctors, medicine, transport facilities, bringing up of food supplies, requisitions in the villages—"

"And how are you planning to do all this?"

"We will be helped, that's certain. But it's we who have to organize it. The British or Americans who liberate us are fighting troops. They won't be equipped to administer a concentration camp right away. That we must do. With their help, of course."

509 saw Lewinsky's head outlined against the cloudy sky. It was bulky and round, without any softness. "Strange, isn't it," he said, "how we take our enemy's help for granted?"

"I've slept," said Berger. "I'm all right again. It was just the stomach, nothing else."

"You're sick. And it's not the stomach," answered 509. "I've never heard of anyone spitting blood from the stomach."

Berger's eyes had opened wide. "I dreamed something extraordinary. It was very clear and real. I was operating. The bright light—"

He looked into the night.

"Lewinsky believes we'll be free in two weeks, Ephraim," said 509 gently. "They're getting news all the time now."

Berger didn't move. It seemed as though he hadn't heard anything.

"I was operating," he said. "I was about to make an incision. A stomach resection. I'd just started and suddenly I didn't know how to go on. I had forgotten everything. I broke out in a sweat. The patient lay there, opened, anesthetized—and I didn't know how to go on. I'd forgotten how to operate. It was terrible."

"Forget it. It was a nightmare. Nothing else. The things I've dreamed! And just think of the things we're going to dream about when we're out of here!"

Suddenly, quite distinctly, 509 smelled eggs and bacon. He tried not to think of it. "It won't all be rejoicing," he said. "That's certain."

"Ten years." Berger was still staring at the sky. "Ten years of nothing. Away. Gone! No work done. I never thought of it until now. It's possible I've forgotten a great deal. Even now I don't quite know how an operation is performed. I can't remember exactly. During the first years in the camp I used to re-enact operations in my mind at night. To keep in touch. Then I gave it up. It's possible I've forgotten it—"

"It leaves one's memory, but one doesn't really forget. It's like languages or bicycling."

"One can lose the technique. The hands. The precision. One can become uncertain. Or lose touch. In ten years a lot has happened. A lot been discovered. I don't know anything about it. I've just grown older—older and more tired."

"Strange," said 509. "Just by chance, a moment ago, I thought of my old profession, too. Lewinsky had asked me about it. He thinks we'll get out of here in a couple of weeks. Can you imagine that?"

Berger shook his head absent-mindedly. "What's happened to time?" he said. "It used to be unlimited. Now you say two weeks. And all of a sudden one asks: What's happened to the ten years?"

The burning town glowed in the valley. Though night had fallen, it was still sultry. Waves of steam began to rise. Lightning flashed. Two more fires glowed on the horizon—distant bombed towns.

"Shouldn't we be glad for the time being that it's possible for us even to think what we're thinking, Ephraim?"

"Yes. You're right."

"We're already thinking like human beings again—about what it'll be like after we get out. When were we able to do that before? Everything else will come right on its own."

Berger nodded. "And if I have to spend the rest of my days darning stockings when I get out of here! Nevertheless—"

The sky was torn by a flash of lightning and thunder slowly followed from afar. "D'you want to go inside?" asked 509. "Can you manage to stand up, or crawl?"

The storm broke at eleven o'clock. Flashes of lightning brightened the sky and for seconds there was cast up a pale moon landscape with the craters and ruins of the destroyed town. Berger was fast asleep. 509 sat in the frame of the door; since Handke had been killed Barrack 22 was once more free for him. He kept the revolver and ammunition hidden under his jacket. He was afraid that in the event of a downpour of rain they might get wet and become useless in the hole under his bunk.

That night, however, it rained little. The storm kept on spreading, dividing itself, and for a long time there were several storms flinging lightning at one another like swords from horizon to horizon. Two weeks, thought 509, and saw the landscape beyond the barbed wire flare up and fade again. It seemed to resemble another world which imperceptibly, during recent weeks, had drawn nearer and nearer, had grown out of a lost no-man's land of hopelessness, and now lay already close to the barbed wire, waiting, with the smell of rain and fields, of destruction and fire, but also with that of growth and forests and green. He felt how the flashes of lightning passed through him, illuminating that world—and how at the same time a long-lost past rose up, pale, distant, almost incomprehensible and inaccessible. He shivered in the warm night. He wasn't as sure of himself as he had pretended to be to Berger. He could remember the past and it seemed to him much, and moved him; but whether it was enough after the years here he didn't know. There had been too much death between then and now. He knew only that life meant getting out of the camp, but soon after that everything became uncertain and overwhelming and blurred, and far beyond it he could not see. Lewinsky could, but he thought as a member of the Party. The Party would take him up and he would be in it; that for him was enough. What was it, then? thought 509, what was this that called, beyond the primitive desire to live? Revenge? With revenge alone, little was achieved. Revenge belonged to the other, the sinister part that had to be settled, but what came after that? He felt a few warm raindrops on his face, like tears from nowhere. Who had any tears left? They had been burned out, dried out years ago. The occasional mute tugging, the diminishing of something which already had seemed almost nothing—this was the only thing that proved there was still something to be lost. A thermometer that long ago had indicated the lowest degree of feeling—and that it was growing colder one realized only by the fact that occasionally a frozen limb, a finger, a foot, dropped off, almost without pain.

The flashes of lightning followed one another faster, and under long rolling thunder the hill opposite lay very clear in the twitching, shadowless light—the remote white house and garden. Bucher, thought 509. Bucher still had something. He was young and he had Ruth. Someone who would leave with him. But would it last? Who cared about that? Who, after all, expected guarantees? And who could give them?

509 leaned back. What nonsense I'm thinking, he thought. Berger must have infected me. We're just tired. He breathed slowly and through the stench of the ground and the barrack he thought he smelled once more the spring and the burgeoning. This came back, every year, with swallows and blossoms; indifferent to war and death and grief and hope. It came. It was there. That was enough.

He pulled the door to, and crept into his corner. The lightning continued flashing all through the night. The ghostly light fell through the broken windows and the barrack appeared to be a ship gliding noiselessly along a subterranean stream between rocky shores, a ship filled with dead who by some dark magic still breathed —and among them a few living who had not given themselves up for lost.

CHAPTER NINETEEN

Only one column had still been working in the town. They had gone on rummaging about in the ruins for bodies and had found eighteen more people. Now they were marching back.

They marched right through the town. The SS no longer took any trouble. They guarded the column but they no longer led them round the town or made detours through the least damaged sections to prevent the prisoners from seeing the devastation. They now led them out by the shortest route.

The streets were ruined. Walls of houses had been thrown from one side to the other as though they had leapt on one another for a petrified rape. In some places the rubble lay many feet high. A piano with its top torn off stood in the street half-buried in mortar and stone. The keyboard was intact and a few children were strumming. They were trying to play the Horst Wessel song. It sounded thin and more than half the strings had snapped. A roofless baker's shop stood open. A queue of people jostled one another outside it. They were dusty and tired and patient. The prisoners marched past them. The SS shouted commands. There was a smell of bread. But even here the sweet putrid stench of corpses came through, mixed with the bitter smell of acids and burning. The unnaturally warm weather was the cause. Water flowed from broken pipes onto the street. A few men in fire-brigade uniform were trying to break up the ground. They had tools with them to repair the water conduits. The pipes were new and glistened and it seemed strange that anyone should still give a thought to such things; it seemed so useless and unimportant amidst all the devastation. A field kitchen had driven up a side street. In front of it, too, stood a long queue of people.

The broken windows in the shops had already been boarded up again with wooden laths and planks and strips of cardboard. There weren't many Nazi uniforms to be seen any more. There were more trousers and boots than tunics. The tunics had already given way to civilian jackets; the lower halves were still Nazi.

The prisoners came to the open section of the town. They crossed one of the bridges that had not been destroyed. At the end of it stood an ancient stone figure that had lost its head and one arm. On the Square beyond it the equestrian statue of Frederick the Great had tumbled off its granite base. It was tipped up so that Frederick the Great now rode straight towards the sky. His outstretched arm pointed at a few clouds glistening in the sun.

The column passed down a tree-lined street that was still entirely undamaged. It was a remnant of forgotten peace amidst the desolation. The trees had put forth their leaves, the houses were massive and without blemish, the sidewalk clean, the windows intact, and behind the windows hung curtains, neatly gathered and pleated. It seemed inconceivable.

A group of boys came marching along the street. They wore uniforms. They were strong healthy boys, sturdy and lively, the kind every mother desires. Seeing the prisoners, they stepped out of their way onto the sidewalk. The prisoners were marching down the middle of the street. The boys stood still and began whispering. One of them was fourteen or fifteen, the others younger. The fifteen-year-old had a calm open face, slender with a narrow skull, blue eyes and a tuft of silky blond hair. He raised his hand and the whole group shouted: "Traitors to the Fatherland!"

They shouted it in high youthful voices. Once more: "You Jewish swine! Traitors!"

It resounded through the streets. For a moment the birds in the trees stopped chirping. A window was opened. Again the boys shouted. Then the fifteen-year-old stepped forward, pulled a revolver from his pocket, took two paces, raised it, aimed quickly at a prisoner marching on the outside and at close range shot him in the face. "One dog less!" he said in a clear voice and stepped back. "Pity I've no more bullets, or I'd finish off a few more!"

The prisoner lay in the gutter. The blood welled up from under his head. Painfully he raised himself onto his arms and turned his face toward the group of boys. His face was old and there were gaps in his teeth, and the blood ran into his mouth and dripped, and the eyes above it grew slowly blind. The good-looking fifteen-year-old did not avert his gaze. He calmly contemplated the wound. Finally the bleeding face sank down. The arms gave. The right foot began to twitch. Then this, too, ceased.

"My God, Helmuth," said one of the boys.

Two SS-men approached. "What's all this? What d'you think you're doing?"

"One traitor less," said Helmuth and brushed back his hair.

"You can leave that to us," snorted one of the SS-men.

"So?" Helmuth stared at him.

"Stop that," said the second SS-man nervously to the first. "Don't start any funny business just now." He turned to the prisoners. "Forward! Get going! On with you!" he shouted at them, pulling out a revolver. "March on, I said. D'you want to leave another one here? Four men in the rear pick up the dead!"

The column marched on. One SS-man stayed behind to take down the dead man's number. "You're a sharp one, what?" he asked Helmuth.

"Werewolf," said the boy, off-handish.

His comrades stared at him in admiration. The window above them was slammed shut so that the panes rattled. The SS-man reached into the dead man's pockets and got up. "Heil Hitler!" said Helmuth, sharply.

The SS-man turned round. "Heil Hitler!"

The prisoners seized the dead man's legs and arms and raised him up. The boys formed a group again. Helmuth took the lead. "Sing!" he ordered.

They marched off. Their high youthful voices could still be heard from afar.

> "When Jewish blood spurts from the knife
> Everything goes twice as well!"

It had already become almost a folksong. They had never learned anything else.

"Bruno," said Selma Neubauer calmly. "Don't be a fool. Think sensibly. Think before others begin thinking. That's our chance. Sell what you can sell. The building plots, the garden, the house here, everything—loss or no loss."

"And money? What's the good of money?" Neubauer shook his head, annoyed. "If your prophecies should come true, what value would money have? Have you forgotten the inflation after the last World War? A billion was worth one mark. Real estate, that was the only thing even then."

"Real estate, sure! But real estate you can put in your pocket."

Selma rose and walked over to a cupboard. She opened it and removed several stacks of linen. Then she took out a box and unlocked it. It contained gold cigarette cases, compacts, a few diamond clips, two ruby brooches and several rings. "Here," she said. "I bought these during the last few years without your knowing. With my money and with what I've saved. To buy them I sold the shares I had. Today they'd no longer be worth anything. The factories are in ruins. But this keeps its value. It can be taken along. I wish we had nothing but such things!"

"Taken along! Taken along! You talk as though we were criminals who had to flee!"

Selma put the things back in the box. She polished a cigarette case with the sleeve of her dress. "The same thing can happen to us that happened to others when you came to power, or don't you think so?"

Neubauer jumped up. "If one were to listen to you," he said, furious and helpless, "one might as well go and hang oneself. Other men have wives who understand them, who are a comfort when they come home from work, who cheer them up—but you! Nothing but prophecies of doom and howls of disaster! All day long! And at night as well! Not even then do I get any peace! All the time, Sell! Sell! Sell! Gloom! Gloom! Gloom!"

Selma didn't listen to him. She stowed away the box and rearranged the linen in front of it. "Diamonds," she said. "Good, clear diamonds. Unset. Only the best stones. One carat, two carat, three carat, up to six or seven, if you can get them. That's the thing. Better than all your Blanks and gardens and plots and houses. Your lawyer has gypped you. I'll bet he took double commission. Diamonds can be hidden. They can be sewn into dresses. Even swallowed. Not so your building plots."

Neubauer stared at her. "The way you talk! One day you are hysterical with fear of a few bombs—and the next you talk like a Jew who'd cut one's throat for cash."

She measured him with a contemptuous glance. She looked at his boots, his uniform, his revolver, his mustache. "Jews don't cut throats. Jews look after their families. Better than many Germanic supermen. Jews know what to do in dangerous times."

"So? What did they know then? Had they known anything they wouldn't have stayed here and we wouldn't have caught most of them."

"They didn't believe you'd treat them as you did." Selma Neubauer dabbed her temples with eau-de-cologne. "And don't forget that money has been blocked in Germany since 1931. Since the Darmstaedter und National Bank got into difficulties. That's why a lot of them couldn't get away. After that you caught them. All right. And now you want to stay here for the same reason. And for the same reason they will catch you."

Neubauer glanced quickly round. "Take care, for God's sake!

Where's the maid? If anyone hears you, we're lost. The People's Court knows no mercy. One denunciation is enough."

"It's the maid's day off. And why can't the same be done to you as you did to the others?"

"Who? The Jews?" Neubauer laughed. He remembered Blank. He had a vision of Blank torturing Weber. "They? They'll be glad if they're left in peace."

"Not the Jews. The Americans and British."

Neubauer continued laughing. "They? They even less! That's none of their business, anyhow. Inner political affairs like our camps don't interest them in the least! With them it's purely a matter of military affairs and foreign politics. Don't you understand that?"

"No."

"They're democrats. They'll treat us correctly if they win—which is still debatable. Soldierlike. Correct. We'll just be honorably defeated. They can't do anything else. That's their ideology! With the Russians it would be a different story. But they're in the East."

"You'll see for yourself. Just stay here."

"Yes, I'll see. And I'm staying here. Would you mind telling me where we could go anyway, if we wanted to get out?"

"With diamonds we could have gone to Switzerland years ago—"

"Could have!" Neubauer banged the table. The beer bottle in front of him trembled. "Could have! Could have! There you go again! Would you mind telling me how? I suppose we could have flown across the frontier in a stolen airplane? You're talking nonsense."

"Not in a stolen airplane. But we could have taken a few vacation trips. Taken over money and jewels. Two, three, four vacation trips. Left something behind each time. I know people who have done it."

Neubauer went to the door. He opened it and closed it again. Then he came back. "D'you realize what you're saying? Sheer high treason! You'd be shot on the spot if one word of it leaked out."

Selma looked at him. Her eyes glittered. "Well—? Wouldn't that be a good way for you to show what a hero you are at the last moment? You could get rid of a dangerous wife into the bargain! Maybe that's just what you'd like—"

Neubauer couldn't stand her gaze. He paced up and down the

room. He wasn't sure whether she'd heard anything about the widow who came to visit him off and on. "Selma," he said finally in a different voice, "what's all this about? We must stand together! Let's be sensible. There's nothing to be done now but hold out. I can't run away. I'm under orders. And where could I flee to? To the Russians? No. Hide in unoccupied Germany? The Gestapo would soon find me there and you know what that means! To the other side, to the Americans and British? That wouldn't do, either. All things considered, it's better to wait for them here. Otherwise it would look as though I had a bad conscience. I've thought it all over, believe me. We've got to hold out, there's no other solution."

"Yes."

Surprised, Neubauer glanced up. "Really? Do you understand at last? Have I proved it to you?"

"Yes."

He looked at her cautiously; he didn't believe in such an easy victory. But Selma had suddenly given up. Her cheeks seemed to sag. Proved, she thought. Proofs! What they have proved they believe—as though life consisted of proofs! There's nothing to be done about them. Clay gods. Believe only what they want to believe. She contemplated her husband for a long time. It was with a strange mixture of pity, contempt, and a remote tenderness that she looked at him. Neubauer grew uncomfortable. "Selma—" he began.

She interrupted him. "Bruno, only one more thing, the last one—I ask you to do."

"What?" he asked suspiciously.

"Have the house and the building plots made over to Freya. Go to the lawyer at once. Just that, nothing else."

"Why?"

"Not for ever. For the time being. If everything goes well, they can be transferred back. You can trust your daughter."

"Yes—yes—but the impression! The lawyer—"

"To hell with impressions! Be practical. Freya was a child when Hitler took over. One can't reproach her for anything."

"What d'you mean by that? Are you suggesting that I can be reproached for something?"

Selma was silent. Again she cast that strange glance at Neubauer.

"We're soldiers," he said. "We act on orders. And an order's an order. Everyone knows that."

He stretched himself. "The Führer commands. We obey. The Führer takes full responsibility for his commands. He has declared that often enough. That's sufficient for any patriot. Or isn't it?"

"Yes," said Selma, resigned. "But go to the lawyer. Have our property made over to Freya."

"Oh, all right. I'll go and talk to him." Neubauer had no intention of doing so. His wife was just hysterical. He patted her on the back. "Just leave it to me. I've always managed so far."

He stamped out. Selma Neubauer went to the window. She watched him get into the car. Proofs! Orders! she thought. That's their way out of everything. All very well as long as it worked. Hadn't she herself played along? She looked at her wedding ring. Twenty-four years she had been wearing it now. Twice it had had to be enlarged. At the time she'd received it she'd been a different person. There'd been a Jew then who had asked her to marry him. A small efficient man who lisped and didn't shout. Josef Bornfelder was his name. In 1929 he had left for America. Clever man. At the right time. She'd heard of him once again through an acquaintance to whom he had written. He was doing very well. Mechanically she turned her wedding ring round and round. America, she thought. There they never have an inflation. They're too rich.

509 listened. He knew the voice. Cautiously he cowered down behind the pile of dead and listened.

He knew that tonight Lewinsky was bringing someone from the labor camp who had to hide for several days; Lewinsky, however, faithful to the old rule that only contact men should know one another, had not divulged who it was.

The man talked in a low voice but very clearly. "We need every man who is on our side," he said. "When National Socialism collapses there will be no organized party to take over the political direction. During these last twelve years they've all been split up or destroyed. What remains of them has gone underground. We don't know to what extent they still exist. It will require determined people to build up a new organization. Throughout the chaos of defeat only one single party will remain intact: National Socialism. I don't mean the camp followers, they join any party—I mean the nucleus. That will go underground in one body and wait until it can emerge again. It's this we've got to fight against; and for that we need people."

It's Werner, thought 509; it must be him; and yet I'm sure he's dead. He couldn't see anything; the night was moonless and turbid. "The majority of the masses outside is demoralized," the voice continued. "Twelve years of terror, boycott, denunciation and fear have seen to that—and on top of it now comes the lost war. With the help of underground terror and sabotage they can still be held for years in fear of the Nazis. They've got to be won back again—the misguided and the intimidated. Strangely enough, opposition to the Nazis has been maintained better in the camps than anywhere outside. Here they have penned us up. Outside, the groups have been dispersed. Outside, it was difficult to maintain contact. Here it was simple. Outside, almost everyone had to pull through by himself; here, one gave the other strength. A result which the Nazis did not foresee." The voice laughed; it was a short, mirthless laughter.

"Apart from those who have been killed," said Berger. "And those who died."

"Apart from those, of course. Still, there are some who have been spared. Each one of these is worth a hundred others."

It must be Werner, thought 509; he could now see the shadowy ascetic head in the dark. He's already analyzing again. He's organizing. He's making speeches; he has remained the fanatic and theoretician of his Party. "The camps must become the cells of reconstruction," said the low clear voice. "In this connection three points are at the moment the most important. The first is: Passive, and in extreme cases, active resistance against the SS, so long as they are in the camp. The second: The prevention of panic and excesses while the camp is being taken over. We must show that we have discipline and are not motivated by excesses of revenge. Later on organized courts will—"

The man paused. 509 had got up and walked toward the group. It consisted of Lewinsky, Goldstein, Berger and the stranger.

"Werner—" said 509.

The man stared into the dark. "Who are you?"

He straightened himself and came nearer. "I thought you were dead," said 509.

Werner looked close into his face. "Koller," said 509.

"Koller! You're alive! And I thought you were dead long ago!"

"I am, too. Officially."

"He's 509," said Lewinsky.

"So you're 509! That makes things simpler. I'm also officially dead."

Both stared at one another through the darkness. It was not a new situation. Many a man in the camp had already found someone whom he had believed dead. But 509 and Werner had known one another from the days before the camp. They had been friends; then their political opinions had gradually driven them apart.

"Are you going to stay here now?" asked 509.

"Yes. For a few days."

"The SS are combing through the last letters of the alphabet," said Lewinsky. "They caught Vogel. He ran into the hands of someone who knew him—a damned junior squad leader."

"I won't be a burden to you," declared Werner. "I'll look after my own food."

"Sure," said 509, with barely perceptible irony. "I wouldn't have expected anything else from you."

"Tomorrow Muenzer will provide some bread. Lebenthal can go and get it from him. He'll produce enough for more than myself. Something for your group, too."

"I know," answered 509. "I know, Werner, that you wouldn't accept something for nothing. Are you going to stay in 22? We could also put you in 20."

"I can stay in 22. You, too, surely. Now that Handke's no longer around."

None of the others was aware that something like a duel of words was going on between the two men. How childish we are, thought 509. An eternity ago we were political opponents—and still neither of us wants to be indebted to the other. I get an idiotic satisfaction from the fact that Werner is seeking shelter with us, and he is hinting at the possibility that but for his group I might have been finished off by Handke.

"I overheard what you were explaining just now," he said. "It's correct. What can we do?"

They were still sitting outside. Werner, Lewinsky and Goldstein were asleep in the barrack. Lebenthal was to wake them in two hours. They had arranged to change places then. The night had turned sultry. Berger nevertheless wore the warm Hussar tunic; 509 had insisted on it.

"Who's the new one?" asked Bucher. "A big shot?"

"He was one, before the Nazis came. Not too big. Medium. A provincial big shot. Efficient. Communist. Fanatic, without a private life and without humor. Now he's one of the underground leaders in the camp."

"Where d'you know him from?"

509 meditated. "Before 1933 I was the editor of a newspaper. We often had discussions. And I often attacked his Party. His Party and the Nazis. We were against both."

"And what were you for?"

"For something which now seems rather pompous and ridiculous. For humaneness, tolerance and the right of the individual. Funny, what?"

"No." Ahasver coughed. "What else is there?"

"This," bleated Lebenthal.

They all fell silent for a while.

"Revenge," said Meyerhof suddenly. "There is still revenge! Revenge for all this! Revenge for every single dead! Revenge for everything that's been done! An eye for an eye and a tooth for a tooth!"

Everyone looked up in surprise. Meyerhof's face was distorted. He had clenched his fists and each time he uttered the word revenge he banged them on the ground. "What's wrong with you?" asked Sulzbacher.

"What's wrong with you all?" retorted Meyerhof.

"He's crazy," said Lebenthal good-naturedly. "He recovered his health and that's made him *meschugge*. Six years ago he was a timid little Bocher who didn't dare to open his beak—then a miracle saved him from the chimney and now he's Samson Meyerhof."

"I don't want any revenge," whispered Rosen. "I only want to get out of here."

"What? And let the entire SS get away without settling our accounts?"

"I don't care! All I want is to get out." Desperately Rosen pressed his hands together and whispered passionately as though everything depended on it, "I want nothing else but to get out! Out of here!"

Meyerhof stared at him. "D'you know what you are?"

"Be quiet, Meyerhof!" Berger had raised himself. "None of us here is what he was or would like to be. What we really still are, will show itself later. Who can know that now? Now we can only wait and hope and maybe pray."

He pulled the Hussar tunic round his shoulders and lay back again.

"Revenge," said Ahasver thoughtfully after a while. "There would have to be a great deal of revenge. And revenge would bring revenge again. Better to see to it that things like this can never happen again."

The horizon flared up. "What was that?" asked Bucher.

A low rumbling answered. "That's not a bombardment," declared Sulzbacher. "One more thunderstorm. It's warm enough for that."

"If it starts raining we'll wake those from the labor camp," said Lebenthal. "Then they can lie out here. They're stronger." He turned to 509. "Your friend, the big shot, too."

There was another flash of lightning. "Did any of those in there hear about a transport leaving here?" asked Sulzbacher.

"Only rumors. The last one was that a thousand men were about to be picked out."

"Oh God!" Rosen's face shimmered pale in the darkness. "They're bound to take us. The weakest. To get rid of us."

He glanced at 509. They all thought of the last transport they had seen.

"It's a rumor," said 509. "There are thousands of latrine rumors nowadays. Let's be calm until an order comes. Then we'll still have time to see what Lewinsky, Werner and those in the office can do for us. Or what we here can do for ourselves."

"Maybe we should let Lewinsky and Werner go on sleeping after all when it starts raining," said Lebenthal.

Rosen shuddered. "Remember how they dragged them out by their legs from under the bunks that time—"

Lebenthal looked at him with contempt. "Have you never seen worse than that in your life?"

"Yes."

"I was once in a great slaughter yard," said Ahasver. "I was there for the kosher slaughtering. In Chicago. Sometimes the animals knew what was going to happen. They smelled the blood. Then they ran around like that—like those people at that time. Anywhere. Into corners. And they were pulled out by their legs in the same way—"

"You were in Chicago?" asked Lebenthal.

"Yes."

"In America? And you came back?"

"It was twenty-five years ago."

"You came back?" Lebenthal stared at Ahasver. "Has anyone ever heard anything like that?"

"I was homesick. For Poland."

"You know—" Lebenthal broke off. It was too much for him.

CHAPTER TWENTY

In the morning the weather turned into a gray milky day. The lightning had ceased but from beyond the forests there still came a muffled, distant rumbling.

"Queer kind of storm," said Bucher. "Usually, when they pass off, you see sheets of lightning and don't hear any thunder. This one's the other way round."

"Maybe it's coming back," answered Rosen.

"Why should it come back?"

"In the mountains thunderstorms sometimes wander around for days."

"There are no mountain gorges here. There's only the one range over there, and that's not high."

"Have you any other worries?" asked Lebenthal.

"Leo," said Bucher calmly, "you better go and see that we get something to chew. Even if it's old shoe leather."

"Any other orders?" asked Lebenthal after a pause of astonishment.

"No."

"All right. Then watch your tongue. And look after your own grub, you puppy! Has anyone ever heard such cheek!"

Lebenthal tried to spit, but his mouth was dry and his denture popped out with the effort. He caught it in the air and put it back. "That's what one gets for risking one's neck for you every day," he said, irritated. "Reproaches and commands! Next thing, Karel will start giving me orders!"

509 came up. "What's going on here?"

"Ask him." Lebenthal pointed at Bucher. "He's giving orders. I wouldn't be surprised if he isn't trying to become a block senior."

509 glanced at Bucher. He has changed, he thought. I didn't realize it so much before. But he has changed. "What's really going on?" he asked.

"Nothing. We were just talking about the storm."

"Why should you care about the storm?"

"No reason. It's just queer that it's still thundering. And at the same time there's no lightning, nor any clouds. Only that gray soup up there. But those are no storm clouds."

"Problems! It thunders without lightning! *Gojim naches!*" Lebenthal squawked from his corner. "*Meschugge!*"

509 looked up at the sky. It was gray and seemed to be cloudless. Then he listened. "It's actually thun—" He broke off. His attitude changed. He suddenly listened with his whole body.

"Another one," said Lebenthal. "*Meschugge* is trumps today."

"Quiet!" whispered 509, sharp.

"So you, too—"

"Quiet, damn it! Be quiet, Leo!"

Lebenthal fell silent. He realized it was no longer a question of the thunderstorm. He watched 509, who was listening intently to the distant rumbling. Everyone now fell silent, straining his ears.

"Listen," 509 said then slowly and very quietly as though he feared something might fly away if he spoke louder. "That's no thunderstorm. That's—"

He listened again. "What?" Bucher stood close beside him. They looked at one another and kept listening.

The rumbling grew a little louder, then faded again. "That's not thunder," said 509. "That is—" He waited another moment, then glanced around as though afraid of something, and still in a very low voice he said, "That, I believe, is artillery fire."

"What?"

"Artillery fire. That's not thunder."

They all stared at each other. "What's going on here?" asked Goldstein from the door.

No one said a word. "Well, are you all frozen?"

Bucher turned toward him. "509 says it's artillery we hear. The front can't be very far away any more."

"What?" Goldstein came closer. "Really? Or are you just daydreaming?"

"Who'd talk nonsense about something like that?"

"I mean, aren't you fooling yourselves?"

"No," said 509.

"D'you understand anything about it?"

"Yes."

"My God!" Rosen's face grew distorted. He suddenly began to sob.

509 continued to listen. "When the wind changes we're bound to hear it more distinctly."

"How far away d'you think they are?" asked Bucher.

"I can't say for sure. Fifty kilometers. Sixty. Not much further."

"Fifty kilometers. That's not far."

"No, that's not far."

"They must have tanks," Bucher continued. "They can go fast. If they break through—how many days d'you think they'll need—maybe only one—" He stopped.

"One day?" repeated Lebenthal. "What are you saying? One day?"

"If they break through. Yesterday we heard nothing. Today they are there. Tomorrow it can be closer. The day after tomorrow—or the day after the day after tomorrow—"

"Don't talk! Don't say such things! Don't drive people crazy!" shouted Lebenthal suddenly.

"It is possible, Leo," said 509.

"No!" shouted Lebenthal and buried his face in his hands.

"What do you mean, 509?" Bucher's face was deathly pale and excited. "The day after tomorrow? Or how many days?"

"Days!" Lebenthal shouted again and let his hands drop. "How can it all of a sudden be only days?" he murmured. "Years, eternities, and now suddenly you're talking about days, days! Don't lie!" He came closer. "Don't lie!" he whispered. "I implore you, don't lie."

"Who'd think of lying at a moment like this?"

509 turned around. Goldstein stood directly behind him. He was smiling. "I can hear it, too," he said. His eyes grew larger and larger and very black. He smiled and raised his arms and one leg as though about to dance, and smiled no longer and fell forward.

"He has fainted," said Lebenthal. "Open his jacket. I'll get some water. There must still be some in the trough."

Bucher, Sulzbacher, Rosen and 509 turned Goldstein around. "Shall we fetch Berger?" asked Bucher. "Can he get up?"

"Wait."

509 bent close over Goldstein. He unbuttoned his jacket and trouser belt. When he straightened himself Berger was there. Lebenthal had let him know. "You were supposed to stay in your bunk," said 509.

Berger knelt down beside Goldstein and examined him. It didn't take long. "He's dead," he declared. "Probably heart failure. It was bound to happen. They completely ruined his heart here."

"But he heard it," said Bucher. "That's the main thing. He heard it."

"What?"

509 put his arm around Berger's narrow shoulders. "Ephraim," he said gently, "I think the day has come."

"What?"

Berger looked up. 509 suddenly realized it was hard for him to speak. "The—" he said and paused and pointed towards the horizon. "They're coming, Ephraim. We can hear them." He looked at the palisades and the machine-gun towers which swam in the milky white. "They've arrived, Ephraim—"

At noon the wind veered round and the rumbling grew more distinct.

It was like a distant electric contact that flashed across into thousands of single hearts. The barracks grew restless. Only a few labor gangs were sent out. Everywhere faces were pressed against the windows. Again and again thin figures appeared before the doors and stood there, craning their necks.

"Has it come nearer?"

"Yes, it seems to be getting more distinct."

In the boot department everyone worked in dead silence. The kapos saw to it that no one spoke. The SS supervisor was present. The knives severed the leather, cutting out rotten parts, and in many hands they felt different. Not like tools; like weapons. Here and there a cautious glance was directed at the kapos, the SS, and the revolvers and the tommy gun which had not been there the previous day. But in spite of the supervisor's strict vigilance, every single man in the department knew precisely what was going on throughout the day. Over the years most of them had learned how to speak without moving their lips; and each time, after the baskets full of the leather strips had been emptied and carried away, the report of the carrier who had been in contact with others outside soon spread through the groups of those within: the rumbling could still be heard. It had not ceased.

The outside gangs were doubly guarded. They marched around the town and then from the west into the old quarter toward the Market Place. The guards were very nervous. They yelled and gave commands without rhyme or reason; the prisoners marched in perfect order. So far they had cleared up only in the new sections of the town; now for the first time they came to the interior of the Old Town and saw the devastation there. They saw the burnt-out remains of the quarter in which the medieval houses of wood had stood. Almost nothing of them was left. They saw it and marched through it and the inhabitants who had stayed behind stood still or turned away as they passed by. They marched on and they no longer felt like prisoners. In a mysterious way they had gained a victory without having been present, and the years of captivity suddenly appeared no longer like years of defenseless defeat, but like years of battle. And the battle was won. They had survived.

They came to the Market Place. The Town Hall had entirely collapsed. They were given picks and shovels to clear away the rubble. They set to work. It smelled of burning; but beneath it they recognized again the other smell, sweetish, putrid, pressing against the stomach, the smell they knew better than any other; the stench of putrefaction. In the warm April days the town smelled of the bodies still buried in the debris.

After working for two hours they found their first body under the rubble. At first they saw only its boots. It was an SS senior squad leader.

"The worm has turned," whispered Muenzer. "It has turned at last! Now we're digging up their dead. Their dead!"

He continued to work with renewed strength. "Look out!" bellowed a guard, approaching. "There's someone lying there, can't you see?"

They shoveled away more rubble. Shoulders emerged and then a head. They raised up the dead man and dragged him aside.

"Carry on!" The SS-man was nervous. He stared at the body. "Go slow from now on!"

In quick succession they dug up three more Party members and laid them with the first. They carried them away by their boots and uniformed arms. For them it was an unprecedented experience; so far they had carried only their comrades in this way, beaten up and dirty, from the bunkers, from the torture chambers, dying or dead, and then during recent days a number of civilians. Now for the first time they were carrying their enemies. They went on working and there was no need for anyone to drive them on. Sweat poured down their bodies, so hard did they work to find more corpses. With strength they had never suspected, they lugged away beams and iron girders, and full of hatred and satisfaction they dug for the dead as though digging for gold.

After another hour they found Dietz. He had broken his neck. His head was pressed so hard into his chest it looked as though he had been trying to bite his own throat. They didn't touch him right away. They first shoveled him completely free. Both arms were broken. They lay there as though they had a joint too many.

"There is a God," whispered the man beside Muenzer without looking at anyone. "There's still a God! There is a God!"

"Shut up!" shouted an SS-man. "What did you say?" He kicked the man in the knees. "What did you say? I saw you talking."

The man got up. He had fallen over Dietz. "I said we ought to make a stretcher for the Herr Senior Group Leader," he answered with an expressionless face. "We can't just carry him like the others."

"You have nothing to say here! Here we still give orders! Got that?"

"Yes."

Still, Lewinsky had heard. *Still give orders.* So they know it, he thought. He raised his shovel.

The SS-man looked at Dietz. Automatically he sprang to attention. This saved the prisoner who believed once more in God. The SS-man turned around and went to get the squad leader. He also assumed something like a military attitude.

"The stretchers haven't arrived yet," declared the SS-man. The answer of the man who believed once more in God had evidently made an impression on him. A high-ranking officer like that really shouldn't be dragged away by his arms and legs.

The squad leader looked around. He noticed a door lying a short distance away in the rubble. "Dig that thing out! We must make shift with that for the time being." He saluted in the direction of Dietz. "Lay the Herr Senior Group Leader carefully on that door over there."

Muenzer, Lewinsky and two others fetched the door. It was a piece of sixteenth century carving representing the discovery of Moses. It had a crack and was charred. They seized Dietz by his legs and shoulders and carried him towards the door. The arms dangled and the head drooped very far back.

"Take care, you lousy dogs!" bellowed the squad leader. The body of the dead man lay on the wide door. From under his right arm smiled the infant Moses in his basket among the rushes. Muenzer noticed it. They forgot to remove the door from the Town Hall, he thought. Moses. Jewish. All this has already happened before. Pharaoh. Tyranny. Red Sea. Deliverance.

"Eight men! Take hold of it!"

Twelve men sprang towards it with unusual speed. The squad leader gazed about him. Opposite stood the half burned-out church of St. Mary's. He deliberated for a moment, but promptly dismissed the thought. One couldn't take Dietz into a Catholic church. He would have liked to telephone for instructions, but the telephone service had been put out of action. He had to do what he hated and feared most—act on his own.

Muenzer said something. The squad leader noticed it. "What? What did you say? Step forward, you lousy dog!"

Lousy dog seemed to be his favorite expression. Muenzer stepped forward and stood at attention. "I said I thought it might be beneath the dignity of a senior group leader to be carried by mere prisoners."

Steadily and respectfully he looked at the squad leader. "What?" shouted the leader. "What? Lousy dog! What's that got to do with you? Who else? We have—"

He fell silent. Muenzer's argument seemed to make sense. The dead man should actually have been carried by the SS; but meanwhile the prisoners could escape.

"What are you standing around here for?" he bellowed. And suddenly he had an idea as to where Dietz could be taken. "To the hospital!"

What could still be done for the dead man in the hospital no one quite knew. It just seemed to be a suitably neutral place. "Forward—" He took the lead. This, too, seemed to him necessary.

At the exit from the Market Place an automobile suddenly appeared. It was a low Mercedes-Compressor. The car came slowly along, picking its way through the wreckage. Amidst all the destruction its smooth elegance had an almost obscene effect. The squad leader stood at attention. A Mercedes-Compressor was the official car for V.I.P.'s. Two high-ranking SS officers sat in the rear, another in front beside the chauffeur. A number of suitcases were strapped to the back; a few smaller ones lay inside the car. The faces of the officers had angry, defiant expressions. The chauffeur was obliged to drive very slowly through the rubble. The car passed close by the prisoners who were carrying Dietz on the door. The officers ignored them. "Drive on!" said the one in front to the chauffeur. "Faster!"

The prisoners stood still. Lewinsky held the door's rear right-hand corner. He looked at Dietz's broken neck, at the smiling carved figure of the child Moses and he looked at the Mercedes and the luggage and the fleeing officers and he took a deep breath.

The car crawled past. "Shits!" said one of the SS-men suddenly, a huge butcher with a boxer's nose. "Shits! Damned shits!" He didn't mean the prisoners.

Lewinsky listened. For a short while the distant rumbling was drowned in the roaring of the Mercedes' engine; then it came through again, muffled and inexorable. Subterranean drums for a funeral march.

"Move on!" commanded the squad leader irritably. "On with you! On!"

The afternoon dragged on. The camp buzzed with rumors. They blew through the barracks and changed every hour. Now the SS had decamped; then someone appeared who insisted that on the contrary they had been reinforced. Now American tanks were allegedly near the town; next moment they were German troops come to defend it.

At three o'clock the new block senior arrived. He was a red, not a green one. "Not one of us," said Werner, disappointed.

"Why not?" asked 509. "He is one of us. A political one. Not a criminal. Or what d'you mean by *us*?"

"You know perfectly well. Why d'you ask?"

They were sitting in the barrack. Werner wanted to wait until after the last whistle before returning to the labor camp. 509 kept himself hidden so as to find out how the new block senior would behave. Beside them a man with dirty white hair lay dying of pneumonia.

"*One of us* is a man who belongs to the camp's underground movement," lectured Werner. "That's what you wanted to know, eh?" He smiled.

"No," answered 509. "That's not what I wanted to know. And it's not what you meant, either."

"For the time being I mean that."

"Yes. For the time being. As long as the emergency coalition here is necessary. And then?"

"Then," said Werner, surprised at so much ignorance, "then, of course, there must be a party to take over. An organized party; not a bunch of people thrown together at random."

"Your Party, you mean. The Communists."

"What other?"

"Any other," said 509. "So long as it's not another totalitarian."

Werner gave a short laugh. "You fool! Only a totalitarian. Can't you read the signs on the wall? All intermediate parties have crumbled. Communism has remained strong. The war will come to an end. Russia has occupied a great part of Germany. It's by far the strongest power in Europe. The time of coalitions is over. This one was the last. The Allies have helped Communism and weakened themselves, the fools! World peace will depend on—"

"I know," interrupted 509. "I know that old song. But do tell me, supposing you won and had the power, what would happen to those who are against you? Or those who are not for you?"

Werner was silent for a moment. "There are many different ways," he said then.

"I know some. Killing, torturing, concentration camps."

"Among others. Depending on what's necessary."

"What an advance over the Nazis! Worth while living for!"

"It is an advance," declared Werner, unperturbed. "It's an advance in aim. And also in method. We don't do anything for the sake of cruelty. Only out of necessity."

"I've heard that often enough. That's what Weber explained to me when he stuck lighted matches under my fingernails. It was necessary in order to extract information."

The breathing of the white-haired man changed into the halting death rattle with which everyone in the camp was familiar. The rattling sometimes stopped; then in the silence the low rumbling on the horizon could be heard. It was like a litany—the last breath of the dying man and the answer from the distance. Werner looked at 509. He knew that in 1933 Weber had tortured him for weeks in order to extract from him names and addresses. Werner's address, too. 509 had held his tongue. Then, later on, Werner had been betrayed by a weak Party member. "Why don't you come to us, Koller?" he asked. "We could use you."

"That's what Lewinsky asked me, too. And that's what we both had discussions about twenty years ago."

Werner smiled. It was a good disarming smile. "We did. Often enough. All the same, I'm asking you again. The day of individualism is over. One can no longer stand alone. The future belongs to us. Not to the corrupt Center."

509 looked at the ascetic head. "When all this is over," he said slowly, "I'd like to know how long it'll take before you're as much my enemy as those up there on the towers have been?"

"Not long. We've had an emergency coalition here against the Nazis. That will disappear as soon as the war is over."

509 nodded. "I'd also like to know how long it would be, if your Party came to power, before you locked me up?"

"Not long. You are still dangerous. But you wouldn't be tortured."

509 shrugged his shoulders.

"We'd lock you up and let you work. Or shoot you."

"That's comforting. That's how I always imagined your golden age to be."

"Your irony is cheap. You know coercion is necessary. It's a defense necessary in the beginning. Later on it will no longer be needed."

"Oh yes," said 509. "Every tyranny needs it. And every year more, not less. That is its fate. And always its end. You see it here."

"No. The Nazis committed the fundamental error of starting a war for which they were not properly prepared."

"That was no error. It was a necessity. They couldn't help it. Had they been forced to disarm and maintain peace, they'd have gone bankrupt. The same will happen to you."

"We'll win our wars. We conduct them differently. From within."

"Yes. From within and toward the inside. You might as well keep the camps here going. And fill them."

"We might," said Werner quite seriously. "Why don't you come to us?" he repeated then.

"For that very reason. If you should come to power outside, you'd have me liquidated. I wouldn't. That's the reason."

The white-haired man rattled now at longer intervals. Sulzbacher came in. "They say German planes are going to bomb the camp tomorrow morning. They'll destroy everything."

"One more latrine rumor," declared Werner. "I wish it was already dark. I must go back."

Bucher glanced at the white house on the hill beyond the camp. It stood in the slanting sun amidst the trees and was undamaged. The trees in the garden had a bright sheen of the first pink and white cherry blossoms.

"Do you believe it at last?" he asked. "You can hear their guns. They're coming nearer every hour. We'll soon get out."

He looked once more at the white house. It was his superstition that all would go well as long as the house remained intact. Ruth and he would live and be saved.

She crouched beside the barbed wire. "And where'll we go when we get out?" she asked.

"Away from here. As far as possible."

"Where?"

"Anywhere. Perhaps my father's still alive."

Bucher didn't believe it, but he didn't know for certain his father was dead. 509 knew it, but he had never told him.

"None of my family's alive," said Ruth. "I was there when they were taken to the gas chambers."

"Maybe they were only sent on a transport. Or they let them survive somewhere else. After all, they let you survive."

"Yes," answered Ruth. "They let me survive."

"We used to have a little house in Osnabrück. Maybe it's still standing. They took it away from us. If it's still standing, we might perhaps get it back. We can go there and take refuge."

Ruth Holland didn't answer. Bucher looked across at her and saw she was crying. He had almost never seen her cry and thought it was because of her dead relatives. Death, however, was such a daily occurrence that it seemed to him exaggerated to show so much grief after so long a time. "We mustn't think back, Ruth," he said with a trace of impatience. "Otherwise, how shall we ever be able to live again?"

"I'm not thinking back."

"Why are you crying, then?"

Ruth Holland wiped the tears from her eyes with her clenched fists. "Do you want to know why they didn't gas me?" she asked.

Bucher sensed vaguely she was about to say something it was better not to know. "You don't have to tell me," he declared. "But you can tell me if you want to. It doesn't make any difference."

"It does make a difference. I was seventeen. At that time I wasn't as ugly as I am now. That's why they let me live."

"Yes," said Bucher without understanding.

She looked at him. He saw for the first time that she had very transparent gray eyes. He had never noticed them before. "Don't you understand what that means?" she asked.

"No."

"They let me live because they needed women. Young ones—for the soldiers. For the Ukrainians, too, who were fighting with the Germans. Do you understand now?"

Bucher sat for a moment as though stupefied. Ruth watched him. "That's what they did with you?" he asked finally. He didn't look at her.

"Yes. That's what they did with me." She was no longer crying.

"It isn't true."

"It is true."

"I don't mean it that way. I mean you didn't want it."

She broke into a short bitter laugh. "That makes no difference."

Bucher now looked at her. Her face seemed to be bereft of all expression; but just this turned it into such a mask of suffering that he suddenly felt, and not only heard, that she was speaking the truth. He felt it as though it was tearing his stomach to pieces; yet at the same time he didn't want to admit it, not yet—he wanted at this moment only one thing—that the face before him should change.

"It isn't true," he said. "You didn't want it. You weren't really there. You didn't do it."

Her glance returned from a void. "It is true. And one cannot forget it."

"None of us knows what we can forget and what not. We all have many things to forget. Otherwise we might as well stay here and die."

Bucher had repeated something 509 had said the evening before. He swallowed several times. "You're alive," he then said with an effort.

"Yes, I'm alive. I move, I speak words, I eat bread which you throw over to me—and those other things live, too. They live! Live!"

She pressed her hands against her temples and turned her head. She's looking at me, thought Bucher. She's already looking at me again. She's no longer talking only to the sky and the house on the hill.

"You're alive," he repeated, "and that is enough for me."

She let her hands drop. "You child," she said, disconsolate. "You child! What, after all, do you know?"

"I'm not a child. No one who's been here is a child. Not even Karel, who is eleven."

She shook her head. "I don't mean that. You believe what you're saying now. But it won't last. Those other things will come back. With you and with me. The memories, later, when—"

Why did she tell me about it, thought Bucher. She shouldn't have told me. Then I wouldn't have known and it wouldn't have existed. But maybe it's better so. "I don't know what you mean," he said. "But I believe that for us there are rules that are different from the ordinary ones. There are men among us here in the camp who have killed people because it was necessary; and these men don't consider themselves murderers—as little as a soldier at the front considers himself a murderer. They aren't, either. It's the same with us. What has happened to us cannot be measured by normal standards."

"You'll think differently about it once we're out of here."

She looked at him sadly. Suddenly he understood why she had been so unusually dejected these last weeks. She had been afraid—afraid even of the liberation. "Ruth," he said, and felt a sudden wave of heat rise behind his forehead. "It's over. Forget it. You have been forced to do things you abhorred. What remains of it? Nothing!"

"I used to vomit," she said slowly. "I vomited nearly every time, afterwards! At last they sent me away." She kept looking at him.

"That's what you'll have—gray hair, a mouth with a lot of teeth missing, and a whore."

He started at the word and didn't answer for a long time. "They have debased us all," he said at last. "Not only you. All of us. All who are here, all who are in all the camps. You in your sex; all of us in our pride and in more than our pride; in our being human. They have trampled about on it, they have spat on it, and they have debased us so much it's hard to understand how we've survived it. I've thought a great deal about it during these last weeks. I've also talked to 509 about it. They've done so many things—to me, too."

"What?"

"I don't want to talk about it. 509 says it isn't true if one doesn't acknowledge it inwardly. I didn't understand him at first. But now I know what he means. I'm not a coward and you're not a whore. All the things they did to us don't mean anything as long as we don't feel like it."

"I feel like it."

"You won't, once you get out."

"Even more."

"No. If that were true, only a few of us would be able to go on living. They debased us; but it's not we who are debased. It's the others who did it."

"Who said that?"

"Berger."

"You have good teachers."

"Yes—and I have learned a great deal."

Ruth leaned her head to one side. Her face was tired. There was still suffering in it; but it was now more relaxed. "There are so many years," she said. "There'll be the life of every day—and then—"

Bucher watched the blue shadows of clouds pass over the hill and the white house. For a moment he was surprised that the house was still there. It seemed to him as though it should have been hit by a soundless bomb. But it was still there. "Shouldn't we wait till we're outside and have tried it before we despair?" he asked.

Ruth looked at her thin hands and thought of her gray hair and her missing teeth, and then she thought that for years Bucher had hardly seen a woman outside the camp. She was younger than he, but she felt many years older; knowledge weighed on her like lead. She didn't believe any of those things which he anticipated with so much certainty—and yet in her, too, there was a last hope to which she clung. "Yes, Josef," she said. "We should wait till then."

She walked back to her barrack. Her dirty skirt flapped round her thin legs. Bucher's eyes followed her and suddenly he felt rage rise in him like a boiling fountain. He knew he was helpless and that there was nothing he could do, and he also knew that he had to get over it, that he himself had to understand what he had said to Ruth. He stared at the ground. An ant was crawling over the earth. It dragged a dead beetle. The beetle was tiny but compared to the ant it was enormous. It depended on how you looked at it. It always depended on that.

Slowly he got up and walked to the barrack. He suddenly couldn't stand the bright sky any longer.

CHAPTER TWENTY-ONE

Neubauer stared at the letter. Then he read the last paragraph again.

> That's why I'm leaving. If you want to let yourself be caught, that's your own business. I want to be free. I'm taking Freya along. Follow us.
>
> Selma.

A Bavarian village was given as an address.

Neubauer gazed about him. He didn't understand it. It couldn't be true. They were bound to return at any moment. To leave him now—that was impossible! Where was the faith of the Nibelungen? Where the Germanic woman who fought side by side with her husband?

Clumsily he sat down in one of the French armchairs. The thing cracked. He got up, gave the chair a kick and let himself drop onto the sofa. That damned trash! Why on earth did he have that stuff rather than honest decent German furniture? It was for her sake he had gotten it. She had read something about them and had thought they were precious and elegant. What had they to do with him—him, the rough, honest retainer of the Führer? He raised his leg for a second kick at the fragile chair but thought better of it. What was the good? One day maybe the stuff could be sold. But who'd think of buying art while the sound of the guns could be heard?

He got up again and walked through the apartment. In the bedroom he opened the wardrobe doors. Before opening them he still had some hope, but at sight of the empty shelves it vanished. Selma had taken her furs and all her valuables. He swept the linen aside; the jewelry box was not there. Slowly he closed the doors and stood for a while in front of the dressing table. Absent-mindedly he picked up the bottles of Bohemian glass, took out the stoppers and sniffed at them without smelling anything. They were presents obtained during those glorious days in Czechoslovakia—she hadn't taken them along. Probably too fragile.

Suddenly he took a few quick steps toward a cupboard, tore it open and began searching for a key. He didn't have to search long. The safe was open and empty. She had gone off with all the security bonds. Even with his gold cigarette case with the swastika in diamonds—a gift from the industry while he was still technical adviser. He should have stayed there and gone on milking those brothers. The idea of the camp had turned out to be a mistake after all. At first, to be sure, one had been able to use it as a convenient means of putting on pressure; but now, as a result, one was saddled with it. All the same, he was one of the most humane Commandants. This was well known. Mellern was no Dachau, no Oranienburg, no Buchenwald—not to mention the extermination camps.

He pricked up his ears. One of the windows stood open and a muslin curtain fluttered like a ghost in the wind. This infernal rumbling from the horizon! It made one nervous. He closed the window. In his haste a curtain got jammed in it. He opened the window again and pulled the curtain in. It got caught on one corner and tore. He cursed and banged the window to. Then he went into the kitchen. The maid was sitting at the table and when he came in she jumped up. Of course she knew everything, that bitch! He helped himself to a bottle of beer from the icebox. He also found half a bottle of Steinhaeger and took both bottles with him into the living room. Then he returned; he had forgotten a glass. The maid was standing by the window, listening. She whipped round as though caught doing some forbidden thing. "Shall I prepare something to eat?"

"No."

He stamped out again. The schnapps was strong and aromatic; the beer cold. Run away, he thought. Like Jews. Worse! Jews didn't do that. They stuck together. He had often noticed that. Cheated! Left in the lurch! That's what one got out of it! He could have gotten more out of life if only he hadn't been such a faithful family man. Faithful—well, as good as faithful, one could say. Really faithful if you considered what he could have had. Those few times! The widow—that hardly counted. A few years ago there'd been a red-haired woman who had come to rescue her husband from the camp— the things she had done in her distress! Actually, the husband had died long before. Naturally, she didn't know that. It had been a gay evening. Later, of course, when she received the cigar box with the ashes, she had behaved like an idiot. All her own fault she'd gotten locked up. An *Obersturmbannführer* couldn't allow himself to be spat at.

He poured himself a second large Steinhaeger. What had made him think of that? Oh yes, Selma. Just imagine the things he could have had! Yes, he had missed many an opportunity. When you thought of all the things others had done! That clubfooted Binding of the Gestapo, for instance! Every day a new one!

He pushed the bottle away. The house seemed as empty as if Selma had gone off with the furniture as well. She had dragged Freya along. Why hadn't he had a son? Not his fault, certainly not! Oh, to hell with it all! He gazed about him. What was he to do now? Try to find her? In that little village? She'd still be on her way. Could take a long time before she got there.

He stared at his shining boots. The shining honor—smeared now by treason. Clumsily he got up and walked out through the empty house.

The Mercedes stood outside. "To the camp, Alfred."

The car crawled slowly through the town. "Stop!" said Neubauer suddenly. "To the bank, Alfred."

He walked out as steadily as he could. People mustn't notice anything! Imagine! Making a fool of him, too! During these last months she had drawn out half the money. When he had asked at the bank why he hadn't been informed they had shrugged their shoulders and talked of a joint account. They were even convinced they'd been doing him a favor. The drawing out of large sums was officially looked upon askance.

"To the garden, Alfred."

It took them a long time to get through. But on arriving at last, there lay the garden, so peaceful in the morning light. Here and there some fruit trees were already in bloom, the narcissus were out, and violets and crocuses in many colors. They lay in the bright green of the leaves like multicolored Easter eggs. No infidelity from them— they arrived on time and were on the spot as was expected of them. Nature was reliable—there was no running away.

He walked into the shed. The rabbits were nibbling behind the wire. There were no thoughts of bank accounts in their clear red eyes. Neubauer stuck a finger through the wire and gently scratched the soft fur of the white Angoras. He had meant to have a shawl made from the fur for Selma. He, the kindhearted fool whom everyone betrayed!

He leaned against the wire and stared through the open door. Surrounded by the peace of the happily nibbling animals, his feeling of outrage turned into a deep self-pity. The radiant sky, a blossoming branch swaying up and down before the door, the gentle animal faces in the shade—everything contributed to it.

Suddenly he heard the rumbling again; it was less regular but louder than before. Irresistibly it broke into his private grief, a hollow subterranean knocking. It knocked and knocked and with it fear returned once more. But now it was a different kind of fear. It was deeper. Now he was alone and could no longer deceive himself by trying to convince others and thereby himself. Now it came over him without any restraint, it gushed into his throat from his stomach and from the throat back to his stomach and into the intestines. I have done no wrong, he thought, without conviction. Only my duty. I have witnesses. Any number. Blank is my witness; just recently I gave him a cigar instead of having him locked up. Anyone else would have confiscated his firm without paying a cent. Blank himself admitted it, he'll testify to that; I've been decent, he'll swear to it. He won't swear to it, a cold other self thought in him, and he turned around as though a voice had spoken behind him. There stood the rakes, the spades, the hoes, painted green, with reliable wooden shafts—if only one were a peasant now, a gardener, an innkeeper, a nobody! That damned branch blossoming there, it had an easy life, it just went on blossoming and had no responsibility. But where should an *Obersturmbannführer* go? From one side came the Russians, from the other the British and Americans, where could one go? It was easy for Selma to talk. Running away from the Americans meant running nearer to the Russians, and what they would do was easy to imagine. They hadn't passed through their devastated country, from Moscow and Stalingrad, for nothing!

Neubauer wiped the sweat out of his eyes. He took several steps. His knees wobbled. One had to do some clear thinking. He groped his way out of the shed. The air outside was fresh. He breathed deeply; but it seemed that with the air he was also breathing in the irregular rumbling from the horizon. It vibrated in his lungs and made him weak. Easily and without retching, he vomited against a tree amongst the narcissus. "The beer?" he said. "Beer and Steinhaeger don't mix." He glanced toward the entrance to the garden. Alfred couldn't see him. He remained standing for a while. Then he felt his sweat drying in the wind. Slowly he walked back to the car. "To the whorehouse, Alfred."

"Where, Herr *Obersturmbannführer?*"

"To the whorehouse!" Neubauer suddenly yelled angrily. "Don't you understand your own language any more?"

"The brothel has been closed. It is now an emergency lazaret."

"Drive to the camp, then."

He got in. To the camp—where else could he go? . . .

"What d'you think of the situation, Weber?"

Weber looked at him unperturbed. "Excellent!"

"Excellent? Really?" Neubauer began searching for cigars; then he remembered Weber didn't smoke them. "Unfortunately I have no cigarettes here. Had a box; they disappeared. Heaven knows where I put them."

He stared disgruntled at the window boarded up with planks. It had been broken by the bombing, and there was no new glass to be had. He didn't know that during the confusion his cigarettes had been stolen and via the red-haired clerk and Lewinsky had provided the Veterans of Barrack 22 with bread for two days. Fortunately his secret notes—all his humanitarian instructions which later had been misinterpreted by Weber and others—had not disappeared. He watched Weber out of the corner of his eye. The camp leader seemed perfectly calm, although he undoubtedly had all kinds of things on his conscience. There had been those recent hangings, for instance—

Suddenly Neubauer grew hot again. He was covered, even doubly so. Nevertheless—"What would you do, Weber," he said amiably, "if for a short period of—of waiting, let us say, the enemy should occupy the country—which," he added hastily, "doesn't necessarily have to mean defeat, as history has frequently proven?"

Weber had listened to him with a hint of a smile. "For someone like me there's always something to do," he answered in a matter-of-fact tone. "We'll come up again—though possibly under other names. As Communists, for instance. For several years there won't be any National Socialists. Everyone will be a democrat. That doesn't matter. At some time or other I'll probably be attached to the police force. Maybe with false papers. Then the work can continue."

Neubauer smiled to himself. Weber's confidence helped him to recover his own. "Not a bad idea. And I? What d'you think I'll be?"

"That I don't know. You have a family, Herr *Obersturmbannführer*. In that case it's not so easy to change and go underground."

"Of course not." Neubauer's good mood disappeared again. "You know, Weber, I'd like to make a round of the camp. Haven't done that for a long time."

When he arrived in the disinfecting ward, the Small camp already knew what was about to happen. Most of the weapons had already been smuggled back into the labor camp by Werner and Lewinsky. Only 509 had held on to his revolver. He had insisted on it and kept it hidden under his bunk.

A quarter of an hour later, from the hospital by way of the latrine, came the astonishing news that the inspection was not to be a penal affair; that the barracks were not to be thoroughly searched; that on the contrary Neubauer was actually being downright benevolent.

The new block senior was nervous. He shouted at everyone and gave orders. "Don't shout so much," said Berger. "It won't get you anywhere."

"What?"

"Just that."

"I'll shout if I want to. Barrack 22, step out! Line up!" The men who could still walk came out and fell in. The block senior ran down the line. "These are not all! There are more!"

"Are the dead to line up, too?"

"Shut up! Bring out the sick!"

"Listen. Nothing is known about an inspection. None has been ordered. You don't have to make the barrack line up in advance."

The block senior was sweating. "I'll do as I like. I'm the block senior. Where's the one who's always sitting about with you here? With you and you." He pointed at Berger and Bucher.

The block senior opened the barrack door to make sure. This was just what Berger had wanted to prevent. 509 was hiding; he had to keep out of Weber's way. "He's not here." Berger stepped into the doorway.

"What? Get out of my way!"

"He's not here," said Berger without moving. "That's that."

The block senior stared at him. Bucher and Sulzbacher stepped in beside Berger. "What does all this mean?" asked the block senior.

"He's not here," said Bucher. "Do you want to know how Handke died?"

"Are you crazy?"

Rosen and Ahasver had joined the others. "Do you realize I can break the bones of the whole bunch of you?" asked the block senior.

"Listen," said Ahasver, and pointed his knobby forefinger in the direction of the horizon. "Still coming nearer."

"He wasn't killed in the bombing," said Bucher.

"It wasn't us who broke Handke's neck. Not us," said Sulzbacher. "Haven't you ever heard of the camp *Vehme?*"

The block senior took one step back. He had heard what happened to traitors and informers. "Do you here belong to it?" he asked, incredulous.

"Be sensible," said Berger calmly. "And don't drive yourself and us crazy. Who'd want at this moment to get on the list of those we're going to get even with?"

"Who has ever mentioned such a thing?" The block senior began to gesticulate. "If nobody tells me anything, how am I supposed to know what's going on? What's it all about? Everybody's been able to depend on me until now."

"Then everything's fine."

"Bolte's coming," said Bucher.

"All right, all right." The block senior hitched up his pants. "I'll watch out. You can depend on me. I'm one of you."

Damn it, thought Neubauer, why couldn't the bombs have fallen here? That would have solved the whole problem! Everything was always going wrong.

"This is the Mercy Division," he said.

"The Mercy Division," repeated Weber.

"Oh, well." Neubauer shrugged his shoulders. "After all—we don't make them work here."

"No." Weber was amused. The idea of making these ghosts work was absurd.

"The blockade," said Neubauer. "Not our fault—the enemy—" He turned to Weber. "It stinks here like a monkey house. Can't something be done about it?"

"Dysentery," answered Weber. "After all, this is a recreation place for the sick."

"The sick, of course!" Neubauer promptly picked up the thread. "Sick, dysentery, that's why it stinks, of course. Would be the same in the hospital, too." He looked about him, undecided. "Couldn't the people be given a bath?"

"The danger of contagion is too great. We have kept this part of the camp rather shut off from the rest. The bathing installations are on the other side."

At the word contagion Neubauer had taken a step back. "Have we enough clean underwear to supply these men? The old things ought to be burned, then, don't you think?"

"Not necessarily. They can be disinfected. We have enough underwear in the clothing depot. We've received large shipments from Belsen."

"Good," said Neubauer, relieved. "Then get them some change of underwear, some clean outfits or anything else we have in the line of clothes. Distribute some chloride of lime and disinfectants. That'll make a different impression right away. Make a note of it." The first camp senior, a fat prisoner, officiously noted it down. "Make a point of extreme cleanliness!" dictated Neubauer.

"Extreme cleanliness," repeated the camp senior.

Weber suppressed a grin. Neubauer turned toward the prisoners. "Have you got everything you need?"

Throughout twelve years the answer had been prescribed. "Yes, Herr *Obersturmbannführer*."

"Fine. Carry on."

Neubauer glanced around once more. The old barracks stood there like black coffins. He meditated and suddenly had an idea. "Have something green planted here," he declared. "This is just the time for it. A few shrubs along the north sides, and a bed of flowers along the south walls. That'll cheer things up. We do have such things in the nursery garden, don't we?"

"We do, Herr *Obersturmbannführer*."

"Well then, start in right away. We can do the same thing with the barracks in the labor camp." Neubauer was warming up to his idea. The gardener in him was breaking through. "What about a bed of violets—no, primroses are nicer, the yellow gives more color—"

Two men slipped slowly to the ground. No one moved to help them. "Primroses—have we enough primroses in the garden?"

"We have, Herr *Obersturmbannführer*." The fat camp senior stood at attention. "There are plenty of primroses there. In full bloom."

"Good. See that that's done. And have the camp band play a bit nearer here now and again, so that these men can also hear it."

Neubauer walked back. The others followed him. He felt somewhat calmer. The prisoners had no complaints. Years without any criticism had accustomed him to accept as facts what he himself wanted to believe. He consequently expected even now that the prisoners should see him as he wanted them to; as a man who was doing his best for them under difficult circumstances. That they were human beings he had forgotten long ago.

CHAPTER TWENTY-TWO

"What?" asked Berger, incredulous. "No supper at all?"

"Nothing."

"No soup?"

"No soup and no bread. Weber's express orders."

"And the others? The labor camp?"

"Nothing. No food for the whole camp."

Berger turned around. "What d'you make of this? We're given underwear but no food."

"We've also got some primroses." 509 pointed at two wretched patches on either side of the door. In them stood a few half-wilted plants. They had been planted there at noon by prisoners from the nursery garden.

"Maybe we can eat them?"

"Don't try it. If they're missing we won't get any food for a whole week."

"What is this all about?" said Berger. "After that fuss Neubauer made, you'd think we might even get an odd potato in our soup!"

Lebenthal came over. "It's Weber. Not Neubauer. Weber's furious with Neubauer. Thinks he's trying to protect himself. Probably is, too. That's why Weber is working against him wherever he can. I got that from the office. Lewinsky and Werner and the others over there say the same. We're the ones who're getting it in the neck."

"This'll mean a lot of dead."

They stared at the red sky. "Weber said in the office we'd better not get swollen heads; he'd see to it we'd be kept short." Lebenthal fished the denture out of his mouth, looked at it casually and put it back again.

Feeble screams could be heard from the barracks. The news had spread. Mussulmen staggered out of the door and examined the food pots to see if they smelled of food and if the others had cheated them. The pots were bare and dry. The screams grew louder. Some men just let themselves drop to the ground and hammered at the foul earth with their bony fists. But most of them crept away or lay around motionless with open mouths and staring eyes. From the doors came the feeble voices of those no longer able to get up. It was no articulate screaming; it was just a weak chorale of despair, a singsong which no longer even had words and supplications and curses to express despair. It was already beyond that; it was the very last remnant of drowning life—a humming and squeaking and whistling and scraping, as though the barracks were enormous boxes filled with dying insects.

At seven o'clock the band began to play. Although it stood outside the Small camp it was close enough to be heard clearly within it. Neubauer's instructions had been promptly obeyed. As usual, the first tune was the Commandant's favorite waltz, "Roses from the South."

"If we've nothing else," said 509, "let's feed on hope. Let's devour all the hope that exists. Let's eat up the rumbling of the guns! We've got to pull through. We will pull through!"

The small group crouched together close to the barrack. It was a cool, misty night. They did not feel the cold too much. During these last hours twenty-eight men had died in the barrack; the Veterans had stripped them of those clothes they could use and put them on to ward off cold and sickness. They didn't want to stay inside. In the barrack death panted, moaned and smacked its lips. They had been without bread for three days, today even without soup. On every bunk life struggled, surrendered and faded out. They didn't want to sleep so near to death. Death was contagious and they feared that in sleep they would be defenseless against it. So they sat outside, covered with the clothes of the dead, and stared at the horizon.

"It's only tonight," said 509. "Only this one night! Do believe me. Neubauer will hear about it and cancel the order tomorrow. They're already at loggerheads. It's the beginning of the end. We've held out so long. Just this one more night!"

No one answered. They crouched close to one another like a group of animals in winter; it was not only warmth they gave one another; it was the multiplied courage to live. That was more important than warmth. "Let's talk about something," said Berger. "But about something that has nothing to do with any of this." He turned toward Sulzbacher, who squatted beside him. "What are you going to do when you get out of here?"

"I?" Sulzbacher hesitated. "Let's not mention it until we've got that far. It's unlucky."

"It's no longer unlucky," answered 509 passionately. "We've avoided mentioning it all these years because it would have devoured us. But now we've got to talk about it. Especially tonight! When else? Let's feed on our hope. What are you going to do when you get out, Sulzbacher?"

"I don't know where my wife is. She was in Düsseldorf. Düsseldorf is destroyed."

"If she's in Düsseldorf she's safe. Düsseldorf's occupied by the British. The radio said so some time ago."

"Or she's dead," said Sulzbacher.

"One always has to consider that. After all, what do we know about the people outside?"

"Or they about us," said Bucher.

509 glanced at him. He still hadn't told him his father was dead,

nor how he had died. There would be time enough when they were out; it would be easier for him to take it then. Bucher was young and the only one who had someone to leave with. He would hear about it soon enough.

"What on earth will it be like when we get out?" said Meyerhof. "I've been in the camp six years."

"I twelve," said Berger.

"As long as that? Were you political?"

"No. From '28 to '32 I had a Nazi as patient. He later became a group leader. Actually, he wasn't my patient; he used to come to my office and was treated there by a friend of mine, who was a specialist. The Nazi came to my office only because we lived in the same house. It was more convenient for him."

"And that's why he had you locked up?"

"Yes. He had syphilis."

"And the specialist?"

"He had him shot. I myself could pretend I didn't know what was wrong with him and make out I thought he was just suffering from some inflammation. Even so, he was cautious enough to have me locked up."

"What'll you do if he's still alive when you get out?"

Berger pondered. "I don't know."

"I'd bump him off," declared Meyerhof.

"Just to be thrown back into prison again, what?" said Lebenthal. "For manslaughter. Another ten or twenty years."

"What are you going to do, Leo, when you get out?" asked 509.

"I'm going to open a store for overcoats. Good semiready-mades."

"In summer? Overcoats? It'll soon be summer, Leo!"

"There are summer overcoats. I could have suits, too. And raincoats, of course."

"Leo," said 509. "Why don't you stay in the food business? There'll be more need for that than for overcoats, and here you were a wizard at it."

"Do you think so?" Lebenthal was clearly flattered.

"Absolutely!"

"Maybe you're right. I'll think it over. American food, for instance. That's going to be a big business. Do you remember the American bacon after the last war? It was thick, white, and as tender as marzipan, with pink—"

"Shut up, Leo! Are you crazy?"

"No. It suddenly crossed my mind. I wonder if they'll send some this time, too? At least for us?"

"Be quiet, Leo!"

"What are you going to do, Berger?" asked Rosen.

Berger wiped his inflamed eyes. "I'm going to get myself apprenticed to a pharmacist. Try something like that. Be a surgeon again—with these hands? After that length of time?" He clenched his hands under the jacket he had flung over himself. "Impossible. I'll become a pharmacist. And you?"

"My wife divorced me because I'm a Jew. I don't know anything about her."

"You're not going to look for her?" asked Meyerhof.

Rosen hesitated. "Maybe she did it under pressure. What else could she have done? I advised her to, myself."

"Maybe she's turned so ugly in the meantime," said Lebenthal, "that it will no longer be a problem for you. Maybe you will be glad to be rid of her."

"We haven't gotten any younger ourselves."

"No. Nine years." Sulzbacher coughed. "How will it be, seeing someone again after such a time?"

"You can consider yourself lucky if there is anyone to see again."

"After such a long time," repeated Sulzbacher. "Won't we all be strangers?"

Among the shuffling of the Mussulmen they heard a firmer step. "Look out!" whispered Berger. "Take care, 509."

"It's Lewinsky," said Bucher. He could recognize people by their step.

Lewinsky approached. "How are you making out? Bad day. No grub anywhere. We have a contact man in the kitchen. He managed to swipe some bread and carrots. The cooked food was only for the big shots. Couldn't get any of that. Here's some bread. And a few raw carrots. It's not much, but we didn't get anything today, either."

"Berger," said 509, "divide it up."

There was half a slice of bread and one carrot for each. "Eat it slow. Chew it till every crumb's gone." Berger handed out the carrots first; then, several minutes later, the bread.

"Feeding on the sly like this makes one feel somehow like a criminal," said Rosen.

"Then don't do it, you idiot!" answered Lewinsky laconically.

Lewinsky was right. Rosen knew it. He was about to explain that the thought had not occurred to him till just now, during this strange night when they had discussed their future in order to stave off hunger, and that it was connected with the future; but he abandoned the idea. It was too complicated. And too unimportant.

"They're wavering," said Lewinsky hoarsely under his breath. "Green ones are wavering, too. Want to play along. We let them. Kapos, block seniors, room seniors. Later on we'll sort them out. Two SS-men as well. Even Hoffmann."

"The lazaret physician! That swine!" said Bucher.

"We know what he is. But we can use him. We're getting news through him. Tonight an order for a transport came through."

"What?" asked Berger and 509 simultaneously.

"Transport. Two thousand men are to be rounded up."

"They're going to evacuate the camp?"

"They want two thousand men. For the time being."

"The transport. That's what we feared," said Berger.

"Take it easy. The red-haired clerk is keeping watch. If they're making a list, you won't be on it. Our men are everywhere now. Besides, there's a rumor that Neubauer is hesitating. He still hasn't passed on the order."

"They won't go by a list," said Rosen. "If they can't get them otherwise, they'll catch them wholesale as they did in our camp. The lists they'll make later."

"Don't get excited. It hasn't got that far yet. The whole thing can change any minute."

"Don't get excited, says he!" muttered Rosen.

"If the worst happens, we'll smuggle you into the lazaret. Hoffmann is now keeping both eyes closed. We've already a number of suspected men in there."

"Did they say anything about women being rounded up, too?" asked Bucher.

"No. They won't, either. There are far too few women here."

Lewinsky got up. "Come," he said to Berger. "That's why I'm here. I came to fetch you."

"Where to?"

"To the lazaret. We'll hide you there for a few days. Maybe only for one or two. We have a room next to the spotted-fever ward; no Nazi dares go near it. It's all arranged."

"And why?" asked 509.

"The crematorium gang. They're doing away with them tomorrow. So the rumor goes. Whether they'll include Berger in it, none of us knows. I think they will." He turned to Berger. "You've seen too much down there. Come with me, for safety's sake. Change your clothes. Put yours on a corpse. Take his."

"You'd better go," said 509.

"And the block senior? Can you arrange things with him?"

"Yes," said Ahasver surprisingly. "He'll hold his tongue. We'll see to that."

"Okay. The red-haired clerk has been tipped off. Dreyer in the crematorium is jittery with fear for himself. He won't look for you among the dead." Lewinsky snorted noisily. "There are too many of them anyhow. I stumbled over them all the way here. It'll take four or five days to have them all burned. By then there'll be more. Everything's already in such a mess no one knows what's going on. The main thing is that they don't find you." A grin flashed across his face. "At such times that's always the main thing. To be out of range."

"Come on," said 509. "Let's look for a corpse that isn't tattooed."

They had very little light. The intermittent, smoldering redness on the horizon wasn't any help. They had to bend low over the dead to see if there were numbers tattooed on their arms. Discovering one about Berger's size, they stripped it.

"Go on, Ephraim!"

They were sitting on the side of the barrack which faced away from the guards. "Quick," whispered Lewinsky, "change your clothes here! The fewer who know about it the better. Give me your jacket and trousers."

Berger undressed. He stood silhouetted against the sky like a ghostly harlequin. During the unexpected distribution of underwear he had been thrown a pair of women's drawers which reached halfway down his legs. Above these he wore a low-cut, sleeveless shirt.

"Report him as dead tomorrow morning!"

"Yes. The SS block leader doesn't know him. We'll cope with the block senior all right."

Lewinsky grinned furtively. "You've really gotten quite smart! Come along, Berger."

"So there's going to be a transport after all!" Rosen's eyes followed Berger. "Sulzbacher was right. We shouldn't have talked of the future. It's bad luck."

"Nonsense! We've gotten something to eat. Berger has been saved. It's not certain that Neubauer will pass on the order. What do you mean—bad luck? Do you want a guarantee for years?"

"Will Berger come back?" asked someone behind 509.

"He's been saved," said Rosen, bitterly. "He won't go with the transport."

"Shut up!" retorted 509 sharply. He turned round. Behind him stood Karel, the boy from Czechoslovakia. "Of course he'll come back, Karel," he said. "Why don't you stay in the barrack?"

Karel shrugged his shoulders. "I thought you might have a bit of leather to chew."

"Here's something better," said Ahasver. He gave him his piece of bread and the carrot. He had saved it for him.

Karel began eating very slowly. After a while he felt the others eyeing him. He got up and walked away. When he returned he was no longer chewing.

"Ten minutes," said Lebenthal, glancing at his nickel watch. "A good job, Karel. I couldn't have managed that. With me it lasted ten seconds."

"Couldn't we swap the watch for some food?" asked 509.

"We won't be able to do any swapping tonight. Not even gold."

"One can eat liver," said Karel.

"What?"

"Liver. Fresh liver. If you cut it out right away, you can eat it."

"Cut it from where?"

"From the dead."

"Where did you get that idea, Karel?" asked Ahasver after a while.

"From Blatzek."

"From which Blatzek?"

"Blatzek in the Brno camp. He said it was better than dying. The dead were dead and would go up the chimney anyway. He taught me a lot. He showed me how to play dead and how to run when they're shooting from behind—zigzag, here and there, up and down. Also how not to get smothered in a mass grave. And how to dig oneself out at night. Blatzek knew a lot."

"You know a lot, too, Karel."

"Sure. Otherwise I wouldn't be here."

"That's true. But let's think of something else," said 509.

"We've still got to put Berger's clothes on that corpse."

It was easy. The body wasn't yet stiff. They piled several more corpses on top of it. Then they crouched together again. Ahasver began murmuring. "You've got a lot to pray about tonight, old man," said Bucher grimly.

Ahasver glanced up. He listened for a while to the distant rumbling. "When the first Jew was slain without trial they broke the law of life," he said slowly. "They said, 'What are a few Jews compared with Greater Germany?' They looked away. They had the Army, which at that time didn't belong to the murderers. The Army could have stopped it all in one day. But they let it happen. For that they are now to be punished by God. A life is a life. Even the poorest one."

He began murmuring again. The others were silent. It turned cooler. They crouched closer together.

Squad Leader Breuer woke up. Drowsily he switched on the lamp beside his bed. Instantly two green lights flashed up on his table. They were two small electric bulbs which had been ingeniously fixed into the eye-sockets of a skull. As soon as Breuer turned the switch a second time, all the other lamps went out—leaving only the skull shining into the darkness. It produced an interesting effect. Breuer was very fond of it. He had thought it up by himself.

On the table stood a plate with some cake crumbs and an empty coffee cup. A few books lay beside it; adventure stories by Karl May. These and an obscene privately printed book on the love life of a dancer represented Breuer's literary education.

He raised himself, yawning. He had a bad taste in his mouth. He listened for a while. The cells in the bunker were silent. No one dared moan; Breuer had taught the inmates discipline long ago.

He reached under the bed, pulled out a bottle of brandy and took a wine glass from the table. He filled it and drank it down. Then he listened again. The window was closed. Even so, he thought he heard the rumbling of the guns. He poured himself another glass and drank it. Then he got up and looked at his watch. It was half-past two.

He pulled his boots over his pajamas. He needed the boots; he was fond of kicking stomachs. Without boots it had little effect. The pajamas were practical; the bunker was very hot. Breuer had enough coal. The crematorium was already running short; but Breuer had laid in a store for his purposes in good time.

He walked slowly along the corridor. The door of each cell had a peephole which enabled one to see in. This Breuer didn't need. He knew his menagerie and he was proud of this expression. Sometimes he also called it his circus; it was then that he fancied himself as a lion tamer with his whip.

He walked past the cells as a wine lover walks through his cellar. And just as the connoisseur chooses the oldest wine, so Breuer decided tonight to deal with his oldest guest. It was Luebbe in Cell Seven. He unlocked it.

The cell was small and unbearably hot. It had a central heating apparatus turned on full blast. A man was chained by the hands and feet to the pipes. He hung unconscious just above the floor. Breuer contemplated him for a while; then he fetched a watering can from the corridor and sprayed the man as though he were a parched plant. The water sizzled on the hot pipes and evaporated. Luebbe didn't stir. Breuer unlocked the chains. The burned hands fell down. He sprayed the remains of the water in the can over the figure on the floor. A puddle formed. Breuer walked out with the can to fill it again. Outside, he stood still. Two cells further on someone moaned. He put down the can, unlocked the second cell and strolled leisurely in. He could be heard muttering; then came the muffled sounds of kicking; then a thumping, shoving, knocking, clanking, and suddenly howls and screams that slowly merged into the gasps of choking. There were a few more hollow thuds and Breuer appeared again. His right boot was wet. He filled the watering can and strolled back to Cell Seven.

"Well, well!" he said. "You're awake!"

Luebbe lay flat on the ground, face down. He was trying with both hands to scrape together the water on the floor to lick it up. He moved clumsily like a half-dead toad. Suddenly he saw the full watering can. With a low squawk he arched himself, lunged round and made a grab for it. Breuer trod on his hand. Luebbe failed to pull it out from under the boot. He craned his neck as far as he could toward the can; his lips quivered, his head trembled, and he squawked with great effort.

Breuer contemplated him with the expert's eye. He realized that Luebbe was almost finished. "Go on, then—guzzle!" he growled. "Guzzle your last breakfast!"

He grinned at his joke and stepped off the hand. Luebbe threw himself at the can with such haste that it rocked. He couldn't believe his luck. "Guzzle slowly," said Breuer. "We have time."

Luebbe drank and drank. He had just gone through chapter six of Breuer's educational program—several days of feeding on nothing but salted herring and salt water; and in addition to this chained to the hot pipes with the heat full on.

"Enough!" declared Breuer at last and pulled away the can. "Get up. Follow me."

Luebbe stumbled up. He swayed and leaned back and vomited water. "You see," said Breuer, "I told you to drink slow. Move!"

He pushed Luebbe in front of him down the corridor into his room. Luebbe fell into it. "Get up!" said Breuer. "Sit down on that chair!"

Luebbe crawled onto the chair. He swayed and leaned back and waited for the next torture. He no longer knew anything else.

Breuer looked at him thoughtfully. "You are my oldest guest, Luebbe. Six months, what?"

The ghost before him swayed. "What?" repeated Breuer.

The ghost nodded.

"A nice time," declared Breuer. "Long. It's the kind of thing that binds men together. Somehow you've grown quite close to my heart. Sounds funny, but that's more or less what it amounts to. After all, I haven't anything against you, personally, you know that. You know that," he repeated after a pause. "Or don't you?"

The ghost nodded again. He was waiting for the next torture.

"It's just that we're against the whole lot of you. The single one is of no interest." Breuer nodded ponderously and poured himself a cognac. "No interest. A pity, I thought you'd have pulled through. We'd only two more chapters to go—the hanging from the feet and my special final one—and then you'd have been through and gotten out, you know that?"

The ghost nodded. He didn't know it for certain, but it was a fact that Breuer occasionally discharged prisoners for whom no express death warrant had been issued after they had lived through all the tortures. In this respect he followed a kind of bureaucratic system; whoever got through was given a chance. It was caused by a reluctant admiration for the victim's ability to withstand so much. There were some Nazis who thought this way, and who as a result considered themselves gentlemen keeping to the rules of fair play.

"Pity," said Breuer. "I'd have rather liked you to get away. You showed courage. Pity I've got to do away with you all the same. You know why?"

Luebbe didn't answer. Breuer lit a cigarette and opened the window. "Because of that." He listened a moment. "D'you hear it?"

He watched Luebbe's eyes following him uncomprehendingly. "Artillery," he said. "Enemy artillery. They're coming nearer. That's why! That's why you'll be done away with tonight, my boy." He closed the window. "Bad luck, what?" He grinned crookedly.

"Just a few days before they could have gotten you out of here! Rotten bad luck, what?"

He was pleased with his idea. It lent finesse to the evening. A spot of spiritual torture as a final touch. "Really, infernal bad luck, what?"

"No," whispered Luebbe.

"What?"

"No."

"Are you that tired of life?"

Luebbe shook his head. Breuer looked at him, astonished. He felt that the ghost sitting before him was no longer the same wreck as a minute ago. Luebbe suddenly looked as though he'd had a day of rest. "Because now they're going to get you," he whispered with torn lips. "All of you!"

"Damn nonsense!" For a moment Breuer was furious. He realized he had made a mistake. Instead of torturing Luebbe he had rendered him a service. But who could have guessed that this creature cared so little for life? "Don't you go and get ideas! I was just fooling you. We won't lose! We're just clearing out of here! The front's being shifted, that's all."

It didn't sound convincing. Breuer knew it himself. He took a swig. Doesn't matter, he thought, and drank again. "Think what you like," he said then. "Whatever happens, you're out of luck. Forces me to finish you off." He felt the alcohol. "Pity for you and pity for me. Was a good life. Well, maybe not for you, if one comes to think of it."

Despite his weakness, Luebbe watched him carefully. "What I like about you," said Breuer, "is that you didn't give in. But I've got to finish you off so that you can't talk. Particularly you, the oldest guest. You first. The others' turns will come, too," he added soothingly. "Never leave witnesses behind. Old National Socialist rule."

He took a hammer out of the table drawer. "I'll get it over quick." He put down the hammer. Instantly Luebbe stumbled up from the chair and tried to snatch the hammer with his burnt hands. Breuer gave him a slight shove with his fist. Luebbe fell. "Well, well," said Breuer good-naturedly. "Still having a try. You're quite right. Why not? Just stay there on the floor. Then it's easier for me." He held a hand to his ear. "What? What d'you say?"

"They'll get you all—all in the same way—"

"Oh, lay off it, Luebbe! That's what you'd like. They won't do that kind of thing. They're much too gentlemanly for that. I'll have quit before, anyhow. And nobody'll think about you any more."

He took another swig. "Would you like a cigarette first?" he asked suddenly.

Luebbe looked at him. "Yes," he said.

Breuer stuck a cigarette between the man's bleeding lips. "Here!" He lit Luebbe's cigarette and with the same match also one for himself.

Both smoked in silence. Luebbe knew he was lost. He strained his ears in the direction of the window. Breuer emptied his glass. Then he put down his cigarette and seized the hammer. "Now, let's get it over with."

"Be damned for ever!" whispered Luebbe. The cigarette did not fall from his mouth; it stuck fast to his bleeding lower lip. Breuer struck several times with the blunt end of the hammer. It was a compliment to Luebbe, who slowly collapsed, that he didn't use the pointed end.

For a while Breuer sat and brooded. Then he remembered what Luebbe had said. In a vague way he felt cheated. Luebbe had cheated him. He should have howled. But Luebbe would never have howled; not even if he had killed him slowly. He would have moaned; but that didn't count, that was only the body. That was like a loud breathing, nothing more. Again Breuer heard the rumbling through the window. Someone would have to howl once more tonight, otherwise something would snap in him. That was it; now he knew it. It couldn't just end like this, with Luebbe. In that case, Luebbe would have won. Clumsily he got up and walked to Cell Four. He was lucky. A terrified voice began to scream, to beg, to wail, and only after a long time did it grow weaker and weaker and finally cease altogether.

Satisfied, Breuer returned to his room. "You see! You're still in our power, after all!" he said to Luebbe's corpse and kicked it with his foot. The kick wasn't hard, but something in Luebbe's face moved. Breuer bent over him; it seemed as though Luebbe were sticking out a gray tongue at him. Then he discovered that the cigarette had gone on burning down to the lips of the dead man; the kick had caused the little pillar of ash to collapse. Breuer was suddenly tired. He didn't feel in the mood to drag out the corpse; so he kicked it under the bed with his feet. There'd be time enough tomorrow. A dark trail remained on the floor. Breuer grinned sleepily. And to think, when I was small, I couldn't even look at blood, he thought. Too silly!

CHAPTER TWENTY-THREE

The dead lay piled up in heaps. The truck no longer came to fetch them. Raindrops hung silvery on their hair and lashes and hands. The rumbling on the horizon had ceased. The prisoners had seen the fire of the guns and heard the explosions until midnight, then everything had grown still.

The sun came up. The sky was blue and the breeze gentle and warm. On the highways outside the town nothing could be seen; not even refugees. The town lay there black and burned out. Through it the river wound its way like a vast glittering snake feeding itself on the corpse of the town. There were no troops anywhere.

For an hour during the night it had rained, a soft downpour, and a few puddles still remained. 509 squatted beside one and accidentally saw his face reflected in it. He leaned closer over the flat clear pool. He could not remember the last time he had seen himself in a mirror; it must have been many years ago. He had never seen one in the camp; and he didn't recognize the face that now stared back at him.

His hair was white-gray stubble. Before coming to the camp it had been thick and brown. He knew it had changed color, he had seen that when tufts of it had fallen to the ground during the haircutting; but loose hair on the floor seemed no longer to have any connection with oneself. In his face he recognized hardly anything; not even the eyes. What flickered there from two sockets above decayed teeth and the too-large nostrils was just something that distinguished him from the dead.

That is me? he thought.

He stared at himself again. He should have realized that he looked similar to the others around, but he had never seriously thought of it. Year after year he had seen them and noticed how they had changed; but since he had seen them every day the change had struck him less than now when seeing himself for the first time in years. It wasn't that his hair was gray and patchy, his face nothing but a mockery of the full healthy face of his memory. What shocked him was that what he saw was an old man.

For a while he sat very quiet. He had thought a great deal during these last few days; but never of the fact that he was old. Twelve years of time was not very long. Twelve years of being locked up was more. But twelve years of concentration camp—who could tell how much that would mean later? Had he retained sufficient strength? Or would he, on getting out of it, break down like a tree rotting within which, in the calm, still seemed healthy, but which crumbled at the first storm? For this was what, in spite of everything, camp life had been—a calm; endless, terrifying, lonely, but nevertheless a calm. Hardly a sound from the outside world had penetrated to the inside. What would happen when the barbed wire fell?

509 stared once more into the shining pool. These are my eyes, he thought. He leaned further over to see them more clearly. Under his breath the water ruffled and the reflection blurred. These are my lungs, he thought, and they are still pumping. He dipped his

hand into the puddle, breaking the surface—and these are my hands which can destroy this image.

Destroy, he thought. But construct? To hate. But can I still do something else? Hatred alone is little. To live, man needs more than hatred.

He straightened himself. He saw Bucher approaching. He has got it, he thought. And he is still young.

"509," said Bucher. "Have you heard? The crematorium's no longer working."

"Not possible!"

"The cremation gang is dead. It seems they haven't chosen a new one yet. I wonder why? Could—"

They looked at each other. "Could they no longer have any use for it? Could they already be—"

Bucher stopped. "Pulling out?" said 509.

"Maybe. This morning they didn't even come for the dead."

Rosen and Sulzbacher came over. "The artillery has stopped," said Rosen. "I wonder what's going on?"

"Maybe they've broken through."

"Or been thrown back. They say the SS intend to defend the camp."

"Latrine rumor. There's a new one every five minutes. If they really defend the camp, we'll be bombed."

509 looked up. I wish it was already night again, he thought. It is easier to hide in the dark. Who knows what may happen yet? The day had many hours, and death required no more than seconds. Many deaths could be hidden in the shimmering hours the sun brought up mercilessly from the horizon.

"There's a plane!" Sulzbacher suddenly shouted.

Excitedly he pointed at the sky. After a while they all saw the tiny speck. "It must be German!" whispered Rosen. "Otherwise there'd be an alarm."

They looked around for a hiding place. There had been rumors that German planes had been ordered to bomb the camp off the face of the earth at the last moment.

"It's only one! Just a single one."

They remained standing. For a bombardment more than one plane would probably have been sent out. "Maybe it's an American observation plane," said Lebenthal, who had suddenly turned up. "They no longer sound the alarm for them."

"How d'you know?"

Lebenthal didn't answer. They all stared at the speck that grew rapidly larger. "That's no German plane," said Sulzbacher.

Now they could see the plane clearly. It came darting straight towards the camp. 509 felt as though from the earth a fist were dragging his intestines to the ground. It was as though he were standing naked on a platform, being sacrificed to a sinister, down-plunging, murderous deity, without being able to flee. He noticed that the others lay flat on the ground and couldn't understand why he had remained standing.

At this moment there came a rattle of shots. The plane pulled itself out of its plunging flight, turned, and circled around the camp. The shots had come from the camp. Machine guns were firing from behind the SS quarters. The plane flew still lower. Everyone stared up at it. And suddenly it moved its wings. It looked as though it were beckoning with them. At first the prisoners thought it had been hit; but it made another round and the wings moved twice again, up and down, like the wings of a bird. Then it rose in flight and sped away. Shots rang out after it. They even began firing from several towers. But soon the machine guns fell silent and only the drone of the engine could be heard.

"It was a signal," said Bucher.

"It looked as though it were beckoning with its wings. Like someone beckoning with his hand."

"It was a signal for us! I'm sure. What else?"

"It wanted to show they know we're here! It was for us! It can't have been anything else. What do you think, 509?"

"I think so, too."

It was the first sign they had received from the outside world since they had been in the camp. The terrible isolation of the years had been pierced. Suddenly they realized that for the world they were not dead. Someone was thinking of them. Unknown rescuers had beckoned to them. They were no longer alone. It was the first visible greeting from freedom. They were no longer the scum of the earth. Someone had sent a plane to assure them that the world knew about them, and would come to their rescue. They were no longer the scum of the earth, despised, spat upon, lower than worms—they were human beings again—for human beings who didn't know them.

What's wrong with me? thought 509. Tears? I? An old man?

Neubauer examined the suit. Selma had hung it in the forefront of his wardrobe. He took the hint. Civilian—he hadn't worn that since 1933. A pepper-and-salt suit. Ridiculous. He lifted it from the hanger and examined it. Then he took off his uniform, walked to the door of the bedroom, locked it, and tried on the jacket. It was too tight. He couldn't button it; not even when he pulled in his stomach. He stepped before the mirror. He looked silly. He must have put on at least thirty or forty pounds. No wonder, after all. Before '33 they'd had to be damned economical.

Strange how determination left one's face when the uniform was gone! One grew wobbly, soft. Felt like it, too. He examined the trousers. They would fit even less than the jacket. No use trying them on. What was the point of it all, anyhow?

He would surrender the camp, correctly. They would treat him correctly—military style. For that, there existed traditions, etiquette, military codes. After all, one was a soldier oneself. As good as a soldier. A wearer of a uniform. High-ranking officer.

Neubauer stretched himself. He might be interned, that was possible. Probably only for a short while. Maybe in a castle in the neighborhood, with gentlemen of the same rank. He deliberated about how he should surrender the camp. Military style, of course. No Hitler salute, with raised arm. No, better not. Soldierly, hand to the cap-peak.

He took a few steps and saluted. Not stiff, not like a junior officer. He tried it once more. It wasn't so easy to produce the proper combination of correctness and elegant dignity. The hand flew too high. Still that damned Hitler salute. Come to think of it, an idiotic way to salute for grown-up men. Throwing up the arm like that—all right for Boy Scouts, but not for officers. Queer how one had done it for so long!

He again tried the military salute. Slower! Not so fast. He watched his reflection in the wardrobe mirror, took several steps back, and strode towards himself—"Herr General, I herewith surrender—"

Something like that. In the old days one handed over the sword at the same time. Napoleon III at Sedan; he remembered that from his schooldays. He had no sword. Revolver? Out of the question! On the other hand, he wouldn't be able to keep any weapons. For occasions like this one regretted not having had proper military training. Should he take off belt and holster beforehand?

He again tried a few steps. Not too close, of course. Halt several yards in front. "Herr General—"

Perhaps even: Herr Comrade. No—not when it was a General. But perhaps a sharp salute and a clasp of the hand. Short, correct. No hand-shaking. After all, the respect of one enemy for another. Officer to officer. Actually comrades all, broadly speaking, even though from enemy camps. One had lost, after a valiant fight. The respect due to the honorably defeated.

Neubauer felt the former post-office clerk rise in him. He was aware of it as an historical moment. "Herr General—"

Dignified. Then the clasp of the hand. Perhaps a brief meal together, as one had been told of chivalrous opponents. Rommel with British prisoners. Pity one couldn't speak any English. Well, there were interpreters enough among the prisoners in the camp.

How quickly one grew accustomed to the old way of saluting! Fundamentally, one had never been a fanatical Nazi. Far rather an official, a loyal official of the Fatherland. Weber and men like him, Dietz and his clique, they were Nazis.

Neubauer fetched himself a cigar. Romeo and Juliet. Better smoke them up. Four or five could be left in the box. Could eventually be offered to the opponent. A good cigar could smooth out many things.

He took a few puffs. What if the opponent wanted to see the camp? All right. If there should be anything they didn't like, he had only acted on orders. Often with a bleeding heart. Soldiers understood that. But—

Suddenly he had an idea. Food; good, plentiful food! That was it. That's what they would look for first. He must immediately give orders for the rations to be increased. In this way he could show that the moment he was not under orders he had done everything in his power for the prisoners. He would even talk it over personally with the two camp seniors. They were prisoners themselves. Later on they would testify on his behalf.

Steinbrenner stood in front of Weber. His face glistened with eagerness. "Shot two prisoners trying to escape!" he reported. "Both in the head."

Weber rose slowly and perched himself lazily on the corner of his table. "At what range?"

"One at thirty, the other at forty yards."

"Really?"

Steinbrenner turned red. He had shot both prisoners from a distance of a few feet—just far enough for the wounds not to show any traces of gunpowder.

"And it was an attempt to escape?" asked Weber.

"Attempt to escape."

Both knew it had been nothing of the kind. It was just the name of a game popular among the SS. They snatched a prisoner's cap, flung it to the rear, then ordered him to pick it up. While passing the SS-man, the prisoner was shot from behind. As a reward, the marksman usually received a few days' furlough.

"Do you want to go on furlough?" asked Weber.

"No."

"Why not?"

"That would look as though I wanted to sneak away."

Weber raised his eyebrows and began slowly swinging the leg on which he sat on the table. The reflection of the sun on the swinging boot strayed over the bare walls like a bright and lonely butterfly.

"So you're not afraid?"

"No." Steinbrenner looked steadfastly at Weber.

"Fine. We need good men. Especially now."

Weber had been keeping an eye on Steinbrenner for some time. He liked him. He was very young and still possessed some of that fanaticism for which the SS had once been famous. "Especially now," repeated Weber. "Now we need an SS of the SS. Do you understand what I mean?"

"Yes. At least I think so." Steinbrenner blushed again. Weber was his model. He felt for him a blind admiration, like that of a boy for an Indian chieftain. He had heard of Weber's courage at the indoor brawls before 1933; he knew that in 1929 he had participated in the murder of five Communist workmen, and as a result had spent four months in prison; the workmen had been dragged out of their beds at night and trampled to death under the eyes of their relatives. He also knew the stories of Weber's brutal interrogations at Gestapo headquarters and of his ruthlessness with enemies of the State. His one desire was to become like his ideal. He had been brought up on the Party doctrine. He had been seven years old when National Socialism came to power and was a perfect product of its education.

"Far too many have been taken into the SS without careful investigation," said Weber. "Now begins the test. Now we will see what class means. The lovely lazy times are over. You know that?"

"Yes." Steinbrenner drew himself up.

"We have a dozen good men here already. Examined under a magnifying glass." Weber gave Steinbrenner a scrutinizing look. "Come back here this evening at eight-thirty. Then we'll discuss things further."

Steinbrenner faced about and marched off, delighted. Weber stood up and walked round the table. One more, he thought. Already enough to put a proper spoke in the Old Man's wheel at the last moment. He grinned. He had noticed long ago that it was Neubauer's intention to represent himself as a whitewashed angel and to throw all the blame on him. To the latter he was indifferent; he had enough on his conscience—but he didn't care for whitewashed angels.

The afternoon dragged on. The SS had practically given up coming to the camp. Though they were unaware that the prisoners possessed weapons, this would not have been the reason why they were cautious; even with a hundred times as many revolvers the prisoners would have stood no chance in an open battle against the machine guns. It was simply the mass of prisoners from which the SS suddenly shrunk back.

At three o'clock the names of twenty prisoners were announced over the loudspeaker—they were to assemble in ten minutes at the gate. It could mean anything—interrogation, or death. The secret camp management arranged for all twenty to disappear from their barracks; seven in the Small camp. The command was repeated. All the summoned prisoners were political. No one obeyed the command. It was the first time that the camp openly refused to obey. Shortly afterwards all prisoners were ordered to the roll-call ground. The secret camp management passed around word for everyone to remain in the barracks. On the roll-call ground it would be easy to mow down the prisoners. Weber wanted to put the machine guns into action but didn't yet dare to proceed so openly against Neubauer. The camp organization knew by way of the office that the order had not been issued by Neubauer but by Weber alone. Through the loudspeaker Weber had announced that the camp would receive no food before all the prisoners had taken up their positions on the roll-call ground and the twenty political prisoners had been handed over.

At four o'clock an order from Neubauer came through. The camp seniors were to come and see him at once. They obeyed the command. The whole camp awaited their return in a state of somber tension.

They returned after half an hour. Neubauer had shown them the order for the transport. This was the second one. Within the hour two thousand men were to be rounded up and leave the camp. Neubauer had declared himself ready to postpone the transport until the next morning. The secret camp organization met at once in the lazaret. They first of all succeeded in persuading the SS physician Hoffmann, who had joined their ranks, to use his influence with Neubauer in order to postpone summoning the twenty political prisoners until the next day and to cancel the roll call. After that the order not to issue any food would be untenable. Hoffmann left at once. The secret management decided that under no condition would they furnish any people for the transport on the following morning. If the SS should attempt to round up the two thousand men, they would sabotage the order. The prisoners were told to try to escape from the roll-call ground into the barracks or onto the camp roads. The camp police, manned by prisoners, promised to be of assistance. It could be assumed that the SS, with the exception of a dozen men, would show no great desire to excel themselves in zeal. This report had come by way of SS Squad Leader Bieder who was considered reliable. The last item was a decision of two hundred Czech prisoners. They declared themselves willing, in the event of the transport being formed after all, to be the first batch—in order to save two hundred others who would not have survived it.

Werner squatted in a hospital smock near the spotted-fever ward. "One day is enough," he murmured. "Every hour works for us. Is Hoffmann still with Neubauer?"

"Yes."

"If he doesn't accomplish anything, we'll have to do it ourselves."

"By force?" asked Lewinsky.

"No. Not by force. Partly by force. But not until tomorrow. Tomorrow we'll be twice as strong as today." Werner glanced out of the window and then picked up his schedule. "Once more. We'll have enough bread for four days if we deal out one ration a day. Flour, barley, noodles are—"

"All right, then, Herr Doctor. I'll take the responsibility. See you tomorrow." Neubauer glanced towards the retreating doctor and let out a slow whistle. You too, he thought. All right with me. The more the better. Can whitewash one another. He put the transport order carefully into his private brief case. Then, on his small portable typewriter, he tapped out his instructions to postpone the transport and added this to the other. He opened the safe, dropped the brief case inside and locked it. The order had been a stroke of good luck.

He took out the brief case once more, and opened the typewriter. Then he slowly typed out a new memorandum—the cancellation of Weber's instructions not to issue any food. To this he added his own order for an ample evening meal in the camp. Small things—but all of value.

An atmosphere of gloom pervaded the SS quarters. The Senior Squad Leader Kammler wondered dejectedly whether he would be entitled to a pension and whether the pension would be paid; he was a rejected student who had learned no profession. The SS-man and former butcher's assistant Florstedt brooded as to whether all the men who had passed through his hands between the years 1933 and 1935 were dead. He hoped so. Of about twenty he was sure. He had finished them off himself with whips, table legs and *sjamboks*. But of some ten others he was not so sure. Squad Leader Bolte, the former commercial clerk, would have liked to have inquired of an expert whether or not the embezzlements of his civilian career had become outlawed. Niemann, the specialist in fatal injections, had a homosexual friend in town who had promised to procure him false papers; but he didn't trust him and decided to keep a last dose ready for the friend. The SS-man Duda wanted to fight his way to Spain and the Argentine; he believed that at such times there was always need for people who shrank from nothing. Meanwhile in the bunker, Breuer was busy killing the Catholic priest Werkmeister by slow and interrupted strangulation. Squad Leader Sommer, an undersized individual who had derived particular pleasure from bringing tall prisoners to the point of uttering terrified screams, was filled with nostalgic melancholy, like a fading maiden after the golden days of her youth. Half a dozen SS-men hoped the prisoners would testify to their good conduct; some still believed in a victory for Germany; others were ready to go over to the Communists; a number were already convinced they had never been real Nazis; and many just didn't think anything at all because they had never learned how—but almost all were positive they had acted under orders and were free of any personal or human guilt.

"More than an hour," said Bucher.

He looked at the empty machine-gun towers. The guards had departed and had not been relieved. This had happened off and on before; but only for short spells and only in the Small camp. Now, however, no guards could be seen anywhere.

The day seemed to have lasted simultaneously fifty hours and only three, so chaotic had it been. Everyone was so exhausted they could hardly speak. At first they had paid little attention to the fact that the machine-gun towers had not been reoccupied. Then Bucher had noticed it. He had also observed that there were no guards in the labor camp.

"Maybe they have already decamped."

"No. Lebenthal has heard they are still there."

They went on waiting. The guards didn't come. They got food. The food carriers reported that the SS were still around. But it looked as though they were preparing to pull out.

The food was handed out. A feeble scuffle started. The starved skeletons had to be driven back. "There's enough here for everyone!" called 509. "More than usual! Much more! You'll all get something."

At last they calmed down. The strongest among them formed a cordon around the cauldron and 509 began with the distribution. Berger was still in hiding in the lazaret.

"Look at that! Even potatoes!" said Ahasver, astonished. "And gristle. A miracle!"

The soup was considerably thicker than usual, and there was almost twice as much of it. There was also a double bread ration. It was still far too little, but for the Small camp it was something unheard of. "Neubauer himself was supervising in the kitchen," reported Bucher. "It's the first time I've seen that since I've been here."

"He's trying to get himself an alibi."

Lebenthal nodded. "They think we're dumber than we are."

"Not even that." 509 put down his empty mug. "They don't take the trouble to think about us at all. They believe we're just what they want us to be, that's all. They do that everywhere. They know everything and always everything better. That's why they've lost the war. They knew everything better about Russia, England and America."

Lebenthal belched. "What a wonderful sound," he said devoutly. "Great God, when was the last time I burped!"

They were excited and tired. They talked and hardly heard what they were saying. They lay on an invisible island. All around them Mussulmen were dying. They died in spite of the more nourishing soup. Slowly they moved their spidery limbs and squawked and whispered on and off or slumbered into death.

Bucher walked as slow and erect as he could across the roll-call ground to the barbed-wire fence that separated the women's barracks from the Small camp. He leaned against it. "Ruth."

She stood on the other side. The setting sun colored her face, giving it a semblance of health as though she'd had many good meals behind her. "Here we stand," said Bucher. "Here we stand, in the open, and for once are not worried."

She nodded. A faint smile passed over her face. "Yes. For the first time."

"As though it were a garden fence. We can lean against it and talk to each other. Without fear. Like a garden fence in spring."

Nevertheless, they were not without fear. Every few moments they glanced behind them and over towards the unoccupied towers. It was too deeply rooted in them. They knew it. They also knew they had to overcome it. They smiled at one another and each one tried to hold out longer than the other without casting a hasty glance to the side.

Others began imitating them. Whoever could, got up and walked around. Some approached the barbed wire closer than was allowed —so close that the guards would have fired had they been there. In this they found a strange satisfaction. It seemed childish, and was anything but childish. They moved about cautiously as though on wooden legs, some swayed and had to hold on to something; heads were raised, the eyes in the wasted faces no longer stared at the ground or into the void—they began to see again. Something almost forgotten moved in their brains—painfully, alarmingly and yet almost nameless. Thus they wandered across the ground, past the mounds of dead, past the groups of listless comrades who were dying or only just able to move or think of food—a ghostly promenade of skeletons in whom, in spite of everything, the last resistance had not died.

The red glow of the setting sun faded. Blue shadows spread over the valley, inundating the hills. The guards had still not returned. The night grew deeper. Bolte didn't appear for the evening roll call. Lewinsky brought news; the SS quarters were buzzing with activity. The Americans were expected within a day or two. The transport was not to be rounded up tomorrow. Neubauer had driven into town. Lewinsky grinned, showing all his teeth. "Not long now! I must go back!" He took with him three of the hidden men.

The night was very calm. It grew vast and was filled with stars.

CHAPTER TWENTY-FOUR

The noise began toward morning. At first 509 heard the screaming. It came from afar through the silence. It was not the screaming of people being tortured; it was the bawling of a drunken mob.

Shots rang out. 509 felt for his revolver. He had it under his shirt. He tried to hear whether it was only the SS who were firing or whether Werner's men were already returning the fire. Then came the barking of a tommy gun.

He crept behind a pile of dead and watched the entrance to the Small camp. It was still dark and so many single dead lay strewn all around the pile that it was easy for him to join them without appearing conspicuous.

The bawling and shooting continued for several minutes. Then it suddenly grew louder and came nearer. 509 pressed himself closer to the corpses. He could see the red bursts from the machine guns.

Bullets spattered everywhere. Half a dozen SS-men came firing down the central road. They fired into the barracks on both sides. Off and on stray bullets thumped softly into the heaps of dead. 509 lay flat and fully covered on the ground.

On every side prisoners raised themselves like frightened birds. They fluttered with their arms and tottered aimlessly about. "Lie down!" shouted 509. "Lie down! Play dead! Don't move!"

Some heard him and let themselves fall. Others stumbled toward the barracks and got jammed together in the doors. Most of those who were lying outside stayed where they were.

The group of SS-men came past the latrine toward the Small camp. The gate was wrenched open. In the dark 509 could see their silhouettes and in the flashes from the revolvers their distorted faces. "Come here!" someone shouted. "Here, to the wooden barracks! Come, let's warm the brothers up! They're probably freezing! Come on!"

"Get going, Steinbrenner. Bring the cans along!"

509 recognized Weber's voice. "Look, there are some in front of the door!" shouted Steinbrenner.

The tommy guns spattered into the dark crowd before the door. It slowly collapsed. "Well done! And now let's start!"

509 heard a gurgling sound as though water were being poured out. He could see dark cans being swung back, and out of them came liquid which splashed high over the walls. Then he smelled the gasoline.

Weber's elite troop had been celebrating its departure. Around midnight the order to pull out had come through and most of the troops had soon marched off; Weber and his lot, however, still had enough schnapps left to get properly drunk. Not liking the idea of simply pulling out, they had decided to storm through the camp once again. Weber had given them instructions to take cans of gasoline along. They intended leaving behind them a blazing beacon that would be remembered for many a day.

They could not do anything to the buildings not made of wood, but in the old Polish barrack they found everything they desired.

"Fire magic! Let's go!" shouted Steinbrenner joyfully.

A match flared up; the next moment a whole box went on fire.

The man holding it flung it to the ground. Another one threw a second box into a can that stood close to the barrack. It didn't catch fire. From the bright red flame of the first box, however, a thin blue streak darted over the ground toward the barrack, up the wall, spread out fanwise and gaseous, then widened into a quivering blue surface. At first it didn't look dangerous, giving the impression rather of a cold electric discharge, thin and fluttering, which would quickly die down. But then a crackling started and in the blue fluttering toward the roof appeared orange heart-shaped kernels of fire—flames.

The door opened ajar. "Shoot down anyone coming out!" commanded Weber.

He had a tommy gun under his arm and was firing. A figure in the doorway fell backward. Bucher, thought 509. Ahasver. They slept close to the door. An SS-man sprang forward, flung aside the bodies still lying before the door, slammed the door to, and sprang back. "Now it can start! Hare hunting!" Sheaves of fire shot up high. Through the bawling of the SS-men the screams of the prisoners could be heard. The door of the next section opened. Men came tumbling out. Their mouths were black holes. Shots rang out. Not one prisoner got through. They piled up before the entrance like a heap of twitching spiders.

At first 509 had lain as though paralyzed. Now he cautiously raised himself. He saw the silhouettes of the SS-men clearly outlined against the flames. He saw Weber standing there, legs wide apart. Slow now, he thought, while everything in him trembled. Slow now, one thing after the other. He took out the revolver from under his shirt. Then, in a short silence between the bawling of the SS and the hissing of the fire, he heard the screams of the prisoners louder than before. It was a high, inhuman screaming. Without thinking, he aimed at Weber's back and fired.

He didn't hear the shot ring out among the other shots. Nor did he see Weber fall. And suddenly he realized he hadn't felt the kick of the weapon in his hand. It was as though his heart had been struck a blow with a hammer. The revolver hadn't gone off.

He wasn't aware that he was biting into his lip. Impotence plunged over him like night, he kept biting and biting so as not to drown in the black fog. Probably gotten wet, useless—tears, salt, rage, a last groping—and then suddenly the relief, the fast gliding of the hand over the smooth surface, a small lever that gave at last, and a flowing, flowing—the revolver's safety catch hadn't been released.

He was in luck. Not one of the SS-men had turned around. They expected nothing from his direction. They stood there and bellowed and kept the doors under fire. 509 raised the weapon to his eyes. In the flickering brightness he could see that the safety catch was now released. His hands were still trembling. He leaned over the mound of dead and supported his arms on them to steady himself. He aimed with both hands. Weber was standing some ten paces in front of him. 509 breathed slowly several times. Then he held his breath, made his arms as rigid as possible, and slowly crooked his finger.

The shot was drowned in the other shots. But 509 had felt the kick very distinctly. He fired once more. Weber stumbled forward, turned half round as though immensely surprised, and then his knees gave way. 509 went on firing. He aimed at the next SS-man who held a tommy gun under his arm. He went on pressing the trigger long after the bullets had been spent. The SS-man didn't fall. For an instant 509 stood there, the revolver in his limp hand. He had expected to be shot at once. But in all the turmoil no one had noticed him. He let himself drop to the ground behind the pile of dead.

At this moment one of the SS-men caught sight of Weber. "Hi!" he shouted. "Storm Leader!"

Weber had been standing a few feet behind them and they had not immediately noticed what had happened. "Storm Leader! What's wrong?"

"He's wounded!"

"Who did it? Which of you?"

"Storm Leader!"

It hadn't occurred to them that Weber could have been hit by anything but a stray bullet. "Damn it, which idiot—"

More shots rang out. But this time they came from the direction of the labor camp. Their flashes could be seen. "The Americans!" shouted one of the SS-men. "Get out! Scram!"

Steinbrenner fired in the direction of the latrine.

"Scram! To the right! Across the roll-call ground!" shouted someone. "Quick! Before they cut us off here!"

"The Storm Leader!"

"We can't drag him along!"

The flashes from the direction of the latrine came closer. "Quick! Away!"

The SS-men ran round the burning barrack, firing as they went. 509 got up. He staggered toward the barrack. Once he fell. Then he pushed open the door. "Come out! They're gone!"

"They're still shooting."

"That's us. Come out! Out!"

He stumbled to the next door and began dragging at arms and legs. "Come out! They're gone!"

Figures broke through the door, stumbling over those on the ground. 509 hurried on. The door of Section A was already on fire. He couldn't get near it. He yelled and yelled, heard shots, a sound of crashing, a piece of burning wood dropped from the roof onto his shoulder, he fell, stumbled up again, felt a violent blow, and came to sitting on the ground. He tried to get up but he couldn't. He heard shouts and saw, as though from very far, people—suddenly a crowd, no longer SS, but prisoners, carrying other prisoners and stumbling over him; he managed to creep away. He had no strength left. He was suddenly tired to death. He wanted to be out of everyone's way. He hadn't hit the SS-man. Maybe not even Weber properly. It had been in vain. He had failed.

He crept on. There was the pile of dead. That's where he belonged. He wasn't worth anything. Bucher dead. Ahasver dead. He should have let Bucher do it. Should have given him the revolver. It would have been better. What, now, had he been good for?

He leaned painfully against the pile. Something was hurting him. He drew his hand across his chest and raised it. There was blood on it. He saw it and it didn't make any impression on him. He was no longer himself. All he could still feel was the heat and hear the screams. Then they too faded away. . . .

He woke up. The barrack was still burning. It smelled of burned wood and charred flesh and putrefaction. The heat had warmed the corpses. They had been lying there for days and begun to drip and stink.

The terrible screaming had ceased. An endless procession of prisoners was carrying away scorched and half-burned survivors. Somewhere 509 heard Bucher's voice. So he wasn't dead after all. Then not everything had been in vain. He glanced round. After a while he noticed something move beside him. It was some while before he recognized it. It was Weber.

He lay on his stomach. He had succeeded in creeping behind the pile of dead before Werner and his men arrived. They hadn't noticed him. One of his legs was pulled up and his arms were outstretched. Blood flowed from his mouth. He was still alive.

509 tried to raise one hand. He wanted to call someone but he was too weak. His throat was parched. Only a rasping sound came out of it. The crackling of the burning barrack drowned it.

Weber had noticed 509's hand move. His eyes followed it. Then they met those of 509. Both looked at each other.

509 didn't know whether Weber recognized him. Nor did he know what these eyes opposite him were saying. He just felt that his eyes had to hold out longer than those before him. He had to outlive Weber. In a strange way it was suddenly infinitely important—as though the validity of everything in which he had always believed, and for which he had fought and suffered, depended on that ember of life behind his forehead smoldering longer than the ember behind the forehead in front of him. It was like a duel and a divine judgment. If he could hold out now, then that which had been so important for him that he had risked his life for it, would also hold out. It was like one last effort. Once more it had been put into his hands—and he had to succeed.

He breathed soft and cautiously, each time just to the limit of the pain. He watched the blood dribbling from Weber's mouth, and he groped to see whether he, too, was bleeding from the mouth. He felt something, but when he looked at his hand there was only a little blood on it and he realized it came from his bitten lip.

Weber's eyes followed 509's hand. Then both looked at one another again.

509 tried to think; he wanted to find out once more what mattered most, and what it was. He wanted it to give him more strength. But his thoughts swam. It had to do with the simplest thing in man and without it the world would be destroyed, this his weary brain still knew. It had to be annihilated, it was evil incarnate; the antiChrist; the mortal sin against the spirit. Words, he thought. They said too little. Why words, still? He had to persevere. It had to die before him. That was all.

Strange that no one saw them. That he himself was not seen he could understand. There were so many dead lying around. But the other! He lay concealed in the shadow of the pile of corpses, that must be it. His uniform was black and the light was not reflected in his boots. Nor were there any longer so many people about. They stood further away and stared at the barrack. In several places the walls had been knocked in. Many years of misery and despair were burning to death there. Many names and inscriptions.

There was a crash. Flames shot up. The roof of the barrack gave way in a rain of sparks. 509 watched the burning boards fly through the air. They seemed to fly very slow. One of them sailed low over the pile of corpses, struck a foot, turned over, and fell on Weber. It landed on the back of his neck.

Weber's eyes began to quiver. Smoke rose from the collar of his uniform. 509 could have leaned over and pushed the board aside. At least, he thought he could have done so; but he wasn't sure whether his lung hadn't been damaged. Blood might then have gushed from his mouth. But this was not the reason why he did not do it. Nor was it revenge; there was now more at stake than revenge. And it would have been far too insignificant a revenge.

Weber's hands moved. His head twitched. The board went on burning his neck. His uniform was singed through. It flickered in small flames. Weber's head moved again. The burning board slipped forward. Instantly his hair began to burn. A hissing sound came from the board; the fire licked round his ears and across his head. 509 could now see the eyes more distinctly. They protruded further from their sockets. Blood gushed in jerks from the mouth which moved without uttering a sound. In the crash of the crumbling barrack no other sounds could be heard.

The head was now naked and black. 509 stared at it. The board slowly burned itself out. The blood ceased flowing.

Everything submerged. Nothing was there but the eyes. The whole world had shrunk to them. They had to go blind.

509 didn't know whether it had lasted hours or minutes—but Weber's arms seemed suddenly to stretch without moving. Then the eyes changed and were no longer eyes. They were only jellylike objects. 509 remained sitting still for a while. Then he carefully supported himself on one arm to push himself forward. He had to be absolutely positive before he yielded. Only in his head did he feel any steadiness left; his body was already weightless and yet at the same time it bore the burden of the whole earth and was almost beyond control. He could not push it forward.

Slowly he leaned over, raised a finger and stuck it into Weber's eyes. They did not react. Weber was dead. 509 tried to sit upright, but now even this he could no longer manage. The leaning forward had caused what he had expected earlier. Something, so deep from within that it might have come out of the earth, welled up and flowed over. The blood flowed easily and without pains. It flowed over Weber's head. It seemed to flow not only from the mouth but from his whole body and back into the earth whence it had risen like a gentle fountain. 509 made no attempt to check it. His arms grew numb. In the smoke he saw Ahasver outlined giantlike against the barrack. So he too is not—he still thought, then the earth that supported him turned into a bog and he sank into it.

They found him an hour later. After the first great excitement had subsided, they had started to look for him. Bucher had finally had the idea to return once more to the barrack and search there, and had found him behind the pile of corpses.

He saw Lewinsky and Werner approach. "509 is dead," he said. "Shot. Weber, too. They're both lying together over there."

"Shot? Was he outside?"

"Yes. He was outside at the time."

"Did he have the revolver on him?"

"Yes."

"And Weber is dead, too? Then he shot Weber," said Lewinsky.

They lifted him and straightened him out. Then they turned Weber over.

"Yes," declared Werner. "It looks like it. He's been shot twice in the back."

He gazed round and saw the revolver. "There it is." He picked it up. "Empty. He has used it."

"We must take him away," said Bucher.

"Where to? The place is littered with dead. More than seventy were burned. More than a hundred wounded. Leave him here till there's more room." Werner stared absent-mindedly at Bucher. "Do you know anything about automobiles?"

"No."

"We need—" Werner checked himself. "What am I talking about? You're from the Small camp, of course. We need men for the trucks. Come, Lewinsky."

"Yes. Great pity about him there."

"Yes—"

They walked back. Lewinsky turned round once more. Then he followed Werner. Bucher remained standing. The morning was gray. The remains of the barrack were still on fire. Seventy men burned. But for 509, he thought, there'd have been more.

He stood for a long time. The warmth coming from the barrack felt like an unnatural summer. It blew over him; he was aware of it, then forgot it again. 509 was dead. It was as though not seventy had died—but several hundred.

The monitors quickly took over the camp. At noon the kitchen was already functioning. Armed prisoners occupied the entrances in case the SS should attempt to return. A committee had been chosen from all the barracks and was already at work. A gang had been formed to requisition food as fast as possible from the surrounding villages.

"I'm going to relieve you," someone said to Berger.

Berger glanced up. He was so tired he could no longer take anything in. "Injection," he said, and held out his arm. "Or else I'll cave in. I can't see straight any more."

"I've had some sleep," said the other man. "I'm going to relieve you."

"We've hardly any anesthetics left. We need some urgently. Haven't the men returned from town yet? We sent them to the hospitals to get some."

Professor Swoboda of Brno, a prisoner from the Czech section, grasped the situation. Here was a dead-tired automaton continuing to work mechanically. "You must go and get some sleep," he said, louder.

Berger's inflamed eyes blinked. "Yes, yes," he declared and bent once more over the charred body.

Swoboda took him by the arm. "Go and sleep! I'll relieve you. You must get some sleep!"

"Sleep?"

"Yes."

"All right, all right. The barrack—" Berger came to for a moment, "the barrack has burned down."

"Go to the clothing depot. There are a few beds prepared for us. Go there and get some sleep. I'll come and wake you in a few hours."

"Hours? Once I lie down I'll never wake up. I've still got to—my barrack—I've got—"

"Come along," said Swoboda energetically. "You've done enough."

He beckoned to someone to help him. "Take him to the clothing depot. They have a few beds ready there for doctors."

He took Berger by the arm and turned him round. "509—" said Berger, half-asleep.

"Yes, yes, all right," answered Swoboda without understanding. "509, of course. Everything's fine."

Berger allowed them to take off his white coat and lead him out. The air outside hit him like a vast wave of water. He staggered and stood still. He felt as though the water went on tumbling over him. "My God, I've been operating!" he said.

He stared at the man helping him. "Sure," answered the man. "Of course you have."

"I've been operating," repeated Berger.

"You certainly have. First you dressed some wounds and smeared them with oil, and then you suddenly started with the knife. In between you were given two injections and four cups of cocoa. Damn lucky they were to have you! With that rush of wounded!"

"Cocoa?"

"Yes. That's what those bastards kept for themselves. Cocoa, butter and God knows what else!"

"Operated. I actually operated," whispered Berger.

"And how! Would never have believed it if I hadn't seen it with my own eyes. Thin as you are! But now you'll have to spend a few hours on a mattress. You're going to get a real bed. A squad leader's. Come."

"And I thought—"

"What?"

"I thought I couldn't do it any more—"

Berger examined his hands. He turned them round, then let them drop. "Yes—" he said. "Sleep—"

The day was gray. The tension increased. The barracks hummed like beehives. It was a strange period of uncertainty, of an unfree freedom with a rapid succession of hope, rumors and dark pressing fear. There was still the danger of SS mobs returning—army troops, or organized Hitler youth. Though the arms from the depot had been distributed, a few well-equipped companies could have engaged the camp in a fatal battle and with some artillery could have wiped them all out in no time.

The dead had been brought to the crematorium. There was no other choice; they had to be piled up like firewood. The lazaret was overcrowded.

In the early afternoon a plane was suddenly sighted. It emerged from low clouds behind the town. A commotion started among the prisoners.

"To the roll-call ground! To the roll-call ground, all those who can move!"

Two more planes dived through from the clouds. They circled

and followed the first. Their engines roared. Thousands of faces stared up at the sky. The planes approached fast.

The monitors had brought a number of men from the labor camp to the roll-call ground. There they formed up in two long lines— describing a gigantic cross. Lewinsky had brought sheets from the SS quarters, and at the end of each crossbar four prisoners held a sheet and waved it.

The planes were now immediately above the camp and circling round it. They came lower and lower.

"Look!" shouted someone. "The wings! They're doing it again!"

The prisoners waved the sheets. They waved their arms. They yelled into the roaring of the engines. Many tore off their jackets and waved them, too. The planes dipped down low. Once more the wings signaled. Then they vanished.

The crowd surged back. Again and again they glanced up at the sky. "Bacon," said someone. "After the last war there were parcels of bacon from overseas—"

Then, down the road, nosing its way along low and dangerous, they suddenly saw the first American tank.

CHAPTER TWENTY-FIVE

The garden lay in a silvery light. The air smelled of violets. The fruit trees on the south wall looked as though they were covered by a cloud of pink-and-white butterflies.

Alfred went ahead. He was followed by three men. They walked in silence. Alfred pointed at the shed. The three Americans spread out soundlessly.

Alfred pushed open the door. "Neubauer," he said. "Come out!"

A grunt answered out of the warm darkness. "What? Who's there?"

"Come out."

"What? Alfred—is that Alfred?"

"Yes."

Neubauer grunted again. "Damn it! Fast asleep! Been dreaming!" He cleared his throat. "Dreamed a lot of nonsense! Did you say 'out' to me?"

One of the Americans had silently crept up beside Alfred. A flashlight was switched on. "Hands up. Step out."

In the pale circle of light could be seen a camp bed on which Neubauer sat, half-dressed. He goggled from puffy eyes, blinking into the bright circle. "What?" he said, thickly. "What's this? Who are you?"

"Hands up!" said the American. "Is your name Neubauer?"

Neubauer half raised his hands and nodded.

"Commandant of the Mellern concentration camp?"

Neubauer nodded again.

"Come out."

Neubauer saw the dark muzzle of the automatic leveled at him. He stood up and raised his hands so fast that his fingers knocked against the low roof of the shed. "I'm not dressed."

"Out with you!"

Hesitatingly Neubauer stepped out. He was in shirt, trousers, and boots. There he stood, gray and drowsy. One of the soldiers frisked him quickly. Another searched the shed.

Neubauer looked at Alfred. "It was you who brought them here?"

"Yes."

"Judas!"

"You are no Christ, Neubauer," answered Alfred slowly. "And I'm no Nazi."

The American who had been in the shed came back. He shook his head. "*Vorwärts,*" said the one who spoke German. He was a corporal.

"Can I put on my coat?" asked Neubauer. "It's hanging in the shed. Behind the rabbit hutch."

The corporal hesitated a moment. Then he went in and returned with a civilian jacket.

"Not that one, please," declared Neubauer. "I'm a soldier. My tunic, please."

"You're no soldier."

Neubauer blinked. "It's my Party uniform."

The corporal went back and brought the tunic. He examined it and gave it to Neubauer, who put it on, buttoned it, straightened himself and said, "*Obersturmbannführer* Neubauer. I am at your disposal."

"Okay, okay. Get going."

They walked through the garden. Neubauer noticed that his tunic wasn't properly buttoned. He undid it and buttoned it up correctly. Everything had gone wrong at the last moment. Weber, the traitor, had tried to do him in by setting some barracks on fire. He had done it entirely on his own; that could easily be proved. In the evening Neubauer had been no longer in the camp. He had learned of it over the telephone. Even so, a damned serious business, just now. And then Alfred, the second traitor. He just hadn't turned up. Neubauer had stood there without a car, when he'd wanted to flee at the last moment. The troops had already left—he couldn't very well have made off into the forest—so he had hidden in the garden. Had thought they'd never look for him there. He had quickly shaven off the Hitler mustache. That bastard, Alfred!

"Sit over on this side," said the corporal and pointed to a seat. Neubauer clambered into the car. This is probably what they call a jeep, he thought. The men were not unfriendly. Correct, rather. No doubt this one was a German-American. One had heard of those German brothers abroad. The Bund, or something like that.

"You speak good German," he said cautiously.

"So I should," answered the corporal, coldly. "I'm from Frankfurt."

"Oh—" answered Neubauer. It really seemed to be a rotten bad day. Even the rabbits had been stolen. As he'd come into the shed, the hutch doors had stood open. That had been an ominous sign. Now they were probably sizzling over the fire of some criminal.

The camp gate stood wide open. Roughly improvised flags hung in front of the barracks. The large loud-speaker blared instructions. One of the trucks had returned with milk cans. The roads were packed with prisoners.

The car with Neubauer stopped in front of the Commandant's headquarters. An American colonel stood there with several officers and gave instructions. Neubauer got out, straightened his tunic and stepped forward. "*Obersturmbannführer* Neubauer. I herewith place myself at your disposal." He gave the military, not the Hitler, salute.

The colonel looked at the corporal. The corporal translated.

"Is this the son of a bitch?" asked the colonel.

"Yes, sir."

"Put him to work over there. Shoot him if he makes a false move."

Neubauer had made a great effort to understand. "Come on," said the corporal. "You've got to work. Over there with you. Start taking the dead away."

Neubauer had still been hoping that things would turn out differently. "I'm an officer," he stammered. "With the rank of colonel."

"So much the worse."

"I have witnesses! I was humane! Ask the people here!"

"I think we'll need a few men to stop your people here from ripping you to pieces," answered the corporal. "That would be okay with me. Get a move on!"

Neubauer cast one more glance at the colonel. But the colonel was no longer taking any notice of him. Neubauer turned around. Two men walked beside him; a third behind him.

After a few yards he was recognized. The three Americans squared their shoulders. They expected an attack and closed in on Neubauer. Neubauer began to sweat. He stared straight in front of him and walked as though he wanted to go simultaneously faster and slower.

But nothing happened. The prisoners remained standing and looked at Neubauer. They didn't throw themselves upon him; they made a lane for him. No one came close. No one said anything. No one yelled at him. No one threw a stone at him. No club fell on him. They just looked at him. They formed a lane for him and looked at him—the whole long way to the Small camp.

At first Neubauer had breathed with relief; then he began to sweat profusely. He muttered something. He didn't look up; but he felt the eyes on him. He felt them focused on him like countless peepholes in a gigantic prison door—as though he were already locked up and every eye was watching him, cold and observant.

He grew hotter and hotter. He walked faster. The eyes remained on him. They became stronger. He felt them on his skin. They were leeches, sucking his blood. He shook himself. But he couldn't shake them off. They came through his skin. They hung onto his veins. "I have—" he muttered. "Duty—I haven't—I was—always—what do they want—?"

By the time they reached the spot where Barrack 22 had stood, he was wet. Six SS-men, who had been captured, were working there with several kapos. Nearby stood some Americans armed with tommy guns.

Neubauer came to an abrupt halt. On the ground in front of him he saw a number of black skeletons. "What—on earth is—?"

"Don't play so dumb," answered the corporal, grimly. "This is the barrack you people set on fire. At least thirty bodies must still be inside. Get going, bring out the bones!"

"This—wasn't done by my orders—"

"Of course not."

"I wasn't here—I know nothing about it. Others did this without my knowledge—"

"Of course. Always others. And these who've been rotting to death here year after year? That wasn't you, either, what?"

"They were orders. Duty—"

The corporal turned to a man standing beside him. "In the next few years those will be the two commonest excuses in Germany— I acted under orders, and—I knew nothing about it."

Neubauer didn't hear him. "I always tried—to do my best—"

"That," said the corporal bitterly, "will be the third one! Get on!" he cried suddenly. "Start! Get the dead out of here! D'you think it's easy not to beat you to pulp?"

Neubauer bent down and began uncertainly to rummage in the debris.

They were brought along in barrows, some on rough stretchers, some supported by their comrades. They were laid down in the corridors of the SS quarters; their lice-infested rags were taken off and burned—then they were brought to the SS bathrooms.

Many didn't realize what was going to happen to them; they sat and lay apathetically in the corridors. Only when the steam escaped from the open doors did some of them come to life. They began to squawk and creep fearfully away.

"Bathing! Bathing!" called their comrades. "You're supposed to have a bath!"

It was of no use. The skeletons clawed into one another and whimpered and pushed like crabs toward the exit. These were the ones who knew bathing and steam only as words for the gas chambers. They were shown soap and towels; it didn't help. These, too, they had seen before. They had been used as a means to induce prisoners to enter the gas chambers. With a piece of soap and a towel in their hands they had died. Only when the first batch of cleansed inmates were carried past them and with gestures and words had confirmed that it was a question of hot water and bathing and not gas, did they calm down.

The steam surged from the tiled walls. The warm water was like warm hands. The prisoners lay in it and splashed about with their bony arms and swollen joints. The crusts of filth softened. The soap slid over the starved skin and dissolved the dirt and the warmth penetrated deeper than merely to the bones. Warm water—they had forgotten what that meant. They lay there and felt it and to many it offered the first notion of freedom and salvation.

Bucher sat beside Lebenthal and Berger. Warmth flowed through them. It was an animal joy. The joy of rebirth, it was life born out of warmth and returned to the frozen blood, to the languishing cells. It was vegetative; a water-sun caressing and awakening seeds they had believed to be dead. As the crusts of dirt on the skin dissolved so did the crusts on the soul. They felt security. The simplest of all securities—warmth. Like cavemen in front of the first fire.

They were given towels. They rubbed themselves dry and contemplated their skin in astonishment. It was still leaden and spotted from starvation, but to them it appeared as white as swans.

They were given clean clothes from the depot. Before putting them on, they fingered and examined them. Then they were led into another room. The bath had stimulated them, but at the same time made them very tired. They walked on sleepily, ready to believe in further miracles.

The room with the beds hardly surprised them. They looked at the rows of beds and were about to move on. "Here," said the American who was leading them.

They stared at him. "For us?"

"Yes. To sleep in."

"For how many?"

Lebenthal pointed at the nearest bed, then at himself and Bucher, and asked, "Two?" Then he pointed at Berger and raised three fingers, "Or three?"

The American grinned. He took Lebenthal and gently pushed him onto the nearest bed; then Bucher onto the second; Berger onto the next, and Sulzbacher onto that beyond. "There," he said.

"A bed for each of us!"

"With a blanket!"

"I give up!" declared Lebenthal. "Pillows, too!"

"Sleep," said the American. "Sleep! As long as you like."

Bucher shook his head. "And these are our enemies!"

They had been given a coffin. It was a light black box of normal coffin size; but it was too wide for 509. It could easily have held someone else as well. It was the first time in years that he'd had so much room to himself.

A grave had been dug for him where Barrack 22 had once stood. They had decided that this was the most appropriate spot for 509. Evening was falling when they brought him there. The crescent moon hung in the hazy sky. Men from the labor camp helped them to lower the coffin.

They had a small shovel. Each in turn stepped up to the grave and threw down some earth. They hadn't much strength. When it came to Ahasver's turn he stepped too close and slipped onto the coffin. They dragged him up again. Other, stronger prisoners helped them fill the grave.

They walked back. Rosen carried the shovel. They approached Barrack 20. A corpse was being taken out of it. Two SS-men were carrying it through the door. Rosen stopped in front of them. They tried to walk around him. The one in front was Niemann, the injection specialist. The Americans had caught him outside the town and brought him back. He was the squad leader from whom 509 had rescued Rosen. Rosen stepped back a bit, raised the shovel and bashed it into Niemann's face. He lifted it again, but the American on guard came up and took the shovel from Rosen's trembling hands. "Come, come—we'll take care of that later."

Rosen was shaking all over. The blow hadn't done Niemann much harm; just scraped some of the skin off his face. Berger took Rosen by the arm. "Come along. You're too weak for that."

Rosen burst into tears. Sulzbacher took him by the other arm. "They'll convict him, Rosen. For everything."

"Beaten to death! They must be beaten to death! Nothing else will help! Otherwise they'll keep on coming back!"

They dragged him away. The American handed the shovel to Bucher. They walked on. "Funny," said Lebenthal after a while. "You were always the one who didn't want any revenge—"

"Let him alone, Leo."

"All right, all right."

Every day prisoners left the camp. The foreign slave laborers well enough to walk were taken away in groups. A number of the Poles remained behind. They didn't want to return to the Russian zone. Almost everyone in the Small camp was too weak to leave; they still needed to be looked after for some time. And many didn't know where to go. Their relatives were dispersed or dead; their property stolen; their home towns destroyed. They were free; but they didn't know what to do with their freedom. They remained in the camp. They had no money. They helped to clean the barracks. They were given beds and food; they waited; they formed groups.

They were the ones who knew that nothing awaited them anywhere. Then there were others who didn't yet believe it. They went in search. Every day they could be seen wandering down the mountain, in their hands a certificate which the civilian administration and the military authorities had given them to obtain ration cards—and in their hearts a few uncertain dates.

Many things had not turned out as they had imagined. The prospect of liberation had been something so enormous that most of them had not thought beyond it. Now it was suddenly there, and beyond it stood not a garden of Eden, with miracles, reunions and a magic rolling back of the years to a time that had been without misery—it was there, and beyond it stretched the desolation of loneliness, of terrible memories, of lostness, and in front of it was a desert and a bit of hope. They wandered down the mountain, and the names of a few places, a few people, a few other camps, and a vague perhaps was all they could hope for. They hoped to find maybe one or two—no one dared to hope for everything.

"We'd better get out as soon as we can," said Sulzbacher. "Things won't change here, and the longer we stay the more difficult it'll become. Before we know where we are we'll be sitting in another camp—for people who don't know where to go."

"Do you think you're strong enough?"

"I've put on ten pounds."

"That's not enough."

"I'll take it easy."

"Where'll you make for?"

"Düsseldorf. Look for my wife—"

"How are you going to get to Düsseldorf? Are there any trains?"

Sulzbacher shrugged his shoulders. "I don't know. But there are two other men here planning to go in that direction. To Solingen and Duisburg. We can stick together."

"D'you know them?"

"No. But it's already a great deal not to be alone."

"You're right."

"That's what I think, too."

He shook hands all round. "Got enough food?" asked Lebenthal.

"For two days. We can report to the American authorities on the road. It'll work out somehow."

He walked off down the mountain with the two who were making for Solingen and Duisburg. He waved once; then not any more.

"He's right," said Lebenthal. "I'm off, too. I'm going to spend tonight in town. I've got to talk to someone who wants to become my partner. We're going to open a business. He has the capital. I the experience."

"Fine, Leo."

Lebenthal took a pack of American cigarettes from his pocket and handed it round. "This'll be the biggest business," he declared. "American cigarettes. Just like after the last war. Mustn't miss the bus."

He contemplated the brightly colored packet. "Better than any money, I tell you."

Berger smiled. "Leo," he said. "You're all right."

Lebenthal glanced at him suspiciously. "I never pretended to be an idealist."

"Don't take it wrong. I didn't mean it that way. You've kept us going often enough."

Lebenthal smiled. He was flattered. "One does what one can. Always a good thing to have a practical businessman around. If there's anything I can do for you—how about you, Bucher? Aren't you leaving, too?"

"No. I'm waiting for Ruth to get a bit stronger."

"Sure." Lebenthal produced an American fountain pen from his pocket and jotted something down. "Here's my address in town. In case—"

"Where did you get that pen?" asked Berger.

"Swapped. The Americans are crazy for souvenirs from the camp."

"What?"

"They collect souvenirs. Revolvers, daggers, badges, whips, flags —it's a good business. I prepared for it in time. Laid in a store."

"Leo," said Berger. "It's a good thing you exist."

Lebenthal nodded without surprise. "Are you staying here for the time being?"

"Yes, I'm staying here."

"Then I'll be seeing you now and again. I'll sleep in town, but come up here to eat."

"I thought you would."

"Sure. Have you enough cigarettes?"

"No."

"Here." Lebenthal took two unopened packs from his pocket and gave one each to Berger and Bucher.

"What else have you got?" asked Bucher.

"Canned food." Lebenthal glanced at his watch. "Well, got to be going—"

From under his bed he pulled out a new American raincoat and put it on. No one made any further comment. Even if he'd had an automobile outside, the others wouldn't have been surprised. "Don't lose the address," he said to Bucher. "Be a pity if we lost touch with one another."

"We won't lose it."

"We're going together," said Ahasver. "Karel and I."

They stood before Berger. "Stay here a few more weeks," said Berger. "You're not strong enough yet."

"We want to get out."

"You know where to?"

"No."

"Then why do you want to go?"

Ahasver made a vague gesture. "We've been here long enough."

He was wearing an old-fashioned gray Havelock, an overcoat with a kind of coachman's collar reaching to his elbows. Lebenthal, already active in business, had gotten it for him. It came from the possessions of a grammar school professor who had been killed in the last bombardment. Karel was dressed in a combination of bits of American uniforms.

"Karel has to leave," said Ahasver.

Bucher joined them. He examined Karel's attire. "What has happened to you?"

"The Americans have adopted him. The first regiment which passed through here. They've sent a jeep to fetch him. I'm going with him some of the way."

"Have they adopted you, too?"

"No. I'm just driving a part of the way with him."

"And then?"

"Then?" Ahasver glanced down into the valley. His coat billowed in the wind. "There are so many camps where I knew people—"

Berger looked at him. Lebenthal has dressed him just right, he thought. He looks like a pilgrim. He'll wander from one camp to another. From one grave to another. But which prisoner had had the luxury of a grave? Then what was he going in search of?

"You know," said Ahasver, "now and again you meet people unexpectedly on the road."

"Yes, old man."

Their eyes followed the two of them. "Queer," said Bucher, "how we all go off in different directions."

"You will be off soon, too?"

"Yes. But we shouldn't lose sight of one another like this."

"Oh, yes," said Berger. "We should."

"We must meet again. After all this here. Some day."

"No."

Bucher looked up. "No," repeated Berger. "We should not forget it. But we also shouldn't make a cult out of it. Or we'll remain forever in the shadow of these cursed towers."

The Small camp was empty. It had been cleaned and the inmates housed in the labor camp and the SS quarters. Streams of water, soap and disinfectant had been used; but the stench of death and filth and misery still hovered over it. Entrances had been cut everywhere into the barbed-wire fences.

"Don't you think you'll get tired?" Bucher asked Ruth.

"No."

"Then let's go. What day is today?"

"Thursday."

"Thursday. Thank God the days have names again. Here they had only numbers. Seven to a week. Each one the same."

They had received their papers from the camp management. "Where shall we go?" asked Ruth.

"Over there." Bucher pointed at the hill on which the white house stood. "Let's go there first and have a good look at it. It has brought us luck."

"And then?"

"Then? We can come back here. There's food here."

"Don't let's come back. Ever."

Bucher looked at Ruth, surprised. "Good. Wait here. I'll get our things."

They didn't amount to much. But they had bread for several days and two cans of condensed milk. "Are we really going?" she asked.

He saw the tension in her face. "Yes, Ruth," he said.

They took leave of Berger and walked toward the gate which had been cut into the barbed-wire fence surrounding the Small camp. They had been outside the camp several times already, though never far—and each time they had felt the same excitement of suddenly being on the other side. The electric current and the machine guns focused precisely on the bare strip of road round the camp still seemed to be there. At their first step beyond the wire enclosure, a shudder passed through them. But then, the world was there, unlimited.

They walked slowly along, side by side. It was a soft, overcast day. For years they had been forced to creep, run and crawl—now they walked calm and upright and no catastrophe followed. No one fired at them. No one yelled. No one pounced on them.

"It's inconceivable," said Bucher. "Each time again."

"Yes. It's almost terrifying."

"Don't look round. Were you going to look round?"

"Yes. It's still sitting in the back of my neck. As though someone were cowering inside my head, trying to turn it round."

"Let's for once try to forget it. For as long as we can."

"Yes."

They walked on and crossed a road. Before them lay a meadow, green and sown over with the yellow of primroses. They had often seen it from the camp. For a moment Bucher thought of Neubauer's wretched, withered primroses outside Barrack 22. He shook it off. "Come, let's walk through there."

"You think it's allowed?"

"I think we're allowed a great deal. And let's try not to be afraid any longer."

They felt the grass under their feet and against their shoes. This, too, they no longer recognized. They knew only the hard earth of the roll-call ground. "Let's go to the right," said Bucher.

They walked to the right. It seemed childish, but it gave them a deep satisfaction. They could do what they wanted. No one gave them orders. No one shouted or fired. They were free. "It's like a dream," said Ruth. "One is only afraid to wake up and to find the barrack and its foulness again."

"I've never had dreams like that. Only others in which I screamed."

"Let's not speak about it any more. Not today."

"No."

"The air here is different." Ruth breathed deeply. "It's live air. Not dead."

Bucher looked at her attentively. Her face was a little flushed and her eyes suddenly shone. "Yes, it's live air. It smells. It doesn't stink."

They stood beside some poplars. "We can sit down here," he said. "No one will scare us away. We can even dance if we want to."

They sat down. They watched the beetles and the birds. In the camp there had been only rats and bluish flies. They listened to the murmuring of the stream beneath the poplars. The water was clear and flowed fast. In the camp they'd never had enough water. Here it flowed freely and wasn't even needed. One would have to grow accustomed to many things anew.

They continued on down the hill. They took their time and rested often. Then came a hollow and when they finally looked back the camp had disappeared.

They sat down and fell silent. The camp was no longer there, nor was the destroyed town. They could see only a meadow and above it the soft sky. They felt the warm breeze on their faces and it seemed to blow through the black cobwebs of the past, pushing them away with gentle hands. This is perhaps how it should start, Bucher thought. From the very beginning. Not with bitterness and memories and hatred. With the simplest things. With the feeling that one is alive. Not that one lives in spite of everything, as in the camp. Simply that one lives. He felt that it was not an escape. He knew what 509 had wanted from him; that he should be one of those who pulled through, unbroken—to bear witness and to fight. But he was also suddenly aware that the responsibility left to him by the dead would cease to be an unbearable burden only when this clear strong feeling of life would be joined to it. It would carry him and give him the double strength: not to forget but also not to be destroyed by memories—as Berger had said on parting.

"Ruth," he said after a while. "I think when one starts as low as we do there must be a lot of happiness ahead."

The garden was in bloom; but when they came close to the white house they saw that a bomb had fallen behind it. It had wiped out the whole back part of it; only the façade had remained undamaged. Even the carved front door was still there. They opened it; but it led to a heap of rubble.

"It never was a house. All this time."

"It is good that we didn't know it was destroyed."

They looked at it. They had believed that as long as it existed, they too would exist. They had believed in an illusion. In a ruin with a façade. There was irony in it, and at the same time a strange comfort. It had helped them, and in the end that was all that mattered.

They found no dead. The house must have been deserted when it was bombed. To the side, under the debris, they discovered a narrow door. It hung askew on its hinges, and behind it was the kitchen.

The small room had only partly collapsed. The stove was intact, and there were even a few pots and pans. The stovepipe could easily be attached and then passed through the open window. "We can light it," said Bucher. "There's enough wood out there to make a fire."

He rummaged about in the wreckage. "There are some mattresses under here. We'll be able to get them out in a few hours. Let's start right away."

"It's not our house."

"It's no one's house. We can safely stay here a few days. For the beginning."

By evening they had two mattresses in the kitchen. They had also found some chalk-covered blankets and an undamaged chair. In the table drawer had been a few forks, some spoons and one knife. A fire was burning in the stove. The smoke passed through the pipe and out of the window. Bucher went on searching in the rubble outside.

Ruth had found a piece of mirror and had put it secretly in her pocket. Now she stood near the window and looked into it. She heard Bucher call, and she answered; but she didn't take her eyes off what she saw. The gray hair; the sunken eyes; the bitter mouth with the large gaps between the teeth. She looked at it mercilessly and for a long time. Then she threw the mirror into the fire.

Bucher came in. He had found a pillow, too. Meanwhile the sky had turned apple-green and the evening was very quiet. They gazed out of the broken window and suddenly they realized that they were alone. They had almost forgotten what it was like. There had always been the camp with its hordes of people, the overcrowded barrack, even the overcrowded latrine. It had been good to have comrades, but it had often been oppressive never to be alone. It had been like a steam roller that had flattened out the Self into a mass Self.

"It is good to be alone for once, Ruth."

"Yes. As though we were the last men."

"Not the last. The first."

They arranged one of the mattresses so that they could look out through the open door. They opened a can of milk and began to eat; then they settled down beside one another in the doorway. Behind the heaps of rubble to both sides shimmered the last light of the day.

(1)